CONVERSATIONS, CHOICES AND CHANCES

Conversations, Choices and Chances

The Liberal Law School in the Twenty-First Century

ANTHONY BRADNEY
Professor of Law, Leicester University

·HART·
PUBLISHING
OXFORD – PORTLAND OREGON
2003

Published in North America (US and Canada) by
Hart Publishing
c/o International Specialized Book Services
5804 NE Hassalo Street
Portland, Oregon
97213-3644
USA

Hart Publishing is a specialist legal publisher based in Oxford, England.
To order further copies of this book or to request a list of other
publications please write to:

Hart Publishing, Salter's Boatyard, Folly Bridge,
Abingdon Road, Oxford OX1 4LB
Telephone: +44 (0)1865 245533 or Fax: +44 (0)1865 794882
e-mail: mail@hartpub.co.uk
WEBSITE: http//www.hartpub.co.uk

British Library Cataloguing in Publication Data
Data Available
ISBN 1–84113–248–9 (hardback)

Typeset by Hope Services (Abingdon) Ltd.
Printed and bound in Great Britain by
Lightning Source UK Ltd

Contents

Preface

There are academics working in contemporary British law schools who 'wake each day with their hair on fire' and there are those who have a different preference: 'sit on your arse for 50 years and hang your hat on a pension.' Energy crackles through the law school. At the same time, sloth, defeat and despair stare out. In this book I have sought to analyse both the reasons for the sense of excitement and adventure that I see in present-day university legal education and for the malaise that runs alongside this excitement. I also offer a goal for law schools, the pursuit of liberal education, which I contend will maintain the excitement and remove the malaise.

Law schools and law students have never been as rich as they are in the present day. Examples of this wealth are obvious. Declining financial budgets do not affect the fact that almost any university library, whatever the recent cuts suffered, is immeasurably richer in material today than almost any library 40 years ago. PCs, the Web and cheap international travel are only three of the things that both make academic life much easier and also much more rewarding, enabling us to travel to worlds, both intellectual and geographical, that few would have been seen before. Even more, the law school is now part of the hubbub of conversations going on in the university. No longer isolated, now it knows that it is precisely a *university* law school. Different voices and strange languages abound and each day things will never be the same again.

Student debt that runs into thousands of pounds does not alter the fact that modern law students, because they are law students, have chances that are open to few of their fellows elsewhere in the university. The university that the student chooses to study in affects what they can do with the rest of their lives but, compared with others in their university, they have a much better chance to select the life they want. Employment rates are high and the range of jobs that law graduates do increases each year. More choices and more chances for students brings with it more responsibility for their decisions. They must attend to the conversations in the university and elsewhere and justify, to themselves and to others, the use that they make of their riches. And, in attending to those conversations, they become aware of still more chances and choices that are open to them; chances and choices not just as workers but as people. Law students are wealthy not only in their employment prospects but also in the way that their enriched understanding of the world can make them better citizens and better people.

Like their parent universities, law schools, no matter how new they are, seem to be ageless institutions, destined to last until the end of time. In fact they can prove to be as fragile as the people who staff them. Not even the citizens of Stamford now remember the university that briefly existed there in the fourteenth century. A never-ending series of governments preaching a religion of money, preoccupied with the possibility of turning universities into personnel departments for British industry, has had an inevitable depressing effect on academic morale. University law schools and the individual academics in them need to consider exactly what they are doing and why they are doing it, if they are to navigate a route through today's uncertain waters. No matter what they do, they cannot hope for calmer seas but they guarantee their own demise if they do not find a chart to guide their voyage. They cannot look to others, either in the university or outside the university, to provide them with their path because there are too many contending voices. Moreover, unreflective obedience to the dictates of others signals only failure, both as an academic and a human being. Each law school and each academic has to decide which, among the sounds they hear, are the clarion calls and which are the songs of sirens. Whether university law schools choose to operate according to the precepts of liberal education, as I suggest in this book, may be a matter for debate (though, in truth, I think that, once one reflects on the matter, the conclusion to that debate is an obvious one); that university law schools need to think more clearly about what they do, and that that thinking needs to be done urgently, are not matters for discussion. Law schools and individual academics can seek to make their place in history or, by failing to take a stance, they can write their lives in the sand. By failing to reflect on what they are and who they are, and by being unwilling to hold fast to the results of that reflection, they will find out what it is like to be the University of Stamford or an academic who once worked there.

The book sets out both a theory of liberal education and a way in which that liberal education can be applied to the law school. It is based partially on my own experience of working as a legal academic over more than two decades, during which time I have, amongst other things, contributed to the development of research and scholarship in a number of diverse fields, developed a variety of courses in one large, old university law school and worked in two professional associations, the Socio-Legal Studies Association and the Society of Legal Scholars (formerly the Society for Public Teachers of Law). More importantly, the book is based upon the increasingly rich vein of research and scholarship that looks at higher education in general and university legal education in particular.

Thinking about and writing about university legal education has become an important activity over the past decades. Some writing is still being produced that does little more than describe the teaching that the author is currently engaged in. Such writing usually does no more than confirm the inconsequentiality of that that the author is doing and ensure that, at least formally, a law school has one less nil return for its RAE entry. Increasingly, however, writing about university education, in both the law school and the wider university, shows the same hallmarks of research and scholarship as benchmark work done elsewhere in the academy; such work attempts to draw connections with previous argument, link with appropriate empirical evidence and analyse the conceptual framework that is being used. Without this body of work, including some work with which I profoundly disagree, this book could not have been written.

This book is dedicated first to my wife, Fiona Cownie, whose decision to spend her life with me has elicited too little gratitude from me and resulted in too little sympathy from other people. Secondly, this book is dedicated to the cats, Amy, Beth, Jo and Meg, who share our lives. The direct way in which they demonstrate their feelings, together with the affection and the loyalty that they show to those with whom they coexist, has provided an example of virtue in action sometimes not found in the behaviour of human beings.

1

The Excitement and the Malaise: Introduction

'BLISS IS IT IN THIS DAWN TO BE ALIVE…'[1]

WRITING IN 1997, in the *Journal of Legal Education*, Donald Weidner suggested that legal academics should '[m]aintain a sense of gratitude for the position of law professor—surely one of the greatest jobs in the world.'[2] That which is true for legal academics in the USA is also true for contemporary British legal scholars. Quite simply, within the British university law school, the world is now a much better place than it ever has been before. No one who has the slightest sense of history could possibly prefer the conditions that prevailed in British law schools 40 or 50 years ago to those that exist today. Foolish common room chatter, in which men (and given the gender conditions of the law school 50 and even 40 years ago it almost necessarily has to be men) look back fondly to a bygone era that once was theirs, shows only that some people suffer from the failure of vision and the enfeeblement of mind that can come with age.[3] For law schools the 'golden age' of British higher education, the 1960s, was more brass than gold, being far too close to a previous

[1] The line that follows, with the same necessary change of tense, is also apt: '[b]ut to be young is very heaven.' Both lines are from William Wordsworth.

[2] D Weidener, 'The Crises of Legal Education: A Wake-Up Call for Faculty' (1997) 47 *Journal of Legal Education* 92 at 103. This attitude towards modern academic life is not unique to those working in law schools. Stanley Aronowitz, a social scientist, entitled his 1998 essay on academic life 'The Last Good Job in America.' The title accurately captures the spirit of the essay (S Aronowitz, 'The Last Good Job in America' in R Martin (ed), *Chalk Lines: The Politics of Work in the Managed University*, Durham, Duke University Press, 1998). Similarly the critic and philosopher Allan Bloom wrote that '[n]one of my disappointments with the university . . . has ever made me doubt that the life it gave me was anything other than the best one available to me' (A Bloom, The Closing of the American Mind (Harmondsworth, Penguin Books, 1988) 245.

[3] But does not necessarily come with age: Hayek was 89 when he published *The Final Conceit*, Nirad Chaudhuri published *Thy Hand Great Anarch!* when he was 90 and *Three Horsemen of the New Apocalypse* when he was 100 and, in 2000, Saul Bellow published *Ravelstein* at the age of 85.

stone age.[4] This present era is the golden age even though the prospects for the future look brighter still.[5]

Forty years ago British university law schools were still small isolated outposts that existed on the outskirts of the academic empire. Academics who inhabited the grander castles of the social sciences, the humanities and the sciences had long regarded those who garrisoned these minor fortifications with a suspicion that bordered on contempt. Veblen, writing in 1918 about American university law schools, observed that:

> [t]he law school's inclusion in the university corporation has the countenance of ancient tradition, it comes down as an authentic usage from the medieval era of European education, and from the pre-history of the American universities. But in point of substantial merit the law school belongs in the modern university no more than a school of fencing or dancing.[6]

Veblen's sentiments found echoes in later British comments. Laski notoriously characterised British legal academics as being largely 'a very inferior set of people who mainly teach because they cannot make

[4] Scott observes that 'the modern university [in the United Kingdom] achieved its apotheosis between 1955 and 1975' (P Scott, *The Crisis of the University*' (London, Croom Helm, 1984) 5.

[5] At this point it is important to note lacunae and limitations in research and scholarship that are pertinent to the arguments in this chapter. First, there is no substantial history of British university law schools similar to that by Stevens in relation to the USA (R Stevens, *Law School: Legal Education in America from the 1830s to the 1980s* (Chapel Hill, University of North Carolina Press, 1983). There has been some writing in this area and some of the primary sources relating to the history are readily available. It is on this material that this chapter rests. Nonetheless a lengthy treatment of the history of British law schools would have made this chapter richer. Secondly we have no study of the attitudes of law teachers which has been carried out in the manner of Evans' studies of those working in departments of modern language or departments of literature (C Evans, *Language People* (Buckingham, Society for Research into Higher Education/Open University Press, 1988); C Evans, *English People* Buckingham, Society for Research into Higher Education/Open University Press, 1993). Here again there have been some more limited and partial studies and this chapter again rests in part on such information as has been published. However, I have also had some access to early conclusions derived from Fiona Cownie's study of legal academics, 'Legal Academics: Culture and Identities' whilst writing this book. This study follows a similar methodology to Evans' work. However, she bears no responsibility for my use of her work.

[6] T Veblen, *The Higher Learning in America* (New York, Augustus M Kelly, Bookseller, 1919) 211. Writing about American law schools at this date, Stevens notes of the case method which predominated in teaching, '[t]here was . . . something lost, intellectually and morally, in the blind obedience to German scientism. In retrospect, the period of high formalism in the life of the case method has about it a touch of the ludicrous'. (Stevens, above n 5, at 122).

a success at the bar.'[7] Academics in law schools were usually peripheral figures in the intellectual life of the university. Lewis Eliot, CP Snow's barrister academic in his 'Strangers and Brothers' series published between 1940 and 1970, brings to his college the contacts made in the outside world of national politics and the civil service but no mention is ever made of him publishing any research.[8] Moreover, whatever the arguable benefits to his college of such links as Lewis had, most academic lawyers during Lewis' time did not mix in such circles; the experience of a local provincial court or a solicitor's office did not have the same cachet within the wider university that Lewis' life, lived partly in 'the corridors of power,' could create.[9] Academic lawyers were

[7] Quoted in, amongst other places, J Bridge, 'The Academic Lawyer: Mere Working Mason or Architect?' (1975) 91 *Law Quarterly Review* 488 at p 492. See also Rowse's typically mischievous comment on law fellows at All Souls College, Oxford in the 1920s. 'Some allowance was made for the fact that law candidates were more specialized, and less likely to come up to the standards of others on the general papers. Somewhat easier to get elected as a lawyer'. (A Rowse, *All Souls in My Time* (London, Gerald Duckworth and Co, 1993) 18.

[8] Twining, in his discussion of the books, cautions against taking 'Eliot too seriously as a representative or a stereotype of English academic lawyers of his period' (W Twining, 'Goodbye to Lewis Eliot: The Academic Lawyer as Scholar' (1980) *Journal of the Society of Public Teachers of Law* 2 at 4). However, he also notes that 'there is more than a core of truth in it' (ibid). It would plainly be wrong to treat any literary work as being simply a piece of descriptive sociology. The canvas of Snow's novels is broader than the events described in them. Thus Trilling has written of *The Master*, the novel which shows Eliot as a barrister-academic in the closest detail, 'the struggle for the Mastership of a Cambridge college serves handsomely as a paradigm of the political life' (L Trilling, *A Gathering of Fugitives* (London, Secker and Warburg, 1957) 130). As Bergonzi observes, 'the dominant interest of 'Strangers and Brothers' lies in the extent and variety of its social observations' and he goes on to suggest that 'future social historians may find a lot to interest them in Snow's novels' (B Bergonzi, 'The World of Lewis Eliot' (1960) 167 *The Twentieth Century* 214 at 215). It is legitimate, however, to add that this is equally true for those interested in the history of the British law school. The 'London Fellows' of All Souls College, Oxford are one example of the kind of law academic portrayed by Snow (J Lowe 'The Warden'(1998) HarperCollins, London p 50). Data on law schools in the 1960s confirms the more general accuracy of Snow's writing. Wilson, in his 1966 survey of United Kingdom law schools, reported that only 17 per cent of academics had PhDs whilst 9 per cent had LLDs (J Wilson, 'A Survey of Legal Education in the United Kingdom' (1966) 9 *Journal of the Society of Public Teachers of Law* 1 at 29). At the same time 78 per cent of legal academics had professional qualifications (Wilson, ibid at 30). Even though Wilson states that 'promotion is to a large extent on published work' the qualifications of legal academics at this time would suggest that they were valued for their professional not their academic experience.

[9] Even Lewis is, for the most part, a marginal figure in his college and the college a marginal part in his life. Only three of the novels in the series, *The Light and the Dark*, *The Master* and *The Affair*, are largely concerned with college life and in only the first two is Eliot a Fellow of the college. Most of the series, including the eponymous *Corridors of Power*, was concerned with Lewis' life outside the college although he holds his college fellowship from very early on in the series.

engaged in the outside world to a much greater extent than their academic colleagues.[10] Harrison's comment on the way administrative tasks were divided in Oxford colleges, '[t]he law fellow was a natural for bursar, the historian for librarian,' illustrates the perceived place of the academic lawyer; lawyer-academics were centrally involved in the administrative not the intellectual life of the university.[11] Where academic lawyers were not peripheral in their university it was rarely their legal scholarship that gave them their status. Thus, for example, John Sparrow, Warden of All Souls College, Oxford between 1952 and 1977, came to the Wardenship from a successful practice at the Chancery Bar.[12] However, none of the 26 books that he published focused on law, Sparrow instead concentrating on literary studies.[13] These early years of British university law schools built an image that has persisted for decades and which may continue to the present day.[14] In 1960 Lawson, then President of the Society of Public Teachers of Law, lamented that '[l]aw is, by and large, not thought of too well in our universities' and doubted 'whether even now it is considered entirely respectable.'[15] Twining, writing about his early career, remembers being asked by an 'official concerned with tertiary education' what he did in his summer vacations and protesting that he did research like any

[10] Rothblatt has written '[t]he modern university faculty member has his professional identification, his standing in the community of scholarship and science, and his special institutional affiliation; but . . . [h]e knows of no single outside referent group' (S Rothblatt, *Tradition and Change in English Liberal Education* (London, Faber and Faber, 1976) 189). This may have been true of other academic disciplines at this time but it was not true for law.

[11] B Harrison 'College Life, 1918–1939' in B Harrison (ed), *The History of the University of Oxford* vol VIII (Oxford, Clarendon Press, 1994) 85.

[12] His first application for silk was rejected at the same time that he was elected to the Wardenship. He retired from practice, and thus made no further applications for silk, on taking up the Wardenship (Lowe op cit p 165).

[13] Lowe, above n 8, at 249–50.

[14] Law has formed part of the teaching profile of British universities from their very first beginnings. However, teaching the English common law is a relatively recent innovation (see further A Bradney, 'English University Legal Education: Elite Education or Mass Education? Some Preliminary Observations' in P Torremans (ed), *Legal Convergence in the Enlarged Europe of the New Millennium* (The Hague, Kluwer, 2000) 290–92). The creation of British university law schools, as opposed to the employment by universities of one or more individual law teachers, is of even more recent origin. University College, London probably has the best claim to be the earliest law British law school, being created in 1826 (J Baker, 'University College and Legal Education 1826–1976' (1977) *Current Legal Problems* 1).

[15] F Lawson, 'The Academic Lawyer as Jurist' (1959-60) 5 *Journal of the Society of Public Teachers of Law* 182 at 184.

other academic.[16] Even much closer to the present day, in writing up his 1980s field-work about academics' views of themselves and their work, Becher, in the first edition of his book *Academic Tribes and Territories*, concluded that

> [t]he predominant notion of academic lawyers [amongst other academics] is that they are not really academics—one critical respondent described them as 'arcane, distant and alien: an appendage to the university world.'[17]

The second edition of the book, co-authored with Trowler, also illustrates the distance between the law school and the rest of the university. Having described academic law as a discipline that is difficult to demarcate from its domain of professional practice Becher and Trowler go on to observe that they were able to find only one discussion that pertained to the culture of law schools.[18] To respond to this by protesting that first the division between practising lawyer and academic lawyer is plain and that secondly there is now a wealth of literature that discusses in various ways the culture of law schools is to miss the point; to two experienced researchers into higher education neither that division nor that literature is obvious. Even in the twenty-first century, the law

[16] W Twining, 'Goodbye to Lewis Eliot: The Academic Lawyer as Scholar' (1980) *Journal of the Society of Public Teachers of Law* 2.

[17] T Becher, *Academic Tribes and Territories* (Buckingham, Open University Press, 1989) 30. Examples of such an attitude could be multiplied almost endlessly. My own university recently laid down a series of academic qualifications that were presumed to be necessary to be appointed to a full-time academic post. It went on to note that there could be exceptions to these general presumptions in the case of professional departments where practice qualifications might be of greater weight. Law was cited as being one such department. In the 25 years that I have been in my department a number of, though a minority of, colleagues have been appointed with practice qualifications. I am unable to think of one who was appointed because of that qualification. As is true in most of the better law departments in the United Kingdom almost everybody appointed to a permanent position in my department now comes after pursuing doctoral studies and having published one or more articles. Despite this fact, when my department was chosen as one of the pilot departments when my university surveyed the way in which academics used their time, one reason given was the fact that the university wanted one of its pilot departments to be a 'professional' department. Of my 40 plus colleagues only one does, what I am assured is, a small amount of practice. At the time of writing this passage three others hold positions in tribunals as chairs or wing-people. Doubtless the experience of my department is not untypical of the way in which many other law schools are regarded by their universities. History can distort a view of present realities.

[18] T Becher and P Trowler, Academic Tribes and Territories (2nd edn, Buckingham, SRHE and Open University Press, 2000) 53. The one piece they refer to is C Campbell and P Wiles, 'The Study of Law in Society in Britain' (1976) 10 *Law and Society Review* 547. (I am grateful to Fiona Cownie who drew my attention to Becher and Trowler's observation.)

school is perceived to be outside the university by others who are within it.

Perceptions are one thing; reality may, however, be very different. Wilson's 1966 survey of British university law schools provides the first detailed account of British legal academics and the law schools in which they were working. Whilst it is largely quantitative rather than qualitative in nature, it gives some clues as to the nature of academic life in the law schools in the years that led up to his study and suggests that the perceptions noted above were not entirely without foundation.

In 1966 there were 25 university law schools; in total there were 614 full-time legal academics.[19] Law schools were thus, by comparison with present-day standards, physically small.[20] Those who worked in them were intellectually isolated from academics in the rest of the university and geographically isolated from their fellows in other law schools. Universities themselves were, of course, much smaller than those of the present day. In 1964 there were only 18,352 full-time academics in British universities.[21] Disciplines and departments other than law were also small. However, those who worked in non-law disciplines could, with a greater or lesser degree of reality, hope to find fellow academics outside their immediate field with whom they could converse about their subject.[22] It was the size of their number plus the peculiarly intractable nature of the dominant paradigm within the law school, doctrinal law as it was then practised, that made academic lawyers so isolated. Law, then, was a language, like Manx or Cornish, that its speakers kept to themselves, insisting on the purely internal,

[19] J Wilson, 'A First Survey of University Legal Education in the United Kingdom' (1965–66) 9 *Journal of the Society of Public Teachers of Law* 1 at 26.

[20] In the absence of suitable survey evidence membership of the Society of Public Teachers of Law has to serve as a proxy for the size of the total academic legal community in the United Kingdom. In 1960 that membership stood at 291 but some of these members either worked outside university law schools are held non-academic positions within those schools ('Report of the General Committee for 1959–60' (1959–60) 5 *Journal of the Society of Public Teachers of Law* 226 at 227; 'Report of the General Committee for 1958–59' (1959-60) 5 *Journal of the Society of Public Teachers of Law* 96, 1971).

[21] A Halsey and M Trow, *The British Academics* (London, Faber and Faber, 1971) 144. The full-time figure in 1997/98 was 67,991 (*Resources of Higher Education Institutions 1997/98* (Cheltenham, Higher Education Statistical Agency, 1999) 202). This is the figure for full-time staff in universities who were wholly funded by their institution. A further 7,923 staff were employed in other higher education institutions.

[22] Thus, eg, see Rogers' description of Ayer at New College, Oxford who, in the 1960s, 'could talk French literature with Merlin Thomas, American politics with Herbert Nicholas, the Spanish Civil War with Raymond Carr' (B Rogers, *AJ Ayer: A Life* (London, Vintage, 2000) 243.

and therefore exclusive, nature of legal reasoning; only those who 'thought like a lawyer' were permitted to think about law.[23] Round themselves, by design or accident, academic lawyers cast a *cordon sanitaire* so that they were protected from questions, methods, concepts and qualifications that they deemed alien to their lives.[24] There were, of course, exceptions; academics in law schools who made a contribution to, and found a place in, the wider academic community. Goodhart, for example, provided an introduction to one of Gluckman's anthropological accounts of the Lozi.[25] Hart was a figure, although not a dominant figure, in the Oxford philosophical circles of his time.[26] Yet these individuals and others like them were not characteristic of an academic tribe that was, at this time, too scattered and unsure of itself even to be a tribe.[27]

What academics did in law schools 40 years ago is slightly mysterious. Comparatively few produced a body of published work that has proved to be of lasting consequence.[28] The problem was not that there was no place in which academics could publish articles. The *Law Quarterly Review* was begun in 1885, the *Juridical Review* only a few years later in 1889. The *Conveyancer* and the *Northern Ireland Legal*

[23] In attributing this character to doctrinal law the phrase 'as it was then practised' is important. First, the dominance of its practice at this time is important. Virtually all writing outside the fields of legal history and jurisprudence was doctrinal and even in these fields of study there were often clear links with doctrinal writing. The law school was, in a decidedly British fashion, vigorously monoglot. Secondly, doctrinal writing at this time had a measure of purity that is far less often found today. Non-doctrinal terminology and literature leaks in to a wide range of doctrinal writing in the present day. Both these points can be seen when comparing the contents of a journal such as the *Law Quarterly Review* during the early years of the 1960s and the last few years of the 1990s.

[24] Nor should one ignore the inhibiting effects of a transport system and a communications industry that was primitive by modern standards.

[25] M Gluckman, *The Judicial Process Among the Barotse of Northern Rhodesia* (Manchester, Manchester University Press, 1955).

[26] There are brief references to Hart in both Rogers' biography of AJ Ayer and Ignatieff's biography of Isaiah Berlin (Rogers, above n 22, at 256; M Ignatieff, *Isaiah Berlin: A Life* (London, Chatto and Windus, 1998) 131, 172, 224, 225, 249, 260 and 272).

[27] The description of different academic cultures as being tribal in nature is usually associated with Becher and the first edition of *Academic Tribes and Territories* but, as he himself notes, this use of the term tribe predates his work by many years (Becher, above n 17, at 22–24; see also Becher and Trowler, above n 18, at 44–47).

[28] Articles which testify to the converse judgement are manifold in number. Deferential statements about the quality of scholarship of previous generations are common. This view, however, is erroneous. The error probably occurs because of an exaggerated sense of courtesy and because the authors concerned choose to recall the noise made by a few rather than the silence of the many. (See, eg, E Griswold, 'The Community of Legal Scholarship' (1965) 81 *Law Quarterly Review* 42).

Quarterly were both first published in 1936 and the first issue of the *Modern Law Review* was in 1937. Still more journals began in the 1950s. However, examination of the contents pages of these journals indicates that many legal academics rarely if ever contributed to them. Some academics wrote for practitioner journals. Indeed, in 1965, Wortley, then the President of the Society of Public Teachers of Law, enjoined academics to write that which was 'saleable.'[29] Yet, even here in the back issues of practitioner journals, there is no rich stream of lost literature to be found. Moreover, as important as the quantity of writing done (or lack thereof) is the form that it took when it was done. Its aim was sometimes more pedagogic than scholarly. In the first issue of the *Conveyancer* an editorial note observed 'in these articles an attempt will be made to examine the whole of the law so as to enable the practitioner to deal adequately with any problem by reference to the volume concerned.'[30] Whatever its merits, such writing was not intended to be a contribution to any Enlightenment-inspired search for knowledge; instead the intention was the possibly worthy but certainly prosaic education of the legal profession. In books the dominant, near exclusive, mode of production at this time was the student or practitioner text with few monographs being published. Each new issue of such texts emphasised the ephemeral quality of that which had been and was being done within the law school, with the new edition always depriving the old of most of its value. Whilst other parts of the university searched for permanence or progress in their writing the law school sought to paint each fleeting moment of Heracleitus' river. Textbooks were palimpsests and slates ready for the rewriting. Present-day academic lawyers have no need to kill their forbearers as usually happens when one generation of academics succeeds another.[31] In terms of lasting research and scholarship they mostly chose an early suicide, if,

[29] B Wortley, 'Some Reflections on Legal Research After Thirty Years' (1965) 8 *Journal of the Society of Public Teachers of Law* 249 at 258–59. Perhaps he considered his own book *Jurisprudence*, which opens with an account of the relationship between anarchism and legal philosophy, to be 'saleable' because it could be marketed as a student text (B Wortley, *Jurisprudence* (Manchester, Manchester University Press, 1967).

[30] (1936) *Conveyancer* 2.

[31] Bloom's 'anxiety of influence' does not just affect poets (H Bloom, *The Anxiety of Influence* (Oxford, Oxford University Press, 1973). '[E]ach new generation [of intellectuals] . . . must murder their intellectual fathers in order to obtain the licence to practise the profession that they learnt from them.' (G Rose, *Mourning Becomes the Law* (Cambridge, Cambridge University Press, 1996) 1.

indeed, they ever lived at all.[32] In this respect it is significant that advances in legal scholarship in the United Kingdom have largely involved distancing oneself from an approach to the study of law, doctrinalism, rather than from the work of specific previous writers.

Forty years on sees a very different picture. In 1995 there were 2,440 full-time law academics.[33] In 2000 there were 85 British university law schools.[34] In the 2001 Research Assessment Exercise 1,451 academic lawyers put forward their published work for assessment.[35] Journals grow in number each year. Where once there were only two or three law publishers now small herds graze. Textbooks continue to be written but now they are published alongside numerous monographs and collections of essays. Indeed, although textbooks are still produced (and in copious quantities) their place in the hierarchy of scholarship and research has at the very least been challenged, and arguably has been supplanted, by the monograph.[36] Law schools have seen the rise of a host of movements such as socio-legal studies, sociology of law, economics and law, feminism, Critical Legal Studies, queer theory and

[32] It might be that these shadowy figures were engaged in innovative teaching practices or the academic politics that attends the founding of new departments. Since we lack any detailed history of British university law departments much is unclear. Even if this is so the points above are not wholly or even largely answered. Those founding new law departments in the present day or those engaged in new teaching initiatives will win few plaudits if they do so wholly at the expense of the pursuit of research and scholarship. A more likely explanation for the absence of a lasting literature from this period may lie in Wilson's comment that 'research in the majority of provincial universities is confined to private research by members of staff' with staff complaining that teaching and administrative loads meant that they could only carry out research during vacation time (Wilson, above n 19, at 23 and 34). The acceptability of this excuse has to be assessed in the light of the fact that '[in] the older provincial universities. . .a number of members of staff are allowed to combine a limited amount of private practice with their teaching commitments' (Wilson, above n 19, at 31–32). Time it seems could be found for practice but not for research.

[33] P Harris and M Jones, 'A Survey of Law Schools in the United Kingdom, 1996' (1997) 31 *The Law Teacher* 38 at 82.

[34] A Bradney and F Cownie, 'British University Law School in the Twenty-First Century' in D Hayton *Law's Futures* (Oxford, Hart Publishing, 2000) 1–2.

[35] http://www.rae.ac.uk. The figure for the previous 1996 exercise was 1,295 (P Birks, 'The Academic and the Practioner' (1998) 18 *Legal Studies* 397 at 406). Both these figures record those lawyers who were assessed by the RAE's law panel. A small number of law academics appear to have been put forward to be assessed by other subject panels in the 1996 exercise (D Vick, A Murray, G Little and K Campbell, 'The Perceptions of Academic Lawyers Concerning the Effects of the United Kingdom's Research Assessment Exercise' (1998) 25 *Journal of Law and Society* 536 at 545). Notwithstanding the very limited numbers involved, the fact that they exist at all does illustrate a striking cultural shift from the intellectual isolation that once characterised law schools.

[36] Vick, Murray, Little and Campbell, above n 35, at 557.

law and literature; movements whose raison d'être has been, in part, to argue that university law schools should not live in an atmosphere that is intellectually isolated from other parts of the university.[37] Virtually every department in the social sciences and the humanities has been raided or visited by those in law schools.[38] Once a dominant paradigm controlled what questions could be asked and what arguments might be put in the law school. Now everything is open to challenge. Some journals have expanded their remit so as to include new kinds of scholarship; others have been started precisely because of these new forms of scholarship.[39]

In this, the early years of the twenty-first century, it can no longer be argued that changes and challenges to traditional practices come only from the margins of the law school. In the contemporary era whole departments are given over to modes of scholarship that would have been unthinkable in a law school in 1960. Some individuals have made their personal reputations, attaining whatever the university has to

[37] The existence of these different movements results in what is sometimes creative tension and sometimes open warfare. Thus, for example, Kramer, in a review of Marmor's *Law and Interpretation* has written that '[f]addish creeds such as Critical Race Theory have yielded little apart from confusion and intellectual flabbiness' ((1998) 57 *Cambridge Law Journal* 612) and later in the same review observed that 'proponents of postmodernist mumbo jumbo and Critical Race claptrap will not read the book and would not be able to understand it if they read it' (at 614). In response to this Goodrich has written about Kramer 'dismissing all legal radicalism with pompous and laconic comments' (P Goodrich, 'The Critic's Love of Law: Intimate Observations on an Insular Jurisdiction' (1999) 10 *Law and Critique* 343 at 353) and described Kramer's style as being 'acerbic and racist' (Goodrich *ibid*). Discord can be destructive (as when, for example, it results in divisions within and between law schools which allow bodies and individuals external to the law school or even the university to more easily impose controls on the law school) but it is also evidence of intellectual energy and excitement; at the very least it demonstrates the fact that people care about such matters enough to assert and defend their views. Equally, '[i]ntellectual communities are held together generally by their disagreements as well as their agreements' (W Phillips, *A Partisan View* (New York, Stein and Day, 1983) 55).

[38] The distinction between 'raided and visited' is important because of the arguments about whether law schools have used or abused the disciplines, methods and concepts that they have found elsewhere in the university (see, eg, R Cotterrell, 'Why Must Legal Ideas be Interpreted Sociologically?' (1998) 25 *Journal of Law and Society* 171; D Nelken, 'Blinding Insights? The Limits of a Reflexive Sociology of Law' (1998) 25 *Journal of Law and Society* 403 and M Travers, 'Putting Sociology Back into the Sociology of Law' (1993) 20 *Journal of Law and Society* 438). Equally important are the arguments about whether we ever do anything else other than abuse other people's work. Thus, for example, Calvino, in an essay on Northrop Fry's *Anatomy of Criticism*, writes 'my argument will be entirely subjective, since everyone mines every book for the things that are useful to him' (I Calvino, *The Uses of Literature* (San Diego, Harvest/HBJ, 1986) 50).

[39] New examples of this kind of journal continue to arise on a regular basis (see, eg, *Legal Ethics*, first published in 1998, or *Entertainment Law*, first published in 2002).

offer by way of prestige and power, by debunking or ignoring that which traditionally was thought to be the height of legal scholarship. Professional associations have either arisen in response to this new order or have had to change their constitutions and their committees to reflect present realities. The academic legal community's assessment of its own diversity is reflected in the membership and the judgements of recent RAE panels.

None of the above is to argue, with Yeats, that all is 'changed, changed utterly.' Change there has been but not an utter change. Much that was in the old order is still to be found in the new dispensation. A few departments and a greater proportion of individuals in the present day would fit easily into the ways of 1960; nonetheless, many departments and great numbers of individual academics would find the culture of the 1960 law school a strange and dispiriting experience. Power now is contested and fragmented. Some individuals will rightly feel their careers and reputations have been affected by having the 'wrong' research interests or theoretical preferences.[40] But such individuals will also be able to see others with the same interests or preferences who have progressed despite or because of those interests or preferences. And what might be the 'wrong' interest or preference at the beginning of the twenty-first century could be precisely that which was dominant as an interest or preference in 1960. In the present intellectual ferment, what is wrong and what is right has become something that is constantly a matter of speculation and assessment in ever-changing clusters of groups which circle round and within law schools.

That the law school now takes part in Steiner's 'carnival of understanding and judgement' has been an established fact for some years[41]; what is still in the process of adding its contribution to the excitement of the twenty-first century law school are the new resources of the IT era.[42] In 1960 research meant the university library's card index

[40] And some will blame their failure on their interests or their preferences when the fault is their application, their ability or their luck.

[41] G Steiner, Errata: An Examined Life (London, Faber, 1997) 20.

[42] See, eg, P Alldridge and A Mumford, 'Gazing into the Future through a VDU: Communications, Information Technology, and Law Teaching' (1998) 25 *Journal of Law and Society* 116; R Widdison, 'Computerised Legal Education: What's in Store?' (1999) 3 *Journal of Information, Law and Technology* and G Greenleaf *et al*, 'Solving the Problems of Finding Law in the Web: World Law and DIAL' (2000) 1 *Journal of Information, Law and Technology* http://elj.warwick.ac.uk/jilt/. For an examination of the impact of IT on lawyers and courts, which will in turn have an impact upon the academy, see R Susskind, *The Future of Law* (Oxford, Clarendon Press, 1996) and R Susskind, *Transforming the Law* (Oxford, Oxford University Press, 1996).

file.[43] In addition *Current Law* noted some but not all new publications according to a system wholly understood only by those who edited the series. For those interested in cases and judgments various citators would assist in tracking down new materials. Books and articles were few in number and even the vast sea of judgments handed down by the higher courts was only partially recorded in the published law reports. Sources of information were poor, even in the very best libraries, and ways of accessing the information were slow, partial and inaccurate. That any real research was done at this time is a testimony to the indefatigable energy of those who did so. Now the very reverse is true. Each week more information is made available and mechanisms for searching for the information become both more accurate and easier to use. In 1960, in the unlikely event that it had been thought profitable to research the judicial career of a particular senior judge, collating the primary material for the study would have required an exhausting search of published law reports together with an examination of unreported cases in something like the Bar Library. Today, obtaining the same primary material takes the time required to write the name of the judge into the LEXIS database and then to print out the list of cases thus obtained.[44] Government departments increasingly open their records via the Web, putting on to their home pages not only documents previously published as hard copy but material that, in 1960, would have been for internal use or that could have been obtained only by special consultation. University libraries can be searched all over the world and, increasingly, journals are available in electronic form. Because of IT, even the poorest university library in 2001 offers better resources than the best did in 1960.[45] Even the study in the individual academic's house can have better resources than the university library of 1960, once it is linked to the Web.[46]

[43] These listed material with varying degrees of sophistication. See the discussion on cataloguing at the Fifty-Third Annual Meeting of the American Association of Law Librarians (1960) 53 *Law Library Journal* 312–26 and P Ward, 'Annotation in Public Library Catalogues: British Practice and Policies' (1962) *Library Association Record* 208.

[44] LEXIS is, of course, fallible, not always containing on its database every case that its contents pages say should be recorded, but the fallibility of LEXIS is probably no more and perhaps is less than that of the individual researcher attempting the same task manually in 1960.

[45] It is not just in IT that the law school's resources have improved. For a description of university law libray holdings in 1957 see J Montrose, 'University Law Libraries' (1957) *Journal of the Society of Public Teachers of Law* 1.

[46] Wealth, however, is both an absolute and a relative matter. Most law school libraries are now wealthier in their resources than any library was in 1960. Some,

Comparing teaching in university law schools in 1960 and teaching in contemporary university law schools is more difficult than comparing research. Research is pre-eminently a public matter. British law schools in 1960 may have contained a series of scholars and researchers who, worse even than Weber, laboured silently away, without their work ever being published in even posthumous form.[47] Such a situation, however, seems unlikely; with research silence almost always indicates absence. By contrast teaching has been, and still is, quintessentially a private matter. Teaching is something that lies almost in liberalism's domain of the private and the intimate; that which I do in my office is a matter for me and my students and for no other. The fact of the acceptance of the notion of privacy in teaching practices makes analysis difficult. What precisely was being done with, or to, students in British university law schools in 1960 is difficult to ascertain. Yet it seems clear that whatever was being done was, in broad terms, the same in most offices, most lecture rooms and most departments throughout the various British university law schools of the time. The standard and almost invariable mixture was one of tutorials, lectures and unseen, written examinations.[48] One cannot gainsay an assertion that academics in 1960 were devoted and diligent teachers; one cannot even prove that they were not more devoted and diligent teachers than are the academics of the present day; one can, however, observe that the devotion and the diligence, if it did exist, produced uniformity. A very different picture now obtains.

Just as plurality and variation, or even division and discord, describe the range of research practices in university law schools in the contemporary era so difference describes teaching practices. Tutorials, lectures and unseen examinations still provide a core around which other methods of learning and teaching revolve but other forms of teaching are now a forceful part of the law school.[49] In part these changes reflect

nevertheless, are wealthier than others in their access to resources that exist at present and, sometimes, the disparity in access is such as to make some libraries that exist now poor when compared with their fellows.

[47] Weber's scholarly reputation largely rests on material published after his death (E Shils (ed), Max Weber on Universities (Chicago and London, University of Chicago Press, 1974) 1).

[48] In his 1966 survey Wilson writes of 'a certain uniformity of practice' (Wilson, above n 19, at 47).

[49] Thus, for example, a 1999 survey of family law teaching concluded that '[t]here was no uniformity of teaching methodology' (F Burton, N Clement, K Standly and C Williams, *Teaching Family Law* (Warwick, National Centre for Legal Education, 1999) 2. See further *ibid* 2–6).

the evolution of the law school and the university over the decades. Teaching in a law school of under 100 students with a staff-student ratio of 1:11.4 is different from teaching in a law school of over 700 students with a staff-student ratio of 1:21.3.[50] Nevertheless, whatever the reason for changes in teaching practices, changes have occurred. Here again, as in the case of research, part of the character of this change has been an increased awareness within the law school of things that are being, and long have been done, in other departments within the university. Things such as take-away examination papers and CAL programmes are not new within the university but they are comparatively new to law schools. The literature that describes and advocates them sometimes draws on the experience of the wider university.[51] Moreover, the literature on teaching in law schools that, in 1960, was occasional and anecdotal has becoming increasingly vibrant and scholarly in the last few years.[52] Equally, just as the law school has seen a variety of contradictory movements in research so the literature on teaching and learning has seen reliance on a range of different and frequently contradictory methods and concepts. For those who would seek a resolution of thought in consensus, the literature on teaching in law schools offers no more hope than the literature on research and scholarship but for those who seek stimulation and sustenance the literature on teaching is, increasingly, as rich as the literature on research.

That there is a greater production within university law departments and greater resources available to them now than there was in 1960 does not, however, necessarily justify the ascription to departments of either the 'excitement' alleged in the title of this chapter or

[50] These figures represent the greatest disparities in Wilson's first and third surveys of university legal education (Wilson, above n 19, at 18 and 27; J Wilson, 'A Third Survey of University Legal Education in the United Kingdom' (1993) 13 *Legal Studies* 143 at 147 and 158). Harris and Jones' later 1996 survey notes that student numbers had grown by 50 per cent between the time of their survey and the previous Wilson survey whilst staff numbers had only grown by 3 per cent (P Harris and M Jones, 'A Survey of Law Schools in the United Kingdom' (1997) 31 *The Law Teacher* 38 at 82). A consequent increase in the size of law schools and a further deterioration in staff-student ratios must therefore have occurred although Harris and Jones give no figures on these points. Some would argue that the nature of the student body has also changed in important ways necessitating a change in teaching practices (see, eg, M Jeeves and A Boon, 'The Common Law in Action Simulation: Reversing the Burden of Proof in Skills Education?' (1990) *The Law Teacher* Special Issue 82). The degree to which such changes have occurred, when the law schools are taken as a whole, can, however, be exaggerated (Torremans, above n 14, at 295–96).

[51] See, eg, M Young, 'Constructing CAL Tutorials' (1996) 22 *The Law Teacher* 145.

[52] See further A Bradney, 'The Rise and Rise of Legal Education' (1997) 4 *Web Journal of Current Legal Issues* http://webjcli.ncl.ac.uk/

Wordsworth's 'bliss' that began this section. Every factory seeks to get ever-greater production from its workers and sometimes gives them better tools so that they can do this; alienated labour is normally the characterisation of work in such conditions and servitude a better description than either 'excitement' or 'bliss' of the atmosphere in which such increased production is achieved. In the second section of this chapter, and in other chapters later in this book, I will note some of the factors that have led commentators to conclude that the circumstances of universities are more akin to a factory than to anything else, with academics being mere workers on a production line. Yet, whatever the eventual balance between excitement and servitude that is to be drawn, no one could truthfully deny the evidence of elements of excitement that clearly pervades British university law schools in the present day. To insist that the welter of increased activity noted above simply stems from loss of tenure and consequent job insecurity, larger numbers of short-term contracts, greater difficulties in promotion or more successfully obtrusive management pressure, is empirically dubious. Indeed, it is possible to conclude that the existence of adverse changes to academic conditions, when combined with the fact that academic law schools are continuing to grow, attracting ever-greater numbers of staff with ever-better qualifications, adds to the argument for the existence of an unparalleled state of excitement within the law school, rather than detracts from it.[53]

In terms of pay there is much less reason to choose academic life than there was in 1960. Average earnings for academic when compared with pay in the manufacturing sector dropped steadily throughout the twentieth century.[54] There is no reason to think that this general trend will stop at any point within the foreseeable future. Salaries in the solicitor's profession, one obvious sector in which those who are legal academics could otherwise find employment, are almost invariably much

[53] A 1995 study found that 22 per cent of the legal academics surveyed had either an MPhil or a PhD in law whilst 4 per cent had an MPhil or a PhD in subject other than law; 35 per cent had a taught postgraduate degree in law and 6 per cent had a taught postgraduate degree in a subject other than law (P Leighton, T Mortimer and N Whatley, *Today's Law Teachers: Lawyers or Academics?* (London, Cavendish Publishing, 1995) 18). By comparison Wilson's 1966 survey found that only 17 per cent of academics at this time had a PhD (Wilson, above n 19, at p 29).

[54] A Halsey, *Decline of Donnish Dominion* (Oxford, Clarendon Press, 1992) 13. See also D Farnham 'University Teachers' Pay' (1987) *Higher Education Review* 35 and C Gradden, "Old" University Academic Staff Salary Movements since 1949 (1998) 52 *Higher Education Quarterly* 394.

higher than the academic salaries.[55] Moreover, work within the solicitor's profession has become increasingly varied, meaning that different parts of the profession, or even different parts of individual firms, are suitable for people with talents and interests that are quite diverse from each other.[56] Plainly many, perhaps most, academics could have found careers within this sector. Others could have taken the intelligence, education, initiative and energy that they will have to display in their academic careers into a large number of forms of employment.[57] People are choosing to become academics in law schools and choosing to stay academics in law schools, notwithstanding ever-poorer pay and deteriorating work conditions.[58] Either they are doing so because they fail to realise the worsening material conditions connected with the job, because (rightly or wrongly) they think that they cannot get other forms of employment or because they find the job attractive. The first two reasons may describe the motivation of a small number of academics.[59] It is implausible, because of the education and intelligence of those involved, to suggest that it explains the motivation of the major-

[55] One recent survey revealed a London firm that paid its trainee solicitors starting their second year of training at a rate that was higher than the professorial minimum salary. Several other firms paid its second year trainees rates of pay which were comparable with the professorial minimum ('Getting in a State', *The Lawyer*, October 2000).

[56] Thus, eg, Lee found that in the largest law firms, although one managing partner required 'proven business skills' in their employed solicitors, another managing partner 'made it clear that brilliant lawyers with few marketing skills could be accommodated' (R Lee, *Firm Views: Work of and Work in the Largest Law Firms* (London, The Law Society, 1999) 64 and 63). Another example of the variation in work available as a solicitor would be the nature of legal aid work on the one hand and large commercial practices on the other hand (see H Sommerlad and D Wall, *Legally Aided Client: Qualitative Perspectives on Quality and Legal Aid* (London, The Law Society, 1999) and Lee, *ibid.*

[57] A law degree has long been a path to a wide range of careers. In 1966 Wilson noted that 'approximately one out of three university law students has no intention of subsequently pursuing a career in the legal profession' (Wilson, above n 19, at p 55). Today the number of career opportunities is even greater than in the past. For a survey of the opportunities see R Lidwell and R Conway, Survey of 1996 *Law Graduates in Careers other than the Law* (Mancheste, Careers Service Trust, 1999).

[58] This is not to argue that everybody is willing to ignore either conditions of service or pay. In 1989 the Committee of Heads of University Law Schools noted the increased number of people leaving academic life (Committee of Heads of University Law Schools (CHULS), *Academic Staff Recruitment and Retention* (London, Committee of Heads of University Law Schools, 1989). Law schools may not be getting as many applicants for lecturing positions as they would like and, in some instances, they may not be getting applications from the kind of people that they would wish to apply. Here, however, I am concerned with the question what makes anyone decide to become, or to stay, an academic in a law school when a crudely materialistic analysis would indicate that they would be better off elsewhere.

[59] Cownie's study of legal academics suggests that this is so (Cownie, above n 5).

ity. Something must be exciting interest; something must be providing a positive reason to join and to stay in university law schools; I would argue that it is that energy and sense of intellectual vibrancy that I have described above.[60]

'DISILLUSIONS AS NEVER TOLD IN THE OLD DAYS'

Many academics in British university law schools, on reading the first section of this chapter, will feel that it does not sit easily with their own intuitive assessment of their or their colleagues lives. Here personal experience and the empirical data on the present state of law schools taken as a whole seems oddly contradictory. When, in an editorial in the *SPTL Reporter*, I wrote that '[t]he phrase "university law school" calls to mind not words such as "opportunity" or "progress" but phrases such as "escape-committee" and "would the last one to leave please turn off the lights?"' comments and responses that I received suggested that I had struck a common chord amongst my colleagues.[61] Excitement there may be in the law school but there is also something else. What that thing is not hard to identify.

In May 2000 Gordon Brown, in time he snatched from his job as Chancellor of the Exchequer, determined that admission tutors at Oxford University had been wrong in their decision not to admit Laura Spence onto a degree course in medicine. The decision, he was reported as saying, was 'scandalous.'[62] Brown's view that he was well qualified to second-guess professional academic decisions is not something that is unique to him. It is an attitude now commonly found in British society. In a letter to *The Times* of 15 August 2000 a parent complained

[60] This is not to ignore the fact that some people are leaving the academic profession because of concerns about both pay rates and general conditions of service (see CHULS, above n 58, at pp 4–9 and Cownie, above n 5).

[61] T Bradney, 'The Future of Law Schools' (1998) 16 *SPTL Reporter* 1.

[62] *The Times*, 26th May 2000. His comment received the 'full endorsement' of the Prime Minister. In the course of preparing a subsequent report on access to higher education the Select Committee on Education and Employment decided not to examine this case. They did, however, note the Chancellor's remarks and asserted that they had not been 'unhelpful' (Select Committee on Education and Employment, *Higher Education: Access* (HCP 205, 2001, para 11). However it should be noted that this observation represented only the majority Labour view on Committee. A minority, including one Labour member, sought to include observations that were both more critical of the Chancellor's remarks and more supportive of Oxford University's admissions process (Select Committee on Education and Employment, *ibid*, at op cit pp lxiv–lxv). Contempt for universities and those working in universities is common but not universal.

that 'the local JobsCentre . . . had difficulty identifying the "skills" which my daughter would transfer [from her 'redbrick university' degree in French] to the workplace.'[63] This, the parent thought, needed 'closer scrutiny.' Such examples can be multiplied many times and are part of the everyday experience of most academics. Academics in 1960 would probably have been more than mildly surprised to find that a Chancellor of the Exchequer would think himself qualified to be an admissions tutor. They would probably have been more amused than surprised at the notion that the Employment Exchange, as it then was, should be regarded as an arbiter of the quality of a university degree.[64] However, in the twenty-first century, in the case of universities, 'new public management' sometimes seems to mean not:

> the importation of private business systems and techniques into public services . . . [and] a set of ideas and values justifying a central role for managers and management within organizations and society[65]

but, rather, management of the universities, at the most micro of levels, by the public, any member of the public, at any time.[66] Plumbers

[63] What is important here is both the fact that the writer thought it a sign of intelligence to put forward the view asserted and that *The Times* thought it worthwhile to publish such comments: that people believe in Father Christmas is not interesting, that they should write to *The Times* and tell the world about their thoughts and that *The Times* would publish these thoughts would be worthwhile considering. Some parents in 1960 might have held views similar to those expressed in the letter quoted but these views were not part of the public discourse on higher education.

[64] They would certainly have seen that, even on the crassest model of utility, a JobsCentre that could not identify the employment skills of a graduate in modern languages in a country that was, on the one hand notorious for its lack of ability at languages and, on the other hand, reliant for its prosperity on its position in the international economy, needed to reconsider the way in which it assessed the employability of its customers. They would probably have also seen that a parent who assessed their daughter's educational achievements on the basis of the views of their local JobsCentre needed extensive tutoring in the meaning of the word 'parent.'

[65] D Farnham and S Horton, 'Public Service Mangerialism: A Review and Evaluation' in D Farnham and S Horton (eds), 'Managing the New Public Services' (London, Macmillan, 1996) 260.

[66] The notion of new public management is both complex and contradictory. See C Hood, 'A Public Management for All Seasons?' (1991) 69 *Public Administration* 3 at 4–5 and Farnham and Horton, above n 65, for attempts to list the essential conceptual features on the notion of new public management. See E Ferlie, L Ashburner, L Fitzgerald, and A Pettigrew, *The New Public Management in Action* (Oxford, Oxford University Press, 1996) 10–15 for an attempt to describe four competing models of new public management. Plainly the notion of new public management has some applicability to changes within the university sector over the last two decades. How applicable the concept is and how effective these changes have been is a matter of controversy (see Ferlie, Ashburner, Fitzgerald and Pettigrew, *ibid*, at 65–66 and Farnham and Horton, above n 65, at 266).

have their particular calling, their own field of expertise, but academics can be second-guessed by their newsagents or their butchers. An individual might query a doctor's clinical judgement by calling for the opinion of another doctor but if an individual doubts an academic opinion they simply substitute their own judgement. In such an atmosphere it is scarcely surprising that some academics feel disenchanted with their vocation. Notions of audit and accountability now find their place alongside and seek to supplant more traditional values of collegiality and autonomy.[67] The general literature on higher education in the United Kingdom is replete with examples of books and articles that address a 'crisis' in the mission of the university. The perceived reasons for this crisis range from questions of resource (or lack of thereof) to arguments about the university's place in the knowledge conditions of a post-modern world.[68] Whatever the reasons for and notwithstanding the possible lack of substance to this 'crisis' one result is that Rose has reported university teachers as being the 15th most stressed occupational group in the United Kingdom out of a total number of 103 occupational groups that he surveyed and had the lowest rating for overall employee well-being.[69]

An atmosphere of audit now pervades higher education. Research is measured by the Research Assessment Exercise; teaching by the Quality Assurance Agency. Universities as individual institutions are assessed by the Funding Councils. Appraisal schemes for individuals, administered on an annual or bi-annual basis, were introduced as a consequence of the pay settlement of 1987.[70] Career barriers, for those fortunate enough to have permanent jobs, exist at the stage of confirmation of probation, progression from lecturer A to lecturer B,

[67] M Power, *The Audit Society* (Oxford, Oxford University Press, 1997) pp 103–4.

[68] A non-exhaustive list of such publications in the year 2000 alone would include R Barnett, *Realizing the University in the Age of Super Complexity* (Buckingham, Society for Research into Higher Education/Open University Press, 2000); P Jarvis, 'The Changing University: Meeting a Need and Needing to Change' (2000) 54 *Higher Education Quarterly* 43; R Barnett, 'Supercomplexity and the Curriculum' (2000) 25 *Studies in Higher Education* 255; P Gumport, 'Academic Restructuring: Organizational Change and Institutional Imperatives' (2000) 39 *Higher Education* 67; C Polster, 'The Future of the Liberal University in the Era of the Global Knowledge Grab' (2000) 39 *Higher Education* 19.

[69] M Rose, *Future Tense . . . Are Growing Occupations More Stressed-out and Depressive?* (Work Centrality and Careers Project, University of Bath (www.bath.ac.uk/~hssmjr) 2001) 31 and 37. See also E Thorsen, 'Stress in Academe: What Bothers Professors' (1996) 31 *Higher Education* 471.

[70] *Times Higher Education Supplement*, 27 November 1987, *Times Higher Education Supplement*, 11 December 1987.

promotion to senior lecturer or reader and finally advancement to a chair.[71] Numerous league tables using different and sometimes competing measures of quality rank both universities and departments.[72] The Quality Assurance Agency judges the law school; so does *The Times* and *The Lawyer*.[73]

Law schools have both suffered from the ills of their parent universities and have had their own particular reasons for feeling a sense of crisis and seeing themselves as being under stress. During the 1980s and 1990s university law schools underwent a string of official and unofficial re-examinations of their role to which they had to respond and the results of which they had to digest.[74] In the end none of these reports sought radically to alter the academic character of the law degree, and thus the law school, that had originally been outlined in the 1971 Ormrod Committee Report.[75] Indeed the final report in this series of inquiries into law schools concluded that 'the degree course [in law] should stand as an independent liberal education in the discipline of law, not tied to any specific vocation,' thus enhancing the autonomy of the law school.[76] Nonetheless this atmosphere of appraisal has caused concern within law schools.[77]

The actual reality of the relationship between the state, society and the universities is a lot more complex than is suggested by the sentiments (deeply felt by many though they are) described in the two paragraphs above. First, such attack as there has been on the university has often couched in the most trivial of terms. Much of the public rhetoric which is to be found in politicians' statements about universities or in

[71] Both Wilson's 1993 survey of law schools and Harris and Jones' 1996 survey reported an increased use of part-time staff by law schools (Wilson, above n 50, at 158; Harris and Jones, above n 50, at 53.

[72] On this phenomenon see M Tight, 'Do League Tables Contribute to the Development of a Quality Culture? Football and Higher Education Compared' (2000) 54 *Higher Education Quarterly* 22 and R Tomlin, 'Research League Tables: Is There a Better Way?' (1998) 52 *Higher Education Quarterly* 204.

[73] '*Now*, league tables are a prominent feature of the higher education scene' Select Committee on Education and Employment, above n 62, at para 1.

[74] *The Royal Commission on Legal Services* (Cmnd 7648, 1979); *A Time for Change: The Marre Committee* (London, General Council of the Bar/The Law Society, 1988) and The Lord Chancellor's Advisory Committee on Legal Education (ACLEC), *First Report on Legal Education and Conduct* (London, ACLEC, 1996).

[75] *Report of the Committee on Legal Education: The Ormrod Committee* (Cmnd 4595, 1971).

[76] ACLEC, above n 74, at para 4.6.

[77] See, eg, P McAuslan, 'The Coming Crisis in Legal Education' (1989) 16 *Journal of Law and Society* 310.

media analyses of higher education is little more than the repetition of a mantra about the need for there to be accountability in the spending of taxpayer's money. Martin Amis correctly suggests that, in the modern era, the invocation of the phrase 'taxpayer's money' is something that is commonly regarded as exempting people from the necessity of exhibiting signs of sanity in their arguments.[78] In political and media circles there has been little if any attempt to specify what is meant by accountability in the context of universities, little evidence of any understanding of the nature of academic culture, little awareness of the way in which new ideas and new learning are created and less interest in how various fanciful schemes for accountability will affect all these matters. In Chapter 7 below I will argue that there are considerable conceptual difficulties and contradictions in ideas like accountability and audit and that, in so far as these ideas mean anything, there are deep-rooted reasons why universities should not be, and indeed cannot be, accountable, in any detailed or micro sense, to anybody but themselves. Once one dispenses with the shallow terminology that is commonly used when discussing these matters it becomes clear that basic ontological and cultural realities will always tend to protect the university from the more obtrusive forms of external intervention.[79] Moreover, in Chapter 8 below I will argue that law schools have reacted to new notions of audit and accountability in a subtle and sophisticated fashion that has largely allowed them to keep, or even gain greater, control of their own agendas in both teaching and research. Further, neither all politicians nor all of the media holds to a monolithic belief that seeks to assert external control over the university and direct it to short-term utilitarian ends. The introduction of section 202, the academic freedom clause, into the Education Reform Act 1988, following backbench pressure in the House of Lords, testifies to the power of academics within at least one House in Parliament.[80] Even the media views universities in contradictory ways. The same issue of *The Times* that published the

[78] M Amis, *Experience* (London, Jonathan Cape, 2000) 82. Amis is wrong to say that this is a failure of intellect that just applies to men. After all, '[p]rivatization [a way of avoiding paying out "taxpayer's money"] is generally regarded as *the* textbook case of Thatcherite policy' (S Letwin, *The Anatomy of Thatcherism* (London, Fontana, 1992) 97.

[79] Which is not to say that these realities will protect them from the effects of the bureaucracy inherent in attempts to intervene.

[80] N Harris, *Law and Education: Regulation, Consumerism and the Education System* (Sweet and Maxwell, London, 1993) 201; N Saunders, 'The Human Rights Act 1998: Research, Freedom of Speech and Academic Freedom' (1999) 11 *Education and the Law*, 187 at 192.

letter suggesting that a JobsCentre should determine the worth of university degrees published an article on the facing page that took as its central theme the notion that '[u]niversities exist to preserve the principle that knowledge is worth pursuing for its own sake, and not just as a means to a commercial end.'[81] Nevertheless, despite these caveats that suggest that the complete picture is more complex, the first paragraphs of this section of the chapter capture some part of the spirit of British universities at the beginning of the twenty-first century. The value of universities is consistently not so much questioned as dismissed and those in universities struggle to find a way to challenge that dismissal. University law schools are, in this respect, in no worse a position than other university departments. They are, however, in some respects in no better a position.

RESISTANCE TO POWER[82]

Both the excitement and the malaise described in the first two section of this chapter need to be put into a theoretical context in order to understand them. Becher and Kogan offer one possible model. They have argued that four different interests compete for control over higher education.

> One group of norms is professional and derives from academic norms and aspirations. Another is governmental and is concerned with the demands of the state, which can range in different times from those of theocracy to those of the economy. A third is that of the market as it seeks particular skills in the workforce and particular forms of knowledge for conversion into wealth production. And, finally, there is that of public and social utility at large, whose interests may lie both in increased educational opportunities and in the maintenance and enhancement of a civilised society.[83]

Using this model one could argue that British university law schools are currently places which exhibit a particularly high degree of academic self-confidence but which find themselves in conflict with both

[81] M Grove, 'Courses that Make us Poorer by Degrees', *The Times*, 15 August 2000. Fiona Cownie drew my attention to the physical opposition of these two pieces.

[82] 'Men at some time are masters of their fates:
The fault, dear Brutus, is not in our stars,
But in ourselves, that we are underlings'
says Cassius to Brutus in *Julius Caesar*.

[83] T Becher and M Kogan, 'Process and Structure in Higher Education' (London, Routledge, 1992) 177.

governmental and market pressures which push them towards a narrower compass of activity than that that they actually wish to engage in. This model is helpful because it explains at least some aspects of the contradictions in the culture of the modern law school and because it also gives an explanation for the historical change in this culture; professional, academic norms that were once weak or even absent from the law school have now become strong and even dominant. But the model is better at explaining changes and contradictions in the direction and focus of the law school than it is at analysing academic lives. In order to understand changes to the latter it is necessary to look at other models.

Elsewhere it has been argued that Foucault's notion of disciplinary technology and:

> the panoptican prison provides a paradigm for understanding not only the processes by which higher education is being restructured, managed and controlled . . .[but also] the rationalist epistemology that underlies government notions of 'administrative efficiency' and 'good' management.[84]

In *Discipline and Punish*, in discussing how he intends to describe the historical move to a disciplinary society, Foucault writes:

> I simply intend to map on a series of examples some of the essential techniques that most easily spread from. . .[one disciplinary institution to another]. These were always meticulous, often minute, techniques, but they had their importance: because they defined a certain mode of detailed political investment of the body, a 'new micro-physics' of power; and because since the seventeenth century, they had constantly reached out to ever broader domains, as if they tended to cover the entire social body. Small acts of cunning endowed with a great power of diffusion, subtle arrangements, apparently innocent, but profoundly suspicious, mechanisms that obeyed economies too shameful to be acknowledged, or pursued petty forms of coercion.[85]

It takes no great imagination to see how the seemingly major and the seemingly minor changes to academic life in recent decades find their place in the description of the 'meticulous, often minute, techniques' of a disciplinary society. The Research Assessment Exercise and the Quality Assurance Agency take their place alongside diaries of attendance at staff development sessions, statements of 'best practice' in

[84] C Shore and S Roberts, 'Higher Education and the Panopticon Paradigm: Quality Assessment as "Disciplinary Technology"' (1975) 27 *Higher Education Review* 8.

[85] M Foucault, *Discipline and Punish* (Harmondsworth, Penguin Books, 1975) 139.

teaching or student management and weekly time-sheets filled in because of Treasury demands. Teaching and even research is routinised and homogenised. Every year during appraisal most academic workers now acknowledge their failure to realise the full potential of their productive capacity in a ritual which only avoids being a Maoist form of self-denunciation because of the privacy which attends it; this acknowledged failure is a necessary failure because our human capacity is to do ever more; the appraisal thus becomes a statement of perpetual penitence; moreover the failure is acknowledged in the sanctity of the confessional which, because this confessional claims to protect our failure from the gaze of others, thus conceals from us the failure of our colleagues and leaves each individual constantly obsessed with their own self and oblivious to the shortcomings of their fellows.[86]

Foucault argues that, in a disciplinary society:

> [d]isciplinary space tends to be divided into as many sections as there are bodies or elements to be distributed. One must eliminate the effects of imprecise distributions, the uncontrolled disappearance of individuals, their diffuse circulation, their unusable and dangerous coagulation; it was a tactic of anti-desertion, anti-vagabondage, anti-concentration. Its aim was to establish presences and absences, to know where and how to locate individuals, to set up useful communications, to interrupt others, to be able to at each moment to supervise the conduct of each individual, to assess it, to judge it, to calculate its qualities or merits. It was a procedure, therefore, aimed at knowing, mastering and using. Discipline organizes an analytical space.[87]

So we fill in forms to explain absence from our departments, to certify adherence to the formulae of corporate image, to mark our holidays or our illnesses and Heads of Department are instructed in the importance of dress codes for their staff. We join the professional associations we are supposed to join, we publish in the places we are supposed to publish in and each lecture contains the required three

[86] Which is not to say that academics find such interviews unacceptable. One survey of academics in Birmingham University found that 70 per cent agreed that they should have an annual interview with their Head of Department and also noted more general agreement with the idea that academics should be appraised in various different ways (D Rutherford, 'Performance Appraisal: A Survey of Academic Opinion' (1988) 13 *Studies in Higher Education* 89 at 95). As Foucault observes in the panopticon each individual interiorises the jailor's gaze and becomes their own overseer (M Foucault, *Power?Knowledge* (New York, Harvester Wheatsheaf, 1980) p 155). Sheep agree to be shorn.

[87] Foucault, above n 85, at 143.

'PowerPoint' slides.[88] It would be easy to fill a book with the petty inanities of modern academic life, prettily connecting them with Foucault's structures.

But to do so, or, rather, to do so alone, would be false.

Foucault did not just write about discipline and power; he also wrote about resistance to discipline and resistance to power:

> [R]esistances to the Panopticon will have to be analysed in tactical and strategic terms, positing that each offensive from one side serves as leverage for a counter-offensive from the other. The analysis of power-mechanisms has no built-in tendency to show power as being at once anonymous and always victorious.[89]

The fact of resistance should not lead to an underestimation of power.[90] But resistance has to be attended to.

> Foucault holds power needs resistance as one of its fundamental conditions of operation. It is through the articulation of points of resistance that power spreads through the social field. But it is also, of course, through resistance that power is disrupted. Resistance is both an element of the functioning of power and a source of its perpetual disorder.[91]

[88] It would be invidious to name the actual law departments that pursue these policies. It is not this book's role to provide an exposé of the malpractices of individual law schools. Every law school I am aware of has faults of the kind noted in the main text. Each example in the text is taken from practices that have been reliably reported to me. Some practices are prevalent through the system. Thus, for example, there is a widespread perception amongst legal academics that there are journals that carry greater weight with RAE panels and some academics report pressure from within their departments to publish in those journals (see, eg, D Wick, A Murray, G little and K Campbell, 'The Perceptions of Academic Lawyers Concerning the Effects of the United Kingdom's Research Assessment Exercise' (1998) 25 *Journal of Law and Society* 536). Other practices are local. My university does not require me to use PowerPoint slides in my lectures. I am aware of one university law school where this is a requirement. The fact that the normal rule in this law school can be waived provided that permission in writing is obtained from central university authorities makes the matter worse.

[89] Foucault, above n 85, at 163.

[90] As the index to Dreyfus and Rabinow's book *Michel Foucault: Beyond Structuralism and Hermeneutics* says under 'resistance' '*See also* Power' (H Dreyfus and P Rabinow *Michel Foucault: Beyond Structuralism and Hermeneutics* (Hemel Hempstead, Harvester Press, 1982) 230). One is the other.

[91] Dreyfus and Rabinow, above n 90, at 147. Nevertheless, despite Foucault's acknowledgement of resistance, his view is 'an essentially dominatory model of power' (L McKay, *Foucault: A Critical Introduction* (Cambridge, Polity Press, 1994) 100); as such it is extremely contentious with many arguing that Foucault underestimates the importance of resistance (see, eg, A Giddens, *The Constitution of Society: Outline of the Theory of Structuration* (Cambridge, Polity Press, 1984) 153–55).

In thinking about resistance in the law school we should note that alongside the literature on new public management in universities there is also a literature on the private life of universities.[92] The first literature talks about the ways in which old discourses can be, and should be, overturned in favour of new hierarchies of both power and value. The second literature talks about the way in which management structures are subverted so that existing cultures can be maintained. Baumant may be right to argue that:

> [t]he image of the world daily generated by present-day life concerns is devoid of genuine or assumed solidity and continuity which used to be the trade-mark of modern 'structures.' The dominant sentiment is now the feeling of a new type of uncertainty—not limited to one's own luck and talents, but concerning as well the shape of the world, the right way of living in it, and the criteria by which to judge the rights and wrongs of the way of living. What is also new about the post-modern rendition of uncertainty (by itself not exactly a newcomer in a world with a modern past) is that it is no longer seen as a temporary nuisance, which with due effort may either be mollified or altogether overcome. The post-modern world is bracing itself for life under a condition of uncertainty which is permanent and irreducible.[93]

Nonetheless, there is also a need to avoid 'scepticism . . . pushed to the point where it becomes just a pretext for strategies of moral and political evasion.'[94] We need to remember that though as substantial a figure as Lyotard may have written that '[a] *self* does not amount to much' he almost immediately qualified that by adding '[n]o one, not even the least privileged among us, is ever entirely powerless over the messages that traverse and position him at the post of sender, addressee or referent.'[95] An analysis of the structures and discourses that pervade public life, including the life of the university, is one thing; a determinist belief in the inevitability of the control of the individual and the failure of all attempts to select an identity is another. There is no serious

[92] For an example of the first literature see D Braun, 'New Mangerialism and the Governance of Universities in a Contemporary Perspective' in D Braun and F Merrien (eds), *Towards a New Model of Governance of Universities* (London, Jessica Kingsley, 1997). For an example of the second literature see P Trowler, *Academic Responding to Change: New Higher education Frameworks and Academic Cultures* (Buckingham, Society for Research into Higher Education/Open University Press, 1998).

[93] Z Baumant, *Postmodernity and its Discontents* (London, Polity Press, 1997) 21.

[94] C Norris, *Uncritical Theory: Postmodernism, Intellectuals and the Gulf War* (London, Lawrence and Wishart, 1992) 86.

[95] J Lyotard, *The Postmodern Condition: A Report on Knowledge* (Manchester, Manchester University Press, 1984) 15.

body of literature that will sustain this latter view.[96] Power is there but so is resistance.

Resistance is both a negative and a positive matter. Resistance is about not doing something but it can also be about doing something. The negative is stronger if there is also the positive. The main thrust of the argument in this book is that the law school has become an almost immeasurably better place for both staff and students, irrespective of race, sexuality, class background or gender, over the last few decades.[97] This does not mean that there is not much work to do or that there are not pressures that would reverse this trend. However, if what we have gained is to be protected, and if we are to make further advances in the face of a hostile political climate, then we need an ideal to which to aspire. This book will argue that that ideal should be the concept of the pursuit of a liberal education. In this context a liberal education will be argued to be a statement about how we facilitate student's learning, a view of the nature of academic research and a comment on the relations that should exist both between individual academics and between academics and their university, their departments and the outside world.

A LIBERAL EDUCATION FOR THE TWENTY-FIRST CENTURY

To push to the fore the notion of liberal education at tertiary level in the twenty-first century might be thought to be perverse or even an archaic position. After all the term ' "liberal education" . . . has almost

[96] The new literatures that have entered the law school are sometimes a source of over-exaggerated scepticism about the possibilities of ethical and political action. They can also be a source for the reverse. Thus, eg, see queer theory which argues that 'while law may be repressive in its relationship to lesbians and gay men (or, indeed, to "queers"), law as a locus of struggle can be dynamic, unstable, and unpredictable . . . opportunities for resistance within the legal realm may be opened up through the spaces in the reasoning left by the law and it is through these gaps that the weakness in the system might be subverted and even queered.' (C Stychin, *Law's Desire: Sexuality and the Limits of Justice* (London, Routledge, 1995), 140.

[97] Although this is not to argue that these matters do not continue to have a dramatic effect on people's experience of the law school. See, eg, N Sam Banks, 'Pedagogy and Ideology; Teaching as if it Matters' (1999) 19 *Legal Studies* 445; R Collier, 'Masculinism, Law and Law Teaching' (1991) 19 *International Journal of the Sociology of Law* 427; F Cownie, 'Women in the Law School: Shoals of Fish, Starfish or Fish Out of Water' in P Thomas (ed), *Discriminating Lawyers* (London, Cavendish Publishing, 2000); C Wells, 'Working out Women in Law Schools' (2001) 21 *Legal Studies* 116.

passed out of our language.'[98] One immediate defence for the approach in this book is quite simply to note that British university law schools have long espoused, and still continue to espouse, the tenets of liberal education as the justificatory background for their pedagogic culture.[99] Whatever else we do, historically we, as a tribe, have signed up to the notion of a liberal education.[100] More importantly, however, I will argue that the historical notions of a liberal education, when properly interpreted in the context of the modern era, provide a backdrop which can both protect and enhance the pluralism of the modern university law school; can protect and enhance what we have and what we are doing. The core concept of a liberal education can provide a framework for the practices of a wide variety of different legal academics, including both those who would not accept liberalism as a political or philosophical credo and even those who would question the necessity of being academic in the setting of a university law school.[101] In suggesting this I do not mean to imply that the notion of a liberal education is simply a warming comfort blanket that will provide succour to all who shelter under it. On the contrary I will argue that it is a challenging agenda that will, in some instances, ask more of even those who are already hard-pressed.

These are times of uncertainty; the barbarians are at the gates; of course, they always have been at the gates but, nevertheless, we must still confront them, as universities continually have done, if the gates are not to fall.[102] In Cavafy's poem the prospect of the arrival of the

[98] R Barnett, 'Recovering an Academic Community: Above but Not Beyond' in R Barnett, *Academic Community: Discourse or Discord?* (London, Jessica Knigsley, 1994) 3). To pray in aid Foucault as a justification for the argument seems even stranger. Nevertheless the connection between Foucault and the argument stands.

[99] J Macfarlane, M Jeeves and A Boon, 'Education for Life or for Work?' (1987) 137 *New Law Journal* 835 at p 836; K Hinett, C Maughan, B Lee and K Stanton, 'Managing Change in Assessment and Learning in Legal Education: A Tale of Two Cities' (1999) 33 *The Law Teacher* 135.

[100] Of course the fact that the tribe has taken this position does not mean that all members of it subscribe to the tenets of the theory of liberal education or even that the tribe will continue to take this view in the future.

[101] For the first see, eg, D Kennedy, 'Legal Education as training for a Hierarchy' in D Kairys (ed), *The Politics of Law: A Progressive Critique* (3rd edn, New York, Basic Books, 1998) 61–62. For an arguable example of the second see H Brayne, N Duncan and R Grimes with R Burridge, A Evans, L Lundy and N Tarr 'Clinical Legal Education: Active Learning in your Law School' (London, Blackstone Press Ltd, 1998) 23.

[102] Minogue notes that 'it is clear that the instituting of universities . . . was the result of one of those fitful enthusiasms for education which had already several times appeared in the courts of barbaric Europe' (K Minogue, *The Concept of a University* (London, Weidenfeld and Nicolson, 1978) 11). Protecting and enhancing universities has only

barbarians provided 'some sort of solution' for those in the city. It was only because they fail to materialise, because it was clear that 'there are no Barbarians any more,' that everybody went 'home again so full of thought.' In the poem, with the absence of the Barbarians, there seems to be little prospect of those thoughts ever amounting to much:

> [I]f life in this imaginary city has reached such a level of despair and futility and overrefinement that the advent of barbarians has become an eagerly awaited solution for both rulers and ruled, what hope can possibly be left for the powerless citizens when even this solution fails to materialize?[103]

In the university law school, however, there is more than despair and futility and the barbarians are real.[104] For the universities, the barbarians (those whose view of the university is antithetical to its previous and present function) can serve a purpose by making suggestions about the use of university resources that make us re-interrogate our own conception of the university. Moreover, since the idea of the university is shaped by history and is therefore not timeless, sometimes this re-interrogation will end in changes to our idea of what the university should be and how it should go about its task. However, that re-interrogation needs to be carried out in the context of an ideal that can be a reality; the pursuit of a liberal education within the law school.

rarely been at the centre of government policy and universities have continually found themselves under threat.

[103] E Keeley, *Cavafy's Alexandria: Study of a Myth in Progress* (London, The Hogarth Press, 1997) 30–31.

[104] I use the term barbarian deliberately and not simply for the sake of the allusion to Cavafy. Much of the writing that radically seeks to change the nature of the university stems from a position that is utilitarian, anti-intellectual and even philistine in its nature. In such cases the term 'barbarian,' 'an uncultured person,' is not an epithet but is simply an objective description.

2

Holistic Education: What is a Liberal Education?

RHETORIC AND REALITY

THE MAJORITY OF contemporary British university law schools and the majority of academics within those law schools hold themselves out as providing a liberal education. Law schools sometimes explicitly say that they are offering a liberal education to prospective students in the publicity material that they circulate to applicants.[1] Individual academics have espoused the value of the law degree as a form of liberal education.[2] More importantly, surveys of both institutions and individuals over the last few decades have invariably come to the conclusion that both British university law schools and individual academics within those law schools generally identify the concept of a liberal education as being the dominant focus for their work.[3] Equally noteworthy is the fact that the Lord Chancellor's Advisory Committee on Legal Education's (ALCEC's) statement that the law degree 'should stand as an independent liberal education in the discipline of law, not tied to any specific vocation' received widespread support in law schools.[4]

Despite all of the above one must be careful about drawing any quick conclusions about the connection between this widespread acceptance of the rhetoric of liberal education within university law schools and the actual reality of the culture of these law schools. The practices to be found in university law schools may undermine their claim to be offering a liberal education. Johnstone, for example, has suggested that:

[1] This was true, eg, of both the Universities of Birmingham and Leicester at the time that this passage was written.

[2] See, eg, B Hepple, 'The Liberal Law Degree' (1996) 55 *Cambridge Law Journal* 470.

[3] See, eg, J Macfarlane, M Jeeves and A Boon, 'Education for Life or for Work?' (1987) 137 *New Law Journal* 835.

[4] ACLEC, *First Report on Legal Education and Training* (London, ACLEC, 1996) 57. For such support see, eg, P Leighton, 'The First ACLEC Report: What Might it Mean for Law Teachers?' (1996) 30 *The Law Teacher* 201 at 205.

> if we look, less at responses to surveys, and more at the everyday discourses and practices of academic lawyers, a rather different picture emerges. If we observe things like careers talks organised by law lecturers, law faculty noticeboards, open days, extra-curricular activities regarded as important, justifications given for the importance of proposed new subjects, and so on, it is difficult to avoid the impression that the majority of university law lecturers are still deeply attached—whatever they say—to a narrow vocationalist image of university legal education.[5]

What either institutions or individuals mean when they say that they support the notion of a liberal education in law is certainly less than clear. Indeed, whether the term liberal education is being used in any positive sense in the law school, identifying adherence to a particular educational agenda, is in itself a moot point. When Bell notes that '[l]aw schools providing undergraduate degrees in law claim to be providing a liberal education, rather than preparation directly for the legal profession' the phrase 'rather than' may be more important than the specific claim to provide a liberal education.[6] For some academics the use of the phrase 'liberal education' seems to be no more than a coded refusal to accept either the Law Society or the Bar Council's right to have any substantial say in the running of the law school; a rhetorical device that is used in the political process of achieving and maintaining autonomy for the academy.[7] One could even go further and suggest that the proposition that the undoubted support that exists for the idea of liberal education in the law school in turn indicates a deep-rooted and well thought out adherence to the ideals that lie behind the notion of a liberal education is almost a counter-intuitive notion. A number of writers have noted, and lamented, the law school's consistent refusal to engage in consideration of educational theory.[8] If legal academics are

[5] G Johnstone, 'Liberal Ideals and Vocational Aims in University Legal Education' [1999] 3 *Web JCLI*.

[6] J Bell, 'Key Skills in the Law Curriculum and Self-Assessment' (2000) 34 *The Law Teacher* 175 at 186.

[7] 'I frequently hear lip-service paid to the ideal of a "liberal arts education in law." Regrettably, once decoded, this often means no more than a desire to expand or maintain the range of dogmatic legal subjects which may be taught, despite the effective control which the legal professions enjoy over the content of approximately half the courses taught in a typical English law degree'. (B Jackson, *The Teaching of Jewish Law in British Universities* (Oxford, Oxford Centre for Post-Graduate Hebrew Studies, undated) 9).

[8] See, eg, F Cownie, 'Searching for Theory in Teaching Law' in F Cownie (ed), *The Law School: Global Issues, Local Questions* (Aldershot, Ashgate, 1999) and J Webb, 'Why Theory Matters' in J Webb and C Maughan (eds), *Teaching Lawyers' Skills* (London, Butterworths, 1996).

as ignorant of educational theory as has been suggested then it seems plausible to suppose that these self-same academics are ignorant of the historical and philosophical tradition that lies behind the phrase 'liberal education'; to feel that the academic claim to teach using the notion of liberal education is one which is only lightly grounded in a knowledge of the tradition that they ostensibly espouse.[9]

The support that exists for the idea of law as a liberal education in the law school cannot, however, simply be dismissed when considering the pedagogical future for the law school; a vaguely held ideal is still an ideal. What academics say they wish to do or not to do are important factors in any inquiry into the law school. Both the literature on the private life of the university referred to in Chapter 1 above and the fate of Thames Valley University as an institution indicate that any suggestions as to the future of the law school which run counter to the present culture of law schools and which fail to attract the support of those working in the law schools are likely to, at best, have a problematic future and, at worst, be doomed to failure.[10] The rhetoric of law schools indicates that the notion of liberal education is part of the cultural mores of the legal academic tribe and as such the notion has a broad degree of acceptance amongst the members of that tribe. Nevertheless, it seems clear that support for liberal education and

[9] Thus, eg, the significance of Hepple's sophisticated account of liberal education in law is diminished by his failure to make any reference at all to that scholarship outside the law school which analyses the nature of liberal education (Hepple, above n 2). This is not to suggest that all legal academics are ignorant of the tradition of liberal education in higher education or that knowledge of that tradition then leads to an acceptance of its validity. Thus, eg, Johnstone has argued that the educational philosophy of Dewey provides a preferable theoretical base to traditional accounts of a liberal education in law in that he synthesises aspects of liberal and vocational education (Johnstone, above n 5). (On Dewey as a philosopher of liberal education see H Giroux, 'Dreaming About Democracy' in D Gless and B Herrnsten Smith, *The Politics of Liberal Education* (Durham, Duke University Press, 1992) 127–28.)

[10] In 1998 a Quality Assurance Agency report on Thames Valley University concluded that 'the University is suffering from a serious breakdown of trust between a substantial proportion of its staff and its management' (*Thames Valley University Quality Audit Report* (Gloucester, Quality Assurance Agency, 1998) http://www.qaa.ac.uk/revreps/instrev/TVU/Contents.htm, para 74). Because of this, and because of a series of problems that had arisen partially because of this breakdown of trust, the Agency recommended a series of changes to the way that the university was run (*Thames Valley University Quality Audit Report*, *ibid*, paras 78 and 79). As a result of this report the Vice-Chancellor of the university, Dr Mike Fitzgerald a former vice chairman of the Committee of Vice-Chancellors and Principals, resigned (*The Times*, 13 November 1998). The fate of Thames Valley provides an illustrative example of the general proposition that universities and their law schools in practice seldom work well when their policies are not in tune with the wishes of their academic staff.

ignorance about liberal education are to be found in equal measure in law schools. Thus, if a case for a more rigorous pursuit of liberal education in university law schools is to be made, there is a need to start with an analysis of the nature of liberal education before there can be any discussion of how it is to be applied to the work of the law school.

THE THEORY OF LIBERAL EDUCATION

Great forests have been sacrificed to make the body of literature that constitutes the tradition of scholarship on or about the nature of liberal education in the universities. It is a literature that crosses national frontiers and that has been written over centuries, finding some of its roots in the arguments of the classic writers of Greece and Rome.[11] Unsurprisingly this great body of literature has produced not a single, highly refined line of thought but, instead, a profusion of different developments which in turn have created a mass of contradictions. Hirst comments that:

> [t]he phrase 'liberal education' has today become something of a slogan which takes on different meanings according to its immediate context. It usually labels a form of education of which the author approves, but beyond that its meaning is often entirely negatively derived. Whatever else a liberal education is, it is *not* a vocational education, *not* an exclusively scientific education, or *not* a specialist education in any sense.[12]

Even where it is possible to identify a positive claim in a statement about liberal education it is important to 'recognize that there is no absolute idea of liberal education, or no dominant form, although there are overlapping purposes.'[13] Various different forms of liberal

[11] For examples of discussion of liberal education outside the context of the Anglo-American educational tradition see S Liedman, 'In Search of Isis: General Education in Germany and Sweden' in S Rothblatt and B Wittrock (eds), *The European University since 1800* (Cambridge, Cambridge University Press, 1993) and K Jaspers, *The Idea of the University* (London, Peter Owen, 1960) 61–68. For discussion of the classical roots of liberal education see M Nussbaum, *Cultivating Humanity: A Classical Defense of Reform in Liberal Education* (Cambridge, Harvard University Press, 1997) especially ch 1.

[12] P Hirst, 'Liberal Education and the Nature of Knowledge' in P Hirst, *Knowledge and the Curriculum* (London, Routledge and Kegan Paul, 1974) 30. To define 'liberal' by what it is not has a long tradition. Johnson, in his Dictionary, defined liberal as being, amongst other things, 'not mean; not low in birth; not low in mind' (S Rothblatt, *Tradition and Change in Liberal Education* (London, Faber and Faber, 1976) 25).

[13] S Rothblatt, 'Liberal Education: A Noble, Troubled and Ironical History' in P Beggen, A Tellings and W van Haaften (eds), *The University and the Knowledge Society* (Bemmel, Concorde Publishing House, 1998) 31–32.

education have been identified. Rothblatt, in the conclusion to a historical survey of the use made of the concept of liberal education in Great Britain, notes that:

> A liberal education can be Truth, Taste, sociability, liberality, humanism, sensitivity, sound critical principles, critical self-awareness, scientific detachment, a glimpse into the permanent realities of existence, civilization, culture—all these have at one historical time or another been identified with the purposes and meaning of a liberal education.[14]

Positions can be taken within the debate about liberal education but it is never possible to say that any one statement reflects what liberal education is; rather authors must contend that their view represents a better or even the best view of liberal education; in this sense their propositions are always normative rather than positivistic.[15] This is not to say that the term liberal education is without content. It does set boundaries. There are some things that are not compatible with a liberal education but there are many choices that can be made from those things that are within the scope of liberal education. In the rest of this chapter I will discuss some of the themes, developed by seminal thinkers in the field of liberal education, that are, in my view, most of use for the work of the law school. This is not intended to be either a history or a survey of liberal education.[16] It is a selective account of liberal education that will provide the substructure for the case that I want to make for the use of liberal education in the law school.

THE LEGACY OF THE NINETEENTH CENTURY

Newman's 1852 lectures on the nature of the university have been described as 'the single most important treatise in the English language'

[14] Rothblatt, above n 12, at 196. See also S Rothblatt, 'The Limbs of Osiris: Liberal Education in the English-speaking World' in S Rothblatt and B Wittrock (eds), *The European and American University since 1800: Historical and Sociological Essays* (Cambridge, Cambridge University Press, 1993).

[15] As is the case with Hirst when, having noted the diversity of ways in which the term liberal education is used, he goes on to argue that liberal education 'is the appropriate label for a positive concept, that of an education based fairly and squarely on the nature of knowledge itself, a concept central to the discussion of education at any level' (Hirst, above n 12).

[16] For a history of the tradition of liberal education in Great Britain see Rothblatt, above n 12.

on their subject.[17] The influence of these lectures on the nature of the university continues to reverberate through British higher education. Thus, for example, although one relatively recent major report on British higher education, the 1997 Dearing Report, makes no explicit references to Newman, it is shot through with discussion of ideas about higher education that are derived, directly or indirectly, from him.[18] It is therefore appropriate to begin an analysis of the nature of liberal education with Newman, even though it is also necessary, when doing this, to remember that what British universities have become is very different from what Newman thought they ought to be. [19]

Newman saw the university as:

> [a]n assemblage of learned men, zealous for their own sciences, and rivals of each other. . .brought by familiar intercourse and for the sake of intellectual peace, to adjust together the claims and relations of their respective subjects of investigation. They learn to respect, to consult, to aid each other. Thus is created a pure and clear atmosphere of thought, which the student also

[17] S Rothblatt, 'An Oxonian "Idea" of a University: JH Newman and "Well-Being" ' in M Brock and M Carthboys (eds), *The History of the University of Oxford* vol. VI (Oxford, Oxford University Press, 1997) 287. For an account of the historical background to Newman's lectures see A Dwight Culler, *The Imperial Intellect* (New Haven, Yale University Press, 1955) chs 6 and 7 and I Ker, *John Henry Newman: A Biography* (Oxford, Clarendon Press, 1988) ch 9.

[18] See, eg, '[I]ts [higher education's] distinctive character must lie in the independent pursuit of knowledge and understanding', and '[the purpose of higher education is] to increase knowledge and understanding for their own sake' (*The National Committee of Inquiry into Higher Education* (The Dearing Report) (London, National Committee of Inquiry into Higher Education, 1997) para 4.4 and para 5.11. Some commentators would deny the present relevance of Newman's work. Smith and Webster have, eg, argued that Newman's work 'Hardly amounts any longer to the prevailing Idea of a university, at least as applying to Britain's hundred-plus university institutions' (A Smith and F Webster, 'Changing Ideas of the University' in A Smith and F Webster (ed), *The Postmodern University? Contested Vision of Higher Education in Society* (Buckingham, SRHE and Open University Press, 1997) 3). For my purposes it is sufficient to argue that Newman's account has some resonance in the present situation of the university and that it offers an ideal form that should more rigorously be followed.

[19] Some commentators see one difference as being the fact that Newman seemed to see the university as being as being a place for teaching not a place for research (J Newman, *The Idea of a University* (New York, Holt, Rinehart and Winston, 1960) xxxix–xl). (See, eg, P Scott, *The Crisis in the University* (Beckenham, Croom Helm, 1984) 3) This point, however, can be exaggerated. Ker cautions against the 'strong element of hyperbole' in Newman (I Ker, *The Achievement of John Henry Newman* (London, Collins, 1991) 3). Nevertheless there are some real differences between Newman's model and the reality of the present day. One obvious difference is the importance that Newman attached to the study of theology in a university (Newman, *ibid*, p 14). There are currently only 24 British universities who offer courses in theology or theology and religious studies (*Degree Course Guides 2000/2001* (Cambridge, Hobson, 2000) Section 19 at 17–20).

breathes, though in his case he only pursues a few sciences out of the multitude.[20]

It is in this atmosphere that he thought a liberal education might be acquired. Newman immediately went on to argue that:

> [h]e [the student] profits by an intellectual tradition, which is independent of particular teachers, which guides him in his choice of subjects, and duly interprets for him those which he chooses. He apprehends the great outlines of knowledge, the principles on which it rests, the scale of its parts, its lights and its shades, its great points and its little, as he otherwise cannot apprehend them. Hence it is that his education is called 'Liberal.' A habit of mind is formed which lasts through life, of which the attributes are, freedom, equitableness, calmness, moderation, and wisdom.[21]

This passage contains the core of Newman's notion of university education. Several points in it are important for my present purposes.

At its centre a university education, for Newman, involved the pursuit of knowledge and, in his view, '[k]nowledge is capable of being its own end.'[22] Newman's position, refusing to accept that what he called the 'Philosophy of Utility' or 'Useful Knowledge' could be the proper objects for university education, a position which was original to him only in the precise form that he expressed it, is repeated by many later writers concerned with liberal education.[23] Another theorist of liberal education, Arnold, writing more generally in 1869, was to 'recommend culture . . . a pursuit of our total perfection by means of getting to know, on all matters that concern us, the best of which has been thought and said in the world' as a focus for life and to reject '[f]aith in machinery' ('machinery' being things of purely instrumental concern such as the pursuit of wealth) as having any 'value in and for itself'; in relation to universities he was to praise Prussian universities as places that properly understood that 'in the university, the idea of science is primary, that of the profession, secondary.'[24] Similarly Housman, in 1892, argued:

[20] Newman, above n 19, at 76.

[21] Newman, above n 19.

[22] Newman, above n 19, at 77. 'Liberal knowledge . . . is understanding and is validated by our willingness to rest in the understanding which it conveys'. (Dwight Culler, above n 17, at 216).

[23] Newman, above n 19, at 89 and 90.

[24] M Arnold, *Culture and Anarchy* (London, Cambridge University Press, 1960) 6; Arnold, *ibid*, 49–50; M Arnold, *Schools and Universities on the Continent* (Ann Arbor, University of Michigan Press, 1964) 254. Walcott writes that '[I]t was in Germany that he [Arnold] had found the finest example of his humanistic ideal of education' (F Walcott,

> a life spent, however victoriously, in securing the necessaries of life, is no more than an elaborate furnishing and decorating of apartments for the reception of a guest who is never to come. Our business here is not to live, but to live happily.[25]

and quoted Aristotle to the effect that 'all men possess by nature a craving for knowledge.'[26]

Essentially the same argument has continued to be put up until and including the present day. Nussbaum's contention that in the USA 'we ask a higher education to contribute a general preparation for citizenship, not just a specialized preparation for a career,' Steiner's suggestion that 'the notion that the asking of questions is the supreme piety of the spirit . . . abstract thought man's pre-eminent excellence and burden,' Russell's assertion that well-educated graduates are those who pursue knowledge for its own sake (and because of that will refuse to obey the instructions of their employers when to do otherwise would be to be untruthful) and Brownsword's suggestion that law schools exist not so as to create good lawyers but so as to produce good citizens, all sit happily with Newman's statements.[27] This having been said all these arguments, like Newman's original statement of his position, are complex ones that deserve further analysis if the precise points that are being made are not to be misunderstood.

The Origins of Culture and Anarchy (London, Heinemann, 1970) 99). Thus Weber wrote '[w]hat is the attitude of the academic man towards his vocation . . . He maintains that he engages in science for science's sake and not merely because others, by exploiting science, can bring about commercial or technical success and can better feed, dress, illuminate, and govern' (M Weber, 'Science as a Vocation' in H Gerth and W Wright Mills (eds), *From Max Weber: Essays in Sociology* (London, Routledge, 1947) 136). On Arnold's notion of culture see W Connell, *The Educational Thought and Influence of Matthew Arnold* (London, Routledge and Kegan Paul, 1950) ch VII. Most of Arnold's writing was concerned with pre-university education but the arguments he put forward are, nevertheless, still relevant to a university system.

25 AE Housman, 'Introductory Lecture' in AE Housman, *Selected Prose* (Cambridge, Cambridge University Press, 1961) 7. See similarly Nussbaum, '[w]e have to think not only how we will earn enough to live, but also about why we live, and what makes life worth living' (Nussbaum, above n 11, at 172).

26 Housman, above n 25, at16.

27 Nussbaum, above n 11, at 294; G Steiner, *Heidegger* (London, The Harvester Press, 1978) 149; C Russell, *Academic Freedom* (London, Routledge, 1993) 27; R Brownsword, 'Teaching Contract: A Liberal Agenda' in P Birks (ed), *Examining the Law Syllabus: The Core* (Oxford, Oxford University Press, 1992) 42. Similar positions have been maintained by many others. Jaspers, for example, suggests that a university education 'prepares each individual to be a member of society' (Jaspers, above n 11, 61).

UTILITY, KNOWLEDGE AND HOLISTIC EDUCATION

Analyses of liberal education have always drawn distinctions between different types of education. Newman's rejection of the pursuit of 'utility' in university education is a theme which is typical of the thought of many who have written about liberal education and which is of particular importance in the context of present-day arguments about the function of the university. Such arguments have both a positive and a negative aspect to them and both aspects are worthy of consideration.

In rejecting the pursuit of utility in education Newman is rejecting anything that narrows education to just one aspect of a student's life.[28] Education, he contends, is there to educate a person not a worker. As Hirst writes:

> the achievement of knowledge is not only the attainment of the good of the mind itself, but also the chief means whereby the good life as a whole is to be found. Man is more than pure mind, yet mind is his essential distinguishing characteristic, and it is in terms of knowledge that his *whole life* is rightly directed. (emphasis added)[29]

Education is not just there simply to transmit either particular skills or information. Rather, the purpose of university education is to convey knowledge where knowledge is understood as being:

> something intellectual, something which grasps what it perceives through the senses; something which takes a view of things; which sees more than the senses convey; which reasons upon what it sees, and while it sees; which invests it with an idea . . . such knowledge is not a mere extrinsic or accidental advantage, which is ours to-day and another's tomorrow, which may be got up from a book, and easily forgotten again, which we can command or communicate at our pleasure, which we can borrow for the occasion, carry about in our hand, and take into the market; it is an acquired illumination, it is a habit, a personal possession, and an inward endowment.[30]

[28] Newman, above n 11, at 81.

[29] Hirst, above n 12.

[30] Newman, above n 19, at 85. What Newman describes is, of course, an ideal demanding that the student becomes 'not so much a creature of impossible virtues as a creature from whom an impossible number of vices have been subtracted' (Dwight Culler, above n 17, at 191). But ideals are what we seek to attain and, in this case, the ideal is perhaps not so much impossible as supremely difficult.

University education is therefore about inculcating into students a certain kind of character or disposition towards life.[31] Those who are educated grasp the pattern of connection that characterises life.[32] In a similar vein to Newman, Arnold writes about culture as 'an endeavour to come at reason and the will of God by means of reading, observing, and thinking'; in a later, less florid and more secular age Leavis talks about literary studies in university, which he sees as, par excellence, a liberal education, as being a 'training in sensibility.'[33] For Newman and for other writers on liberal education, a student may learn a great mass of technical information and still be wholly uneducated if they have not acquired the character and knowledge of connections that goes with that learning; if students cannot, in Nussbaum's phrase, 'call their minds their own' they will not, however much they know, be learned.[34] The student who has successfully inculcated the precepts of a liberal education should:

> have looked into themselves and developed the ability to separate mere habit and convention from what they can defend by argument. [Thus] [t]hey have ownership of their own thought and speech, and this imparts to them a dignity that is far beyond the outer dignity of class and rank.[35]

The focus of liberal education on the search for what might properly be called knowledge and the concomitant acquisition of a particular habit of mind can result in a misunderstanding about the value of purely vocational or professional knowledge or skills in the tradition of liberal education and about the place of factual or technical information in the curriculum. Nothing in any of the work of the writers cited above would lend support to the proposition that professional knowledge or professional skills are to be despised and some of these writers would see consideration of such things as being part of the proper pur-

[31] Newman, above n 19, at 86. In turn this concept of a disposition towards life that is acquired through a liberal education can be recast in terms of propositions about the skills and abilities, such as critical thinking, communication and the facility to make relevant judgements, that are acquired through a liberal education (see Hirst, above n 12, at 34).

[32] Newman, above n 19, at 101.

[33] Arnold, above n 24, at 89; F Leavis, *Education and the University* (London, Chatto and Windus, 1943) 38.

[34] Nussbaum, above n 11, at 293. In a somewhat different sense Hirst argues that to acquire a liberal education is '[t]o learn to see to experience the world in a way otherwise unknown, and thereby come to have a mind in a fuller sense' (Hirst, above n 12, at 40).

[35] Nussbaum, above n 11.

pose of a university.[36] What is at issue for writers concerned with liberal education is the way in which such things are considered and the priority that students should give to such forms of learning. Moreover, a liberal education necessarily involves the acquisition of technical information and, in order to be successful, a student must show that they can master such information.[37] Once again what is at issue is why particular information is selected for study and what use that information is then put to. Both professional knowledge and technical information have value but in a liberal education they are acquired, if at all, not for the value that they have in their own terms but because they can facilitate the wider learning that constitutes a liberal education.

For Newman, Arnold, Housman and others the centrality given to knowledge in education stems in part from their perceptions about the nature of being human. Newman cites Cicero as authority for the proposition that once immediate physical needs are met we naturally turn towards the consideration of knowledge.[38] Arnold looks to Montesquieu and Housman to Aristotle for the argument that curiosity is at the heart of human nature.[39] For them a liberal education represents a systematising of that process which occurs for us all. We need to make sense, to order, that which is around us if we are to act at all; nothing is what it is unless we make it so; the external world is not given to us but constructed by us; as Rushdie writes '[e]ven a baby is faced with the problem of defining itself.'[40] As Steiner puts it, '[m]ore

[36] Thus, eg, Jaspers begins his discussion of the purpose of university education with the observation that '[t]he student comes to the university in order to study the arts and sciences and prepare himself for a profession' (Jaspers, above n 11, at 52); equally Hirst argues that a liberal education might be organised around 'programmes that are in the first place . . . either theoretical or practical' (Hirst, above n 12). Newman does not doubt that 'most people will have to specialize for the sake of their livelihood; he simply adds that for the sake of their intellectual health they ought to correct this specialization by a broad general culture' (Dwight Culler, above n 17, at 192).

[37] 'The problem [for liberal education] is to produce *specialists* who are in touch with a humane centre' (emphasis added) (Leavis, above n 33).

[38] Newman, above n 19, at 79. The fact that we are concerned with university education is of the essence here. We must first be able to provide our sustenance from day to day before we can consider questions about knowledge. But in a modern society those who attend a university, whether it be a university in a mass system or an elite system, have long since passed the educational stage where they have done that which is necessary to equip themselves to acquire those things that are necessary for life. For university students the question is not, will they be able to survive, but, instead, how materially rich will they, or will they choose to, become?

[39] Arnold, above n 24, at 44: Housman, above n 25, at 16. Much more recently Nussbaum sees Marcus Aurelius and Plato as sources for the same proposition (Nussbaum, above n 11, at 63).

[40] S Rushdie, *Midnight's Children* (London, Jonathan Cape, 1981) 129.

than *homo sapiens*, we are *homo quaerens*, the animal that asks and asks.'[41] Anything that we do represents a whole series of explicit or implicit personal and individual answers to questions about how the world is ordered and connected and how we value and evaluate these connections. We have a 'complete and profound responsibility' for our answers to these questions whether we are aware of this or not.[42] Some of these questions are seemingly more important than others; they are the kind we answer when we choose a partner (or not) or vote in an election (or not). Other questions may appear to be trivial. However a liberal education makes us aware that there are no such things as purely technical questions; that everything we do, every choice we make, however mundane, arcane or trivial, has deep-rooted consequences both for us and for others.

In Frost's poem 'The Road Not Taken' a person observes:

> Two roads diverged in a wood, and I—
> I took the one less travelled by,
> And that has made all the difference.

Initially in the poem this choice between two roads seems to be a matter of no importance. There is nothing that clearly points to one road being a better path or indeed to any difference between the paths.

> . . . the passing there
> Had worn them really about the same,
> And both that morning equally lay
> In leaves no step had trodden black.

Yet, despite all this, the choice of road makes 'all the difference.'

> Oh, I kept the first [not taken path] for another day!
> Yet knowing how way leads on to way,
> I doubted if I should ever come back.

Each choice we make makes all the difference and has to be made in the context of the fact that it makes all the difference and the driving imperative of a liberal education is to show that this is so. Shopping for mange-tout in February and drawing up a will for a person whose only means of support is the state old age pension are both deeply value-laden and political acts; the first because shopping for out-of-season vegetables is only possible because of the global economy with the pos-

[41] G Steiner, *Grammars of Creation* (London, Faber and Faber, 2001) 16.
[42] J Sartre, *Existentialism and Humanism* (London, Eyre Methuen, 1973) 30.

itive and negative consequences that that has for those countries supplying the mange-tout and the latter because of what a will says about support for notions of personal property and the heritability of personal property.[43] Confining one's shopping to vegetables that are in season and refusing to draw up the will would, of course, also be equally deeply value-laden and political acts. It is of the essence of a liberal education that all actions are politically and ethically charged. The value of a liberal education lies both in making us understand these questions and in our being more skilled and subtle in giving our answers. Factors such as the culture we are born into, the gender we are assigned or that we choose, the wealth of our parents and the material conditions of our era all influence the way in which we assess the world. But because, no matter what the circumstances of our birth, we are not determined by that birth, a liberal education can help us to make our sense of the world; it can help us 'call . . . [our] minds . . . [our] own'; it can, in Newman's words, put 'the mind above the influences of chance and necessity, above anxiety, suspense, unsettlement, and superstition, which is the lot of the many.'[44]

An education in knowledge naturally takes a priority over a training which is concerned with wealth creation or the intricacies of a particular career, profession or vocation because, until we have at least a tentative grasp of our answers to questions about the nature of the world, we can have no way of assessing how we wish to live in the world or how we will be able to account the way in which we live in the world a success or not. Wealth, careers and the like are, as Arnold aptly puts it, mere machinery because they are there to be used for a purpose and until we have decided what our personal purpose is the machinery can be of no use to us. However, the fact that they are mere machinery does not mean that they do not have a use or that they do not require learning.[45] Moreover, in acquiring a method for answering questions that pertain to knowledge we also acquire information, skills and habits that are of direct and indirect assistance in careers, professions and vocations:

> [T]he man who has learned to think and to reason and to compare and to discriminate and to analyze, who has refined his taste, and formed his

43 See, eg, P McMichael, 'Global Food Politics' in F Magdoff, J Bellamy and F Buttel (eds), *Hungry for Profit: The Agribusiness Threat to Farmers, Food, and the Envirnment* (New York, Monthly Review Press, 2000) and P Proudhon, *What is Property?: An Inquiry into the Principle of Right and Government* (London, Reeves, 1902).

44 Nussbaum, above n 11; Newman, above n 19, at 104.

45 Newman, above n 19, at 85.

judgment, and sharpened his mental vision will not indeed at once be a lawyer . . . but he will be placed in that state of intellect in which he can take up any one of the sciences or callings.[46]

Equally, although the acquisition of knowledge is a study of the general, 'it requires a great deal of reading, or a wide range of information'; it is dependent on a learning of particulars from which the general may be drawn and this learning of particulars may include information that proves to be useful in a profession, vocation or occupation.[47] Indeed, that learning of information may specifically be learning within an individual professional area such as law or medicine.[48] What liberal education requires is not that the information that a student acquires in the process of education be of no vocational significance but that it should not be acquired because of any such significance but, instead, because of its wider possibilities in the search for knowledge.[49] In later chapters I will argue that the study of law in its widest sense and even the study of legal practice in its most mundane sense can be the basis for a liberal education providing that that education is not primarily concerned with making the student a practising lawyer.

THE END OF KNOWLEDGE, LIBERAL EDUCATION AND POST-MODERNISM

Newman thought the university should teach 'universal *knowledge*.'[50] However, now we are told that:

[46] Newman, *ibid*, at 125. See also Newman's comment that a liberal education 'educates the intellect to reason well in all matters' (*ibid*, at 95). This view of the relationship between a liberal education and later employment has constantly been restated. See, eg, JS Mill, 'Inaugural Lecture Delivered to the University of St Andrews' in *Collected Works of John Stuart Mill* vol XXI (Toronto, University of Toronto Press, 1984) 218 and A Flexner, *Universities: American, English, German* (New York, Oxford University Press, 1930) 30–31.

[47] Newman, above n 19, at 97.

[48] Newman, *ibid*, at 126.

[49] Dwight Culler argues that Newman, having first suggested that knowledge needs no end but itself, later 'accepts the criterion [of utility] and merely claims that liberal knowledge is useful too' (Dwight Culler, above n 17, at 222). This, I think, is a misreading of Newman. What he argues is that utility is not something by which knowledge should be judged but that, in fact, knowledge does have utility. One should not judge a book by its cover but when its cover has beauty one should acknowledge that fact.

[50] Newman, above n 19, at xxxvii.

> [t]he postmodern condition has split one big game of modern times into many little and poorly co-ordinated games, played havoc with the rules of all of the games, and shortened sharply the lifespan of any set of rules.[51]

Post-modernism has it seems, on this account, cut away any ground that a liberal education might be founded on.[52] 'The grand narrative' it has been argued 'has lost its credibility' as a way of understanding how forms of knowledge are transmitted and maintained.[53] If this is so, whether we conceive of the roots of liberal education as lying in liberalism or, more generally, in an Enlightenment-inspired search for an overarching philosophical explanation of the world, post-modernism, in denying the possibility of a foundational significance being properly attached to any series of arguments, exposes, it seems, basic theoretical shortcomings in the idea of liberal education. 'Knowledge' is, it appears, in fact more local, more specific and more ephemeral than the form of understanding propounded by theorists of liberal education; language more problematic and less transparent. Thus Readings asks:

> if the assumption that we speak a common language lights the way to terror, in what terms can we speak of community? What is the nature of the social bond, if it cannot simply be the object of free choice and rational assent in communication? And what are the implications for the University, the institution supposed to incarnate this model of communicational community?[54]

The arguments above cannot be ignored. Post-modernism provides a challenge for the traditional notion of a university education on a number of different levels.[55] However, a challenge is, in itself, neither a victory nor a defeat but, instead, an invitation to a contest. The post-modern argument asks theorists of liberal education to once again

[51] Z Bauman, 'Universities: Old, New and Different' in A Smith and F Webster (eds), *The Postmodern University? Contested Vision of Higher Education in Society* (Buckingham, SRHE and Open University Press, 1997) 21.

[52] As to what post-modernism is: 'More a collection of often warring tribes than a unified nation, there is perhaps an identifiable core theme or sensibility which is shared by "postmodern" authors, namely a reaction against certainty or "central control" mechanisms, whether these are sought for or postulated as operating in the human subject, in human society, in texts, in history, in truth or in meaning' (T Murphy, 'Postmodernism, Legal Theory, Legal Education and the Future' (2000) 7 *International Journal of the Legal Profession* 357 at 363.

[53] J Lyotard, *The Postmodern Condition: A Report on Knowledge* (Manchester, Manchester University Press, 1984) 37.

[54] B Readings, *The University in Ruins* (Cambridge, Harvard University Press, 1996) 184–85.

[55] Some indication of the range of levels can be found in the papers collected in Smith and Webster, above n 51.

reconsider and restate their positions. That argument can become a refutation of notions of liberal education only when the argument is seen as being uncontested and uncontestable. In fact the post-modernist position has been the subject of fierce internal debate amongst those who would see themselves as its advocates and has been contested from outside by those who would deny the validity of its basic premises. Moreover, we need to distinguish between two different ways in which post-modernism can challenge notions of a liberal education. First, post-modernism can be an attack on particular parts of particular programmes for a liberal education put forward by individual proponents of the approach. Challenges of this form, whilst important, are not challenges to the core of the idea. Secondly, post-modernism can be seen as an attack on the very idea of a liberal education. Whether post-modernism can ever be successful as the latter seems open to doubt.

In responding to post-modernist attempts to reconceptualise established disciplines within the university as being no more than mere historically and culturally located discourses Norris has argued that:

> the interconnected values of truth, criticism, mutual understanding (so far as is humanly possible), and respect for differences of moral and intellectual viewpoint possess a validity transcending particular circumstances of time and place.[56]

Any attempt to deny these values is, Norris argues, by its very nature self-refuting.[57] Norris' position in this and other works that he has produced in not wholly hostile to the post-modernist position but does point to inherent limitations to how far its arguments can be taken, lest, if taken too far, they become:

> a half-baked mixture of ideas picked up from the latest fashionable sources, or a series of slogans to the general effect that truth' and 'reality' are obsolete ideas, that knowledge is always and everywhere a function of the epistemic will-to-power, and that history is nothing but a fictive construct out of the various 'discourses' that jostle for supremacy from one period to the next.[58]

If 'truth, criticism, mutual understanding (so far as is humanly possible), and respect for differences of moral and intellectual viewpoint'

[56] C Norris, *Deconstruction and the 'Unfinished Project of Modernity'* (London, The Athlone Press, 2000) 104.

[57] Norris, *ibid*, ch 5.

[58] C Norris, *Uncritical Theory: Postmodernism, Intellectuals and the Gulf War* (London, Lawrence and Wishart, 1992) 31.

can be saved then so can liberal education for in the end, in essence, liberal education teaches no more than a respect for using these values as a way of acquiring whatever may be available by way of an understanding of the world, even if both that world and that understanding are, in some sense, post-modern in their nature.[59] If universities can continue to be places:

> where conceptions of and standards of rational justification are elaborated, put to work in the detailed practices of enquiry, and themselves rationally evaluated, so that . . . the wider society [can] learn how to conduct its debates, practical or theoretical, in a rationally defensible way

then the provision of a liberal education also continues to be a possibility but the university can only continue to be such a place if:

> the university is a place where rival and antagonistic views of rational justification, such as those of the genealogists and the Thomists, are afforded the opportunity both to develop their own enquiries, in practice and in the articulation of the theory of that practice, and to conduct their intellectual and moral warfare.[60]

In this sense the development of post-modernism is not antithetical to the pursuit and practice of liberal education. Instead, notions of liberal education can only flourish in the present era if the study of post-modernism flourishes. Post-modernism, of course, may controvert some aspects of traditional theories of liberal education. Thus, for example, if post-modern contentions prove to be correct Newman's 'universal knowledge' is no longer a viable goal. However, Nussbaum's goal for liberal education, that it seeks to facilitate critical self-reflection about one's self and one's traditions, inculcate an awareness of ties of recognition and concern for others and teach an ability to empathise, insofar as this is possible with those others, remains an achievable aim.[61] And the paths to Newman's universal knowledge and Nussbaum's democratic world citizenship are much the same.

[59] Norris, above n 56, at 104.

[60] A MacIntyre, *Three Rival Versions of Moral Inquiry* (London, Gerald Duckworth, 1990) 222.

[61] M Nussbaum, *Cultivating Humanity: A Classical Defense of Reform in Liberal Education* (Cambridge, Harvard University Press, 1997) 9–11.

LIBERAL EDUCATION, ELITE GROUPS AND MASS EDUCATION

Notwithstanding its historical significance in the development of university education in Great Britain it might, nevertheless, be argued that the concept of a liberal education is incompatible with the present era of mass higher education.[62] Newman repeatedly referred to a liberal education as being an education that is suitable for 'gentlemen.' At one point in his lectures, for example, he asserted that a:

> Liberal Education makes . . . the gentleman. It is well to be a gentleman, it is well to have a cultivated intellect, a delicate taste, a candid, equitable, dispassionate mind, a noble and courteous bearing in the conduct of life;—these are the connatural qualities of a large knowledge; they are the objects of a University.[63]

Statements of this type do not seem to be in keeping with an educational system that is seeking ever-increasing rates of participation in university education or, more generally, with a society that largely rejects the desirability of notions of social stratification.[64]

In part Newman's arguments about the class focus of the university do no more than repeat the traditions within which he was working and respond to the social and economic realities of his time. When Blackstone lectured on the place of English common law within the universities he had considered the law's impact upon students who were 'gentlemen of independent estates and fortune.'[65] During the eighteenth and nineteenth centuries, when 'landed and professional families' provided the vast majority of undergraduate students, it

[62] See, eg, J Webb, 'Post-Fordism and the reformation of Legal Education' in F Cownie (ed), *The Law School: Global Issues, Local Questions* (Aldershot, Ashgate, 1999) 246. The argument can also be put in wider terms; that a liberal education is 'elitist' and for this reason is objectionable. For an examination (and rejection) of this argument see J O'Neill and Y Solomon, 'Education, Elitism and the Market' in B Brecher, O Fleischmann and J Halliday (eds), *The University in a Liberal State* (Aldershot, Avebury,1996).

[63] Newman, above n 19, at 91.

[64] The present government is committed to achieving a 50 per cent participation rate in higher education (*Education and Skills: Delivering Results: A Strategy to 2006* http://www.dfee.gov.uk/delivering-results/contents.shtml Objective 3) On rates of participation in university education see, *The National Committee of Inquiry into Higher Education* (The Dearing Report) (London, National Committee of Inquiry into Higher Education) 101.

[65] W Blackstone, 'On the Study of Law' in W Blackstone, *Commentaries on the Laws of England* vol 1 (London, T Cadell and J Butterworth, 1825) 6.

would have been strange to think of university education in any terms other than that of the education of gentlemen.[66] However, closer examination of Newman's text suggests that he saw himself not just as providing an education that fortuitously, because of prevailing social conditions, would be undertaken by gentlemen but, rather, that a university education was an education that was fit for such gentlemen and that it was not fit for those who were not gentlemen.[67]

Newman began his examination of the notion of liberal education by contrasting 'liberal' with 'servile' where the latter meant 'bodily labour, mechanical employment, and the like, in which the mind has little or no part.'[68] Later in his lectures he noted of the 'particular and practical,' which were not knowledge and thus were not the proper focus for the university:

> life could not go on without them; we owe our daily welfare to them; *their exercise is the duty of the many, and we owe to the many a debt of gratitude for fulfilling that duty.*[69]

By these two steps Newman separated the provision of liberal education from the life of the great majority of the population and allocated it instead to a small minority; a minority who he was quite content to see thrive because, in part, of the work of that majority.

Newman's distinction between those who had received the benefits of a liberal education and those who had not was not simply a class distinction:

> There are men who embrace in their minds a vast multitude of ideas, but with little sensibility about their real relations with each other. These may

[66] Rothblatt, above n 17, at 298. The Catholic University in Ireland that Newman was to create found that '[t]he middle class could not afford a university education' (I Ker, *John Henry Newman: A Biography* (Oxford, Clarendon Press, 1988) 442). Newman also saw a liberal education as being gender specific. His discussion relates only to that education which is fit for 'boys,' 'youths' or 'men.' Here again he reflects the prevailing spirit of his times. This reflects both the historical reality of the time and a degree of misogyny on Newman's part. Newman said of his introduction to his lectures 'Ladies, too, had been present and I *fancied* a slight sensation in the room, when I said, not Ladies and Gentlemen, but Gentlemen' (Ker, *ibid*, at 379).

[67] And, in thinking so, Newman trod a well-worn historical path. For the Greeks a liberal education was an education fit for a free man not a slave (Hirst, above n 12, at 31). However the historical record is discordant. In her 'classical defense of reform in liberal education' Nussbaum cites Marcus Aurelius's thoroughly democratic proposition that '[w]herever it is possible to live, it is possible to live a virtuous life' (Nussbaum, above n 61, at 64).

[68] Newman, above n 19, at 80.

[69] (emphasis added). Newman, above n 19, at 85.

> be antiquarians, annalists, naturalists; they may be learned in the law; they may be versed in statistics; they are most useful in their own place . . . If they are nothing more than well-read men, or men of information, they have not what specifically deserves the name of culture of the mind, or fulfils the type of Liberal Education.[70]

However, although people in this category had, for Newman, failed to have a liberal education inculcated into them, they could, in principle, have received its benefits. Who successfully attained a liberal education once they had entered onto a course of study was, for Newman, a matter of individual disposition but whether or not a person was fitted to enter onto such a course depended on their social class. Newman was very clear that the purpose of a university was not to produce 'that antique variety of human nature and remnant of feudalism . . . called "a gentleman".'[71] However a new variety of 'gentlemen' was precisely what Newman sought to educate.

Historically, a liberal education at university in Great Britain, as in many other countries, has been reserved for a small, socially elite group. For some of its proponents a liberal education has been seen precisely as being an education that was suitable only for such a group.[72] This his-

[70] Newman, above n 19, at 102.

[71] Newman, *ibid*, xxxviii. Unsurprisingly for someone living in a Protestant country who had been ordained a Catholic priest five years prior to giving the lectures and was to become a Cardinal 27 years later, the classic British gentleman was not something that was attractive.

[72] This is not a universal truth. Housman, for example, noted that the basis of education, the craving for knowledge, 'is a craving no less native to the being of man, no less universal through mankind, than the craving for food and drink.' (Housman, above n 25, at 16. See also *ibid*, at 18). Arnold's views on the importance of the search for culture were held alongside the view that 'to live in a society of equals tends in general to make a man's spirits expand, and his faculties works easily and actively; while to live in a society of superiors . . . in general tends to tame the spirits and to make the play of the faculties less secure and active' (M Arnold, 'Popular Education in France' in M Arnold, *Democratic Education* (Ann Arbor, University of Michigan Press, 1962) 8). Equally, however, the view that a liberal education should be reserved for a small social elite is not an idea that is entirely confined to previous eras of history. Bloom's analysis of American universities in the 1980s, arguing for the importance of the preservation of the distinction between higher and lower forms of culture, is perhaps more in keeping with Newman's position than that of Arnold (A Bloom, *The Closing of the American Mind* (Harmondsworth, Penguin Books, 1987)). (The background to the publication of this book is discussed in J Atlas, *Saul Bellow* (London, Faber and Faber, 2000) 531–34). One commentator has interpreted Bloom's analysis as 'nothing less than an effort to make explicit what women, blacks and working-class students have always known: the precincts of higher learning are not for them' (H Giroux, 'Dreaming about Democracy' in D Gless and B Herrnstein Smith, *The Politics of Liberal Education* (Durham, Duke University Press, 1992) 124).

torical truth does not mean, however, that this is the only way in which a liberal education at university can be conceived or that it is the only way in which it has been practised.

LIBERAL EDUCATION AS A MASS EDUCATION

The principles of liberal education have permeated university education in the USA to a much greater extent than anywhere else in either the modern or any previous era. This is true not only in the case of elite institutions but is also true for the system when it is taken as a whole.[73] The USA also has a participation rate in higher education that surpasses that of any other country in the world.[74] If any system of university education qualifies as a mass system it is the system that is to be found in the USA.[75] Moreover, neither its adherence to the principles of liberal education nor its high participation rates are new phenomena.[76] Here, in the USA, a liberal education is not conceived of as being an education for a small social elite. It is, instead, a general education for 'democratic citizenship' where, at least for some commentators,

[73] Thus, eg, Nussbaum's study of liberal education in the USA is based on an 'examination [of] a "core" group of institutions chosen to represent different types of US colleges and universities' (Nussbaum, above n 61, at x).

[74] In 1996 the USA had 5,341 tertiary level students per 100,000 head of population, a higher proportion than any other country (*World Education Report 2000* (Paris, UNESCO, 2000) 157). Indeed it could be argued that the American system of tertiary education is the very antithesis of an elite education since 'it differs from all others in offering access to some point of the system to almost everyone who wants to go to college or university without their having to show evidence of academic talent or qualifications' (M Trow, 'American Higher Education: Past, Present and Future' (1989) 14 *Studies in Higher Education* 5).

[75] None of these propositions should be read without qualifications. American universities may, for example, enjoy a high participation rate but rates of participation vary widely depending on the ethnic background of students (A Zusman, 'Current and Emerging Issues Facing Higher Education in the United States' in P Altbach, R Berdhal and P Gumport, *Higher Education in American Society* (3rd edn, New York, Prometheus Books, 1994) 343). Notions of liberal education are still important within undergraduate education in American universities but such interest has waned since 1963 and with 'the stagnant economy of the 1970s, students shifted en masse from the liberal arts towards vocationally oriented subjects' (C Kerr, *The Uses of the University* (4th edn, Cambridge, Harvard University Press,1995) 144; D Bok, *Higher Learning* (Cambridge, Harvard University Press, 1986) 39). Nevertheless, despite these and other caveats, the American system's adherence to notions of liberal education is stronger than in most and probably any other systems of higher education.

[76] See, eg, A Flexner, *Universities: American, English, German* (Oxford, Oxford University Press, 1930) 64.

that citizenship implies not just participation in the political processes of one particular nation-state but an involvement with the world as a whole.[77] It is difficult to see anything being much further removed from Newman's concept of liberal education as being an education for a gentleman than this vision of liberal education as an education for democratic world citizenship yet, at the same time, it is difficult to think of any more successful tertiary system of liberal education than that that is to be found in the USA.

ELITE VALUES AND MASS EDUCATION

Whilst there is no necessary connection between providing a liberal education and the propagation of a social elite there is such a connection between a programme of liberal education and the inculcation within students of what are sometimes seen as being elite social values.

The cast of mind that a liberal education creates results in a certain kind of character or, at least, leads to a predisposition to a certain kind of character. Sceptical inquiry, notions of individual autonomy and a requirement to justify one's actions all tend to promote a particular way of viewing the world and one's place in that world. '[F]reedom, equitableness, calmness, moderation, and wisdom' result from a liberal education, wrote Newman.[78] In a similar fashion Housman believed that it would be compel a student to 'take leave of delusions.'[79] In principle the type of character that a liberal education leads to is not linked with any particular social class nor to any particular occupation. A warehouse labourer, as much as a university lecturer, will benefit from a liberal education at the highest level and will be able to live a better life because of that education. However, the scepticism, sense of the importance of individual judgement and assurance of autonomy that are integral to those who have successfully pursued a course of liberal education are attitudes and values that are usually associated with those in professional and senior managerial occupations. Doctors, for example, have the concept of clinical freedom, judges the notion of judicial independence and academics the idea of academic freedom.[80]

[77] Nussbaum, above n 61, ch 2.

[78] Newman, n 19 above, at 76.

[79] AE Housman, 'Introductory Lecture' in AE Housman, *Selected Prose* (Cambridge, Cambridge University Press, 1961) 19.

[80] Not all professional or senior managerial occupations have notions of individual integrity that are specific as these. However, the very notion of a profession is often

Nothing in the warehouse labourer's job mirrors any of these ideas.[81] The values that a liberal education produces can thus be regarded as being elite values in the sense that, historically, such values have been held by those occupying elite roles within society. However, the historical fact that these values have been held by social elites does not mean that they are only suitable for social elites. On the contrary, precisely because they are values that lead to a richer and fuller life, they are values that are suitable for everybody.[82]

The idea that a liberal education predisposes students to a particular kind of character has to be treated with some caution. Traditionally it has been argued that liberal education is not in itself an education in character.[83] Indeed, for a liberal education to seek to inculcate into students one particular kind of character would be a profoundly illiberal procedure since it is of the essence of liberalism that value choices (and character is precisely the cumulation of a number of value choices) should not be imposed on individuals.[84] Newman emphasised that '[k]knowledge is one thing, virtue another; good sense is not conscience, refinement is not humility, nor is largeness and justness of view faith.'[85] For him the business of the university was the pursuit of knowledge not virtue. However, the acquisition of knowledge brings with it a richer appreciation of the world that in turn builds both a critical and sceptical nature. Newman himself observed both that '[t]he educated mind may be said to be in a certain sense religious; that is, it has what may be considered a religion of its own' and that:

thought to carry with it some notion of individual integrity in the pursuit of the occupation (see, eg, G Millerson, *The Qualifying Associations* (London, Routledge and Kegan Paul, 1964) 4).

[81] I use the illustrative example of the warehouse labourer simply because that was my occupation for several years after I first graduated from law school. Nothing, apart from illustrative importance, attaches to it as an example.

[82] Whether employers outside the usual ranks of graduate employers will regard such an education as making the student 'habituated to employment or otherwise organizationally acceptable' (R Jenkins, 'Black Workers in the Labour Market: the Price of Recession' in R Roberts, R Finnegan and D Gallie (eds), *New Appproaches to Economic Life* (Manchester, Manchester University Press, 1985) 170) is a different question. Indeed, whether the usual graduate employers, including the legal professions, will continue to regard such an education as making the graduate 'habituated to [new forms of] employment' is itself a matter for debate: as is the question of whether the views of employers are of any consequence.

[83] Hirst, above n 12, at 51.

[84] See, eg, J Rawls, 'The Priority of Right and Ideas of the Good' (1988) 17 *Philosophy and Public Affairs* 251 at 262.

[85] Newman, above n 19, at 91.

> [k]knowledge, the discipline by which it is gained, and the tastes which it forms, have a natural tendency to refine the mind and to give it an indisposition, simply natural, yet real, nay more than this, a disgust and abhorrence, towards excesses and enormities of evil.[86]

Following this argument a liberal education does not determine which values a person must choose but it does determine the method by which those values are chosen and defended and, given the way in which those values must be defended, arguably it may delimit a range of values from which the individual can legitimately make their choice.[87]

Newman's ambivalence about the place of morality in a liberal education necessarily is reflected in later debate on the nature of liberal education.

Particular moral leanings have been identified in the work of some individual theorists of liberal education. Thus, for example, Trilling writes of Leavis, who perceived university education as being, amongst other things, an education in 'sensibility':

> Dr Leavis's own critical sensibility is characteristically a moral one, not only in the sense that he happily affirms the value of common morality but also in the sense that, having perceived life to be of a certain weight and pressure, he requires of art that it react to experience with a proportionate counterthrust of commitment, endurance and intelligence.[88]

From the first date he published his arguments there have been some who have viewed Leavis' 'common morality' with suspicion. In his book on the nature of the university Leavis identified a 'humane centre' to civilization and saw one of the purposes of university education as being putting students in contact with that centre.[89] TS Eliot, responding to an earlier sketch of Leavis' ideas, where Leavis had used the phrase 'humane culture' instead of 'humane centre,' asked '[w]hy

[86] Newman, *ibid*, at 137 and 142. There are many other similar statements in Newman's lectures. For example, a liberal education will, according to Newman, free the mind of 'superstition' (Newman, *ibid*, at 104).

[87] There is an obvious comparison here with Weber's view that, whilst the social sciences can study value-judgements, 'whether the person expressing these value-judgements *should* adhere to these ultimate standards is his personal affair; it involves will and conscience, not empirical knowledge' (M Weber, ' "Objectivity" in Social Science and Social Policy' in M Weber, *The Methodology of the Social Sciences* (New York, The Free Press, 1949) 54).

[88] L Trilling, 'Dr Leavis and the Moral Tradition' in L Trilling, *A Gathering of Fugitives* (Boston, Beacon Press, 1956) 102.

[89] F Leavis, *Education and the University* (London, Chatto and Windus, 1948) 28.

should we want humane culture? Why is one conception of humane culture better than another?'[90] Criticism of this general type has continued to the present day. In more recent analyses the moral schemata that is undoubtedly imbedded in Leavis' work has been seen as being redolent of class attitudes rather than as having the universal nature that Leavis claimed for it.[91] Leavis's work, for some, is far from liberal in its attitudes and can be seen as simply imposing a set of ethical, political and social values on students by sheer weight of social authority rather than through any reasoned argument.[92]

Criticism of the kind above would seem to emphasise the importance of liberal education focusing on the fact that it is an education in knowledge not virtue. Yet, other writers have taken a contrary view, arguing that a moral focus is necessary if a liberal education is to be effective as an education. Stryker, for example, has written that:

> [g]iven the close connection between knowledge and power . . . liberal education's disavowal of all moral responsibility seems an illegitimate move. Universities educate, but their education is productive of power; for universities then to view the exercise of that power, and the nature of the society in which it is used, as outside the field of their concern, is surely an improper abrogation of responsibility. A blindness to the moral dimension of the university's mission does not nullify the institution's role in supporting the wider society and, through the education it offers, facilitating the policies society seeks to enact. Institutions of higher education and those teaching within them thus become implicated in any social injustice, despite liberal education's conception of itself as neutral.[93]

Stryker's arguments are articulated in the context of the Holocaust and the role of German universities and those educated in German universities in producing the Holocaust. The argument is, however, a

[90] Quoted in I MacKillop, *FR Leavis: A Life in Criticism* (London, Allen Lane, The Penguin Press, 1995) 240. Eliot was fundamentally opposed to Leavis' humanist position, his view being that 'humanism is, I think, merely the state of mind of a few persons in a few places at a few times' (TS Eliot, 'The Humanism of Irving Babbitt' in TS Eliot, *Selected Essays* (London, Faber and Faber, 1951) 473). However, his criticism is telling, even if one is more sympathetic than he was to the humanist position.

[91] For further discussion of this point see A Bradney, 'Liberalising Legal Education' in F Cownie (ed), *The Law School: Global Issues, Local Questions* (Aldershot, Dartmouth, 1999) 15–17.

[92] Whilst I accept there is some justice in these criticisms it remains the case that Leavis is a literary critic of immense significance whose work is a valuable resource for the law school. See further Bradney, above n 91, at 4–14.

[93] L Stryker, 'The Holocaust and Liberal Education' in B Brecher, O Fleischmann and J Halliday, *The University in a Liberal State* (Aldershot, Avebury, 1996) 9.

much wider one that can be put in relation to any social or individual injustice within the society in which a university is located.[94] Indeed it is possible go further than this and, more simply, argue that, if a liberal education is concerned with showing the connections and structures that pervade the world around us, it cannot ignore those connections and structures that relate to values and choices of values.

A liberal education can take account of both those who would argue in the same vein as Stryker and the cautionary observations of Newman. It can be an education that is, in part, an education about virtue without it being an education in virtue; a liberal education can note the questions about values and the various answers that might be given without, as Leavis arguably does, insisting on one particular answer to those questions. Stryker would plainly want to argue that some answers pertaining to values are unacceptable in the context of a liberal education. This is not an illiberal position. The answers about values that the student gives must adhere to the principles of sceptical enquiry and individual responsibility that are inherent in the notion of a liberal education. Nonetheless this still leaves an extremely broad range of legitimate responses from each individual student. In this sense a liberal education can be an education in values, the range of values that it inculcates will be elite values but the particular value choices made by the student will be personal to them and the education that is provided be for a mass audience.

A LIBERAL EDUCATION AND THE STRUCTURE OF THE ACADEMIC COMMUNITY

Discussion of liberal education, both in relation to the university as a whole and with regard to the law school, has traditionally concentrated on the relationship of liberal education to teaching and research. Analysis of liberal education has meant analysis of what it is that should be taught and what it is that should be included in the notion of research. Nevertheless, despite the fact that hitherto it has mainly been ignored, the notion of a liberal education also carries within it implicit, though largely undeveloped, notions of how a university ought to be organised.

[94] Or, if we use Nussbaum's concept of democratic world citizenship, in the context of any social or individual injustice in the world taken as a whole.

Here again it is worth beginning consideration of this issue by looking at Newman's lectures. Newman's lectures were largely concerned with what it was that should be taught in the university and with the impact that a liberal education would have on the student. He did not, however, entirely neglect the question of how the university should be organised. As we have already seen, in his lectures Newman stated that a university was:

> [a]n assemblage of learned men, zealous for their own sciences, and rivals of each other . . . brought by familiar intercourse and for the sake of intellectual peace, to adjust together the claims and relations of their respective subjects of investigation. They learn to respect, to consult, to aid each other.[95]

When this short passage is read in the context of Newman's general arguments about the nature of liberal education some of the key ideas about the administrative structure of a university that is concerned with a liberal education can be elucidated. First, Newman talks about 'an assemblage of learned men.' There is nothing here that speaks of a hierarchy within the university nor anything that allows for a distinction between the views and wishes of this 'assemblage' and the policies of some separately reified notion of the university or that allows for external control of the assemblage. The university is, and is only, this 'assemblage of learned men.' Secondly, these people are 'zealous for their own sciences.' They are concerned with their own bodies of knowledge and have no interests other than that concern. Their concern for their own subjects is limited only by the fact that, finally, they 'respect . . . consult . . . [and] aid each other.' In sum, in more modern terminology, for Newman the university is a community that is essentially non-hierarchical, individualistic yet also co-operative, where its members are concerned with the propagation of knowledge; in short it is a collegial enterprise.[96] In turn from this image of the university can

[95] Newman, above n 19, at 76.

[96] I am not suggesting that either in these lectures or at any other time, Newman fully thought through the implications of the notion of a liberal education for the administrative structure of the university. Indeed comments that he made outside his lectures suggest that he might have failed to understand the full implications of a university being an 'assemblage of learned men.' In a letter to Archbishop Cullen regarding the establishment of the new Catholic university in Ireland Newman wrote that he did not mind who was appointed as a Professor because 'they [the Professors] will not have anything to do with the government [of the university]' (C Dessain and V Blehl, *The Letters and Diaries of John Henry Newman* vol XV (London, Nelson, 1964) 117). The letter does not make it clear whether Newman thought this would be a permanent feature of the position of

be derived arguments about the necessity for academic freedom, so that members of the university can pursue their interest in their 'sciences' unhindered, and arguments about the obligation on academics to pursue those interests irrespective of, and even in direct opposition to, the wishes of others whilst, at the same time, respecting their obligation to 'respect . . . consult . . . [and] aid' others within the academic community.

The concept of the administrative structure of a university delineated above is an ideal form for a university; no historical example of a university has ever realised this form.[97] It is an aspiration that the liberal university struggles to live up to in the knowledge that it is unlikely to succeed and in the knowledge that the model, both of social life and of social values, that is implicit within the image is one which is largely misunderstood, and rejected where understood, in the larger society outside the university. Yet the organisational model of the university that Newman suggests springs almost inevitably from any concept of a liberal education at tertiary level and is not unique to his vision of the academy. Thus, for example, in German universities in the nineteenth century:

> the university was seen as an institution where pure knowledge . . . could emerge; and this required an academic community where all were more or less equally able to participate in the common endeavour.[98]

Similarly in 1946, in the aftermath of the Second World War, Jaspers wrote '[t]he university is a community of scholars and students engaged in the task of seeking truth . . . It is a body which administers its own affairs regardless of whether it derives its means from endowments, ancient property rights or the state.'[99] The precepts of liberal education make the various elements of this organisational model almost inevitable. Critical inquiry by both staff and students can pros-

professors or whether it was to be so only during the time that the university was 'provisional.' Ker notes that in Newman's constitution for the Catholic university that he created in Ireland he included professors in the government of the university but excluded Heads of Colleges; hardly an exemplary form of collegiality (I Ker, *John Henry Newman: A Biography* (Oxford, Clarendon Press, 1988) 410). Whatever the full complexities of Newman's position his comments provide an instructive starting point for enquiry into the nature of administration within the university.

[97] K Jaspers, *The Idea of the University* (London, Peter Owen, 1960) 83; M Kogan and S Hanney, *Reforming Higher Education* (London, Jessica Kingsley, 2000) 28–29.

[98] R Barnett, 'The Idea of Academic Administration' (1993) 27 *Journal of Philosophy of Education* 179 at 180.

[99] Jaspers, above n 97, at 19.

per in an atmosphere of intolerance and repression but it is less likely to do so than it is in an atmosphere of openness.[100] One can pursue one's own research ends in an hierarchical structure where those who have authority are opposed to one's work and will not cooperate in its production but such research is more likely to be stunted than stimulated by the experience. Research and teaching can be carried on as a solitary pursuit, and in the liberal paradigm are always to some extent solitary matters, but formal and informal interchanges with other scholars and teachers usually facilitate the production of worthwhile work. Research can, for a time, be carried out by tight disciplinary groups who have no intellectual interests or contacts outside their circle but, in the end, all boundaries tend to collapse and interchange with others outside one's field proves to be fruitful.[101]

The degree to which the essential organisational structure of the university differs from the organisation of other institutions and businesses in society can be over-emphasised. In his description of organisational structures Mintzberg, for example, categorises the university as a 'professional bureaucracy'; a form of organisation he regards as being 'common in universities, general hospitals, school systems, public accounting firms, social-work agencies, and craft production firms.'[102] He goes on to note that, as an organisational form, a 'professional bureaucracy':

> is unique among the five configurations [of organisation] in answering two of the paramount needs of contemporary men and women. It is democratic . . . And it provides them with extensive autonomy.[103]

The support that exists among some management theorists for the basic precepts that are inherent in the traditional organisational form of the university is an important corrective to recent suggestions that the form is either inefficient or ineffective.[104] An organisational type

[100] It is important to remember that intolerance and repression are not to solely to be seen in terms of a remembrance of regimes like the Nazi Germany that was the context for Jaspers' essay. A failure to take work seriously because it is representative of forms of scholarship that are seen as being too new or too old is also a form of intolerance and repression as are the petty, but important, inhumanities of racism and sexism.

[101] Steiner's response when asked what his field of research was, 'cow's have fields . . . passions in motion are the privilege of the human mind,' is always worth remembering (G Steiner, *Errata: An Examined Life* (London, Weidenfeld and Nicolson, 1997) 155).

[102] H Mintzberg, *Structure in Fives: Designing Effective Organizations* (Englewood Cliffs, New Jersey, Prentice-Hall, 1983) 189.

[103] Mintzberg, above n 102, at 205–6.

[104] This challenge to the traditional university form is exemplified by the Jarrett Report's call for vice-chancellors to be given the role of chief executives (*Report of the*

that meets both the functional needs of the institution that is the university and the human needs of its staff is plainly a hugely attractive proposition.[105]

This traditional notion of the structure of the liberal university has often been associated with a social image of what that structure represents:

> This 'community of scholars' is usually pictured as a close-knit personal group, probably sharing their knowledge together over a long period, the typical image often being a (perhaps idealised) view of the cloistered scholarly community of an Oxford or Cambridge college.[106]

In the present era this picture of the university is viewed with scepticism and even hostility by many academics. It is a picture that reflects the life of very few academics not just in the limited sense that it is an ideal that is not realised in the lives of those academics but in the wider sense that it does not even reflect the aspirations they have for themselves or their institutions. Cloisters may be an accurate reflection of the ecclesiastical origins of universities in the Western tradition and the lives of unmarried Fellows in Oxbridge colleges in the nineteenth

Steering Committee of Efficiency Studies in Universities (London, CVCP, 1985) 36). For a discussion of attempts to change the organisational structure of universities see C Prichard, *Making Managers in Universities and Colleges* (Buckingham, Open University Press, 2000) particularly at 20–28. For the idea that the university can be seen as being a role model for other forms of organisations in the future see, eg, C Handy, *The Future of Work* (Oxford, Basil Blackwell, 1984) 86–88.

[105] Historically many staff have been excluded from the collegiate life of the university. 'Administrators' have been characterised as the university's civil service and thus excluded from the centre (Barnett, above n 98). Other staff have been entirely disregarded. In principle the division between academic and non-academic staff is neither necessary nor desirable in the context of an institution devoted to liberal education. However the corollary of giving porters an equal say in the running of the institution is an equal devotion to the pursuit of knowledge and the needs of the institution; the right to claim overtime is one of the first casualities of such a change. It is not entirely clear that such staff would welcome Kennedy's suggestion that they 'should have some version of the faculty's unscheduled work experience' if this was the consequence of the bargain (D Kennedy, 'Utopian Proposal or Law School as a Counterhegemonic Enclave' (mimeograph, 1980) 5–6. On the demands made on academic staff if they work in a liberal law school see further Chapter 8 below.

[106] R Finnegan, 'Recovering "Academic Community": What Do We Mean?' in R Barnett (ed), *Academic Community: Discourse or Discord?* (London, Jessica Kingsley Publisher, 1994) 178–79). Even when universities outside Oxbridge began to be built in the nineteenth century they were initially designed in a style that copied the architecture of 'the Oxford model' (R Lowe and R Knight, 'Building the Ivory Tower: the Social Functions of Nineteenth Century Collegiate Architecture' (1982) 7 *Studies in Higher Education* 81 at 88).

century but they seem to have little to do with the family circumstances of the modern academic. Indeed for some the idea of the cloister, and the notion of separation from the outside world that it brings, might suggest 'what women, blacks and working-class students have always known: the precincts of higher learning are not for them.'[107]

The most disturbing part of the organisational claims for the liberal university is the notion that it should be separately organised according to a set of values which are fundamentally different to those which prevail in most other organisations in modern society. Put simply, how can one argue that universities in the twenty-first century necessarily have a special mode of organisation which involves a separate set of values at a time when:

> [h]igher education is being told: be like us, have our values, and in fact become part of us. Indeed, it is being told: for too long, you have been apart from us, holding yourself distinct and separate. In future, you must become one of society's institutions, responsive to its claims and expectations.[108]

Notions of democracy and inclusiveness plus a rejection of social elitism all seem to argue for a university which, in its organisational form, mirrors itself on the prevailing patterns outside the university and by so doing brings itself closer to the community in which it finds itself. Moreover the notion of collegiate governance, the epitome of the organisational form of liberal education, is something that does not even have historical resonance in law schools in the new universities (a significant section of the legal academy) where a managerial ethos has always been more prevalent.[109] Many other models for the organisation of university governance are on offer. For some commentators a change from collegiality to one of these other models is both something that has the air of historical inevitability and is, at the same time, a

[107] H Giroux, 'Dreaming about Democracy' in D Gless and B Herrnstein Smith, *The Politics of Liberal Education* (Durham, Duke University Press, 1992) 124.

[108] R Barnett, 'Recovering an Academic Community' in Barnett, above n 106, at 11.

[109] Evans, writing about the then Polytechnic of North London, observed 'PNL . . . does not suffer from the confusion between the two organizational modes, collegiality and hierarchy . . . the dilemma has been resolved . . . PNL has line management'. (C Evans, *English People* (Buckingham, Open University Press, 1993) 107.) It is also noteworthy that polytechnics, before they became 'new universities,' showed an early willingness to designate their vice-chancellors or directors as chief executives (J Fielden, 'The Shifting Culture of Higher Education' in P Wrights (ed), *Industry and Higher Education* (Bristol, The Society for Research into Higher Education and the Open University, 1990) 77. (See also Kogan and Hanney, above n 97, at 195) However, even in new universities there is considerable opposition to notions of managerialism (M Henkel, *Academic Identities and Policy Change in Higher Education* (London, Jessica Kingsley, 2000) ch 11.

socially expedient course of action.[110] However, the present political unpopularity of collegial governance, its historical association with practices that fostered social divisiveness and its connection with old rather new university law schools are all matters that are conceptually separable from the question of its inherent suitability for the university enterprise. The fact that collegiate governance does not exist in new university law schools can be explained by the historical development of those institutions; its absence from these institutions cannot, however, be justified by this history. Such governance provides the best background for providing a liberal education whatever the founding date of the university. Collegiate governance is associated with traditional universities and traditionally British universities have taken their students from a small social elite; that does not mean that universities have traditionally taken their students from a small social elite because of they practiSed collegiate governance. The political unpopularity of collegiate governance arises partly because it represents an opposition to forms of social organisation that are seen as being conducive to business efficiency. For many, such business efficiency will be seen as being reflective of cultural attitudes which seek to maximise human performance by ignoring the humanity of those who are performing; that will make collegiate governance as an organisational ideal more, not less, attractive. Notwithstanding all of the problems noted above the organisational form of the university law school, the way in which it manages itself, the way in which staff and students treat each other, is as vital to the notion of liberal education as the form that teaching takes or the reason for which research is done. If that enterprise is characterised in terms of liberal education then the organisational pattern follows.[111]

[110] See, eg, P Ramsden, *Learning to Lead* (London, Routledge, 1998) 22–29.

[111] Further discussion of some of the issues raised in this section of this chapter is to be found below in Chapters 6 to 8.

3

Missions for Law Schools: The Liberal University Law School

'THE BUSINESS AND BUSY-NESS OF THE UNIVERSITY'

PELIKAN, IN HIS 1992 analysis of the role of the university, observed that:

> ultimately the question of the business of the university is not the university as business, nor all the other kinds of 'business' and 'busy-ness' at a university, but rather: In what kind of 'business' must the university be engaged if it is to have a right to be called 'university,' and by whose definition of the word university?[1]

Pelikan's remark is particularly pertinent for British university law schools at the beginning of the twenty-first century. At a time when discussion within and about the law school frequently centres on trivia such as the minutia of teaching observations or the intricacies of examination procedures Pelikan reminds us that what really matters is what we think we are trying to do when we conduct the business of the university. Until and unless we satisfactorily identify what that business is, and thus identify what the business of the law school is, discussion of other matters is entirely redundant. A university law school works well only if it knows what it is doing and if its chosen function accords with the role of the university. If either of these things is absent, the law school will necessarily fail, even though that failure may be accomplished in a seemingly efficient and smooth manner, with the law school producing, perhaps because it has effective bureaucratic procedures in place or because it has enthusiastic and energetic staff, both a myriad of graduates and a host of publications. For even the highly

[1] J Pelikan, *The Idea of the University: A Reexamination* (New Haven, Yale University Press, 1992) 75.

productive law school the question will always be, are these *university* graduates, are these *university* publications; are these things properly the product of a university?

Chapter 2 articulated one answer to the question, what should the business of the university be? The business of the university is the pursuit of liberal educational goals and this determines what it should do in its teaching, its research and its governance. In many ways this is the traditional answer to the question, what is the business of the university. However, the final decades of the twentieth century saw many invitations to the university to radically reconsider the nature of its business. In some instances these invitations seemed almost to be instructions. Liberal education, it seems, fell out of fashion, with other educational objectives being favoured instead. This phenomenon was global rather than local. It was, and is, a feature of debate about higher education in the United Kingdom but it was, and is, also a feature of debate about higher education in Australia, North America, Africa and elsewhere.[2] No country, no university, seems to have been untouched by the debate. Moreover, it is a debate that has spread through all the various disciplines of the university and has penetrated even the most unlikely quarters. Thus, for example, scholars of Italian have been asked whether they would like to turn their attention from the study of Dante to the provision of language tuition for putative business people seeking access to Italian markets.[3] The law school has not been

[2] On debate about universities in general see, eg, D Mahoney, 'Establishing the University as the Sole Provider of Higher Education: the Australian Experience' (1992) 17 *Studies in Higher Education* 219; P Altbach, 'Problems and Possibilities: the US Academic Profession' (1995) 20 *Studies in Higher Education* 27 and X Dao, 'Policy-Making on the Improvement of University Personnel in China under the National reform Environment' (1991) 16 *Studies in Higher Education* 103. On debate about the role of the law school see, eg, S Woolman, P Watson and N Smith, ' "Toto, I've a Feeling We're not in Kansas Any More": A Reply to Professor Motala and Others on the Transformation of Legal Education in South Africa' (1997) 114 *South African Law Journal* 30.

[3] At the time of writing this passage Hobson's guide to degree courses in the United Kingdom says of Italian: '[i]f you choose to study for a degree in Italian . . . there are three major questions to ask yourself about what you do when you graduate. First, how directly do you want to use your language in your future career? Second, should you train in other areas such as commerce, finance or management and use your Italian in these settings? Third, would you prefer to use your skills and abilities developed through Italian in a job that does not require you to speak the language?' (*Degree Course Guides 2000/2001* vol 2 (Cambridge, Hobsons, 2000) pt 11 p 70). Sayers, writing soon after the end of the Second World War, recommended reading Dante's Divine Comedy because it 'had much in common with our own distracted times, and his vivid awareness of the deeps and heights within the soul comes home poignantly to us who have so recently rediscovered the problem of evil, the problem of power, and the ease with which

excluded from this debate. Indeed, at times, it has been at its forefront. This chapter will look at some of these invitations to the university to consider a new kind of business and to see whether the pursuit of liberal educational goals is a credible goal in the light of the prevailing political and intellectual climate.

'NOW, UNDER CONDITIONS THAT SEEM UNPROPITIOUS'

In the United Kingdom the 1997 Dearing Report on higher education provides an excellent illustrative example of the tenor of recent debate about the business of the university, showing why liberal educational objectives do not seem to be in keeping with the spirit of the times.

Like the Robbins Report, published over 30 years earlier, Dearing set down a number of different purposes for higher education. The report asserted that:

> The four main purposes of higher education are:
> — to inspire and enable individuals to develop their capabilities to the highest potential levels throughout life, so that they grow intellectually, are well-equipped for work, can contribute effectively to society and achieve personal fulfilment;
> — to increase knowledge and understanding for their own sake and to foster their application to the benefit of the economy and society;
> — to serve the needs of an adaptable, sustainable, knowledge-based economy at local, regional and national levels;
> — to play a major role in shaping a democratic, civilized, inclusive society.[4]

The Robbins Report had provided a pluralistic account of the function of the university but '[o]f the four aims of higher education laid down by Robbins, only one, "instruction in skills," depart[ed] from the path of the liberal ideal.'[5] In Robbins the notion of a liberal education was central to the arguments that were put forward. A superficial

our most God-like imaginings are "betrayed by what is false within" ' (D Sayers, 'Introduction' in Dante, *The Divine Comedy: 1 Hell* (Harmondsworth, Penguin Books, 1949) 10). There could scarcely be a bigger gulf between these two views as to why one might study Italian.

[4] National Committee of Inquiry into Higher Education, *Higher Education in the Learning Society* (The Dearing Report) (London, National Committee of Inquiry into Higher Education, 1997) 72.

[5] B Salter and T Tapper, *The State and Higher Education* (Ilford, Woburn Press, 1994) 11.

analysis seems to indicate that Dearing continued this tradition. Dearing's list of purposes for higher education included some that are central to a liberal education (such as, for example, 'the increase of knowledge and understanding for its own sake'). Moreover, since, as we saw in the last chapter, the pursuit of a liberal education does not preclude the pursuit of other educational objectives alongside a liberal education, it could be argued that the purposes for higher education as set out by Dearing are wholly in keeping with the notion that universities exist to provide a liberal education. Providing graduates who are employable, one of Dearing's objectives, is not, in itself, contrary to the work of any of the liberal theorists discussed in the previous chapter; what matters is that those employable graduates are also graduates who have acquired a liberal education. Closer examination of the report, however, especially when that examination takes account of the pronouncements about universities of various governments over the last few decades, suggests a rather different interpretation of the contents of the report.

Although Dearing discussed liberal educational objectives for higher education the main bulk of the argument in Dearing related to objectives that are far-removed from the kind of concerns discussed in Chapter 2 above. Dearing was aware that students are more than potential workers:

> Education and training must be embraced by people at all levels of achievement and, to varying degrees, throughout working life and thereafter to enhance leisure and the quality of life.[6]

However, Dearing's focus was on how higher education would contribute to the development of the British economy and how graduates would be, by virtue of their being graduates, better workers. As Barnett has observed 'the Report . . . very much places itself on the side of the economic conception of the learning society.'[7] The focus is not on how graduates would be better citizens or better persons. Knowledge, in Dearing, is rarely valued as a good in itself. Thus, even when Dearing discusses:

> [h]igher education institution's distinctive continuing role within a democratic society . . . as independent, questioning institutions unconstrained by any particular political or commercial agenda[8]

[6] Dearing Report, above n 4.

[7] R Barnett, ' "In" or "For" the Learning Society' (1998) 52 *Higher Education Quarterly* 7 at 15.

[8] Dearing Report, above n 4, at 75.

that discussion moves quickly, in the space of one paragraph, from the liberal proposition that:

> [i]t is a distinctive feature of an advanced civilization to seek the advancement of knowledge for its own sake and to satisfy natural human curiosity about the nature of the world

to the commercial proposition that

> [t]he very notion of pure research makes it difficult to predict when an observation becomes useful or applicable. Unless such research is carried out in higher education institutions, it is unlikely to be pursued anywhere else.[9]

The tone of the Dearing Report reflected its terms of reference and these terms in turn reflected British government rhetoric over the past few decades.

In 1985 the then Conservative administration issued a Green Paper on higher education that stated that:

> The Government believes that it is vital for our higher education to contribute more effectively to the improvement of the performance of the economy.[10]

Elsewhere in the paper it was said that universities should be:

> concerned with attitudes to the world outside higher education, and in particular to industry and commerce, and to be aware of 'anti-business' snobbery

and that the universities should 'go out to develop their links with industry and commerce.'[11] 'The future health of higher education,' the paper asserted, 'depends significantly upon its own success in generating the qualified manpower this country needs.'[12] In a subsequent debate on the Green Paper the then Minister for Education, Sir Keith Joseph, said that the Government did value 'education for pleasure and general culture and the financing of scholarship and research as an end in itself' but also observed that there was a need for an improvement in the economic performance of the country, and a need for a greater contribution by higher education to that performance, if these things that were valued were to be affordable.[13] Newman had used Cicero as a

[9] Dearing Report, above n 4.

[10] *The Development of Higher Education into the 1990s* (Cmnd 9524, 1985) para 1.2.

[11] *Ibid*, at para 1.6.

[12] *Ibid*, at para 2.2.

[13] Hansard, House of Commons, vol 79 para 857. Joseph's view of the universities reflected his general view 'that education was a major reason for Britain's economic decline' (A Denham and M Garnett, *Keith Joseph* (London, Acumen Publishing, 2001) 367).

source for the proposition that, once immediate physical needs had been met, human beings naturally turned towards the consideration of knowledge.[14] In 1985, when the United Kingdom's total household disposable income stood at £225.1 billion, an amount which had increased in the decade leading up to 1985 by 24 per cent even when inflation was taken into account, Joseph seemed disposed to doubt whether Cicero's basic precondition for the pursuit of knowledge had been, or would continue to be, met.[15] The suggestion that Joseph regarded the pursuit of knowledge, not as an expression of humanity's insatiable curiosity, but rather, as a luxury that could be afforded by only the most wealthy in society, is irresistible.[16]

In the debate that followed Joseph's statement only three MPs disagreed with the analysis of the function of higher education that the Green Paper and the Minister had put forward. Although their disagreement was expressed in vehement tones none of these dissentient voices spoke on behalf of their parties.[17] Giles Radice, who was the Shadow spokesman on education, did not query the function for higher education set out in the Green Paper when he responded to the Minister's statement.[18] Other MPs challenged or supported various points in the Minister's speech depending on their political complexion but, with the exception of the three dissenters, no one challenged Joseph's vision of the role of higher education. However, in contrast,

[14] J Newman, *The Idea of a University* (New York, Holt, Rinehart and Winston, 1960) 79.

[15] *Social Trends No 17* (London, Her Majesty's Stationary Office, 1987) 85.

[16] One contemporary commentator described Joseph's views as a ' bleak accountant's view of higher education' and turned to Newman to rebut Joseph's arguments (D Watt, 'Keith Joseph's Idea of a University' in F Mount (ed), *The Inquiring Eye: A Selection of the Writings of David Watt* (Harmondsworth, Penguin Books, 1988) 247).

[17] Enoch Powell said that it was 'barbarism to attempt to evaluate the contents of higher education in terms of economic performance or to set a value upon the consequences of higher education in terms of a monetary cost-benefit analysis' (Hansard, House of Commons, vol 79 col 861). Gordon Wilson described Joseph's attitude as 'philistinic' and Eric Heffer reminded him that as a fellow of All Souls he should know that 'man does not live by bread alone' (Hansard, House of Commons, vol 79 paras 864 and 865). Nothing unites these three voices in opposition to the prevailing consensus on the purpose of higher education. Powell, a former Professor of Greek at the University of Sydney and at the time of his speech an Ulster Unionist MP, had consistently taken the liberal view of education, sometimes explicitly linking his arguments to Aristotle's proposition about humanity's inherent craving for knowledge (see, eg, 'A View on Education' in R Collings (ed), *Reflections of a Statesman: Speeches of Enoch Powell* (London, Bellew Publishing, 1991). Wilson was an MP for the Scottish Nationalist Party. Heffer was a member of the Labour Shadow Cabinet but did not hold the education portfolio.

[18] Hansard, House of Commons, vol 97 cols 859–860.

outside Parliament the Green Paper was widely criticised. Joseph was reported as being 'upset' by the hostile reception that the Paper received.[19]

In 1987 the Conservative Government published a White Paper on higher education that started by saying that the Government:

> fully recognizes the value of research, and especially basic research, together with those areas of learning and scholarship which have at most an indirect relationship to the world of work. The encouragement of a high level of scholarship in the arts, humanities and social sciences is an essential feature of a civilised and cultured country.[20]

However, the White Paper followed the pattern established by the earlier Green Paper by immediately going on to observe that 'there is an urgent need, in the interests of the nation as a whole . . . for higher education to take increasing account of the economic requirements of the country.'[21] Following the publication of this White Paper the Conservative Under-secretary of State for Higher Education was reported as saying 'knowledge for its own sake was no longer of prime concern.'[22]

The depth of political consensus between the two main political parties as regards the proper purposes of the university is demonstrated by comparing the 1985 Conservative Green Paper and 1987 White Paper with a number of Labour Party documents relating to higher education. In its 1997 paper, *Higher Education in the 21st Century*, the Labour Party gave the same assurance of its attachment to broad educational goals for higher education that the Conservative Party had given whilst it had been in government. In a foreword to that paper David Blunkett, then the Secretary of State for Education and Employment, stated that:

> [o]ur universities and colleges must have the opportunities to offer world class higher education so that all students . . . can develop their full intellectual and personal potential.[23]

However, once again the emphasis of the paper and the Party's broader educational policies seemed to be on much narrower educational objectives. Later in the paper it was said that:

[19] Denham and Garnett, above n 13, at 401.
[20] *Higher Education: Meeting the Challenge* (Cm 114, 1987) 1.
[21] *Ibid*, at 1–2.
[22] *Times Higher Education Supplement*, 17 June 1988, 6.
[23] *Higher Education in the 21st Century* (London, DfEE, 1997) 2.

> [t]he Government endorses the need to extend opportunities for lifelong learning. This will help to ensure that people are equipped with the skills and knowledge they will need to respond to the technological and other changes taking place in our increasingly competitive global economy. The regular updating of those skills will be essential if the economy is to grow and if individuals are to find fulfilment both in and outside work.[24]

Lest anyone doubted which mattered more, the graduate's life inside work or the life that was outside work, the Labour Party had expanded on its views in an earlier paper that was the basis of its submission to the Dearing Committee. In *Lifelong Learning* the Party had noted that:

> [a]ddressing the needs of the future, rather than the needs of the labour market of today or yesterday, will be crucial in ensuring that the new knowledge gained and skills applied are relevant to the new century.[25]

Again there was the same obeisance to broader educational aims, though even this was slanted towards economic objectives.

> We must ensure that colleges, universities and other bodies offering post-compulsory education and training, including private providers, are accountable, as well as responsive to their students and the needs of the wider community, including industry and commerce.[26]

But the paper went on to conclude that:

> [a]ll students should be prepared for the world of work . . . The Dearing Committee should consider whether [all] students might undertake a vocational skills module as part of their course.[27]

Under Labour's plans both academics and students would be required to comply with the economic educational agenda of the Labour Party, irrespective of whether or not that approach formed part of their own personal goals, beliefs and ambitions. You might, thus, as a person, be an anarchist in your politics but, as a student, you would learn how to be a capitalist during your education. You might wish to go to university because you enjoyed studying your subject but, under the Labour Party's proposals, the state would temper that enjoyment by requiring you to contemplate and prepare for your years of waged

[24] *Higher Education in the 21st Century* (London, DfEE, 1997) at 8.
[25] *Lifelong Learning* (London, Labour Party, 1996) 2.
[26] *Ibid*, at 4.
[27] *Ibid*, at 27–28.

labour.[28] This vision of the university is the university seen as 'the primary institution outside the nuclear family for the training of subjects of the modern nation-state'; 'a bureaucratic arm of the unipolar capitalist system.'[29] One would have to go back to the period between 1939 and 1960, the years when conscription was in force, to find another example of a British political party attempting to press unwilling adults into direct servitude to its objectives. Griffith has described the Conservative administration's 1987 attempt to redirect higher education in general towards economic goals as being 'totalitarian' in nature; here, with its attempt to prescribe not just the direction of the system as a whole but the behaviour of each and every member of that system, the totalitarian spirit took on a new degree of vigour and a more precise form of expression.[30] The Labour Party's later Green Paper on education, *The Learning Age*, began with the uncompromising statement that:

> [l]earning is the key to prosperity—for each of us as individuals, as well as the nation as a whole. Investment in human capital will be the foundation of success in the knowledge-based global economy of the twenty-first century. That is why the Government has put learning at the heart of its ambition.[31]

Its 1998 paper, *Higher Education for the 21st Century*, devoted one whole chapter to 'Higher Education's Links with the Economy'; no similar attention was paid to any broader, more liberal educational objective.[32] Yet it is important to remember that the Labour Party differed from the Conservative Party only in its language. Its approach might be cruder but its goals were the same. The Conservative Party of both Thatcher and Major had seen 'an unbridgeable gulf in values and

[28] Pitcher and Purcell in their large-scale study of the reasons why students choose the subjects they study at university found that the majority of students had chosen their course because they thought they would enjoy it rather than because of any possible career advantage (K Purcell and J Pitcher, *Great Expectations* (Manchester, Higher Education Careers Service, 1996) 11). Engineering students were fairly evenly split between those who chose their subject for reasons of enjoyment and reasons of career advantage. Business studies students and law students were the only students who were very much more likely to choose their subject because of perceived career advantages with 72.2 per cent of law students selecting their course for this reason (Purcell and Pitcher, *ibid*).

[29] B Readings, *The University in Ruins* (Cambridge, Harvard University Press, 1996) 45 and 46.

[30] J Griffith, 'The Threat to Higher Education' (1989) 60 *The Politcal Quarterly* 50 at 53.

[31] *The Learning Age* (Cmnd 3790, 1998) 7.

[32] *Higher Education for the 21st Century* (London, DfEE, 1998).

conceptions of the nature and purpose of university education' when it looked at the views of the academic profession and because of this had simply sought to ignore the profession.[33] The Labour Party saw the same divide and took the same approach.[34]

The economy is referred to seven times in the Annex to the terms of reference for the Dearing Report. This has lead Kogan to query whether there is in fact any governmental support for the role of higher education 'in developing the powers of the mind, and in advancing understanding and learning.'[35] Trow, commenting on the Dearing Report, wrote that:

> I have been reading the Report . . . as a symptom or a statement of a broadly shared view, cutting across party lines, of the role and nature of this country's system of higher education: of its proper structure, its function in and for society, and its guiding values and principles.[36]

The historical record analysed above seems to bear out these views. Moreover, this shared approach is one that is largely opposed to the notions of a liberal education whether they be related to the pedagogical aims of the university, its research goals or its style of governance.

The more local politics of the law schools and their relationship with the legal professions suggests a more complex picture with regard to the reception of notions of liberal education than the view that one gains from looking at the broader panorama of political attitudes towards the universities taken as a whole. It is true that a series of official and unofficial reports through the three final decades of the twentieth century had called for a closer connection between the law schools

[33] M Trow, 'American Perspectives on British Higher Education under Thatcher and Major' (1998) 20 *Oxford Review of Education* 111 at 113.

[34] Indeed those who were education ministers and shadow ministers were sometimes perceived of as being insufficiently rigorous in their hostility to the universities by their own central party organisations. 'The Policy Unit took the view that Shepard's and Blunkett's nominations [for the Dearing Committee] were too close to the universities and insufficiently reflective of Government and business interests to be politically acceptable. The composition of the Inquiry was adjusted accordingly and several businessmen and sector administrators were drafted in'. (D Robertson, Who Won the War of Dearing's Ear?' (1998) 30 *Higher Education Review* 7 at 9.) Businessmen thus gained a considerably increased range of influence on the contents of the report (Robertson, *ibid*, at 19). On the other hand '[t]here were no FRS and no FBAs, the accepted indicator of eminence in the humanities and social sciences' (M Kogan, 'The Treatment of Research' (1998) 52 *Higher Education Quarterly* 48 at 49). These groups consequently had much less influence on the final report.

[35] Kogan, above n 34.

[36] M Trow, 'The Dearing Report: A Transatlantic View' (1998) 52 *Higher Education Quarterly* 93 at 94.

and the legal professions; in the modern idiom this could be seen as being a call for a closer connection between the academic world and 'the world of work.'[37] Yet, at the same time, there were also a number of reports and statements from outside the universities that supported the idea of a liberal education in university law schools.[38] However, it would be difficult to argue that these latter statements suggest a depth of support for liberal education in the legal professions that would be such as to indicate a willingness to voice significant opposition to government plans for university law schools.

In previous chapters I have argued that an educational policy that runs counter to the occupational culture of the universities is going to be, at best, difficult to implement; that one of the reasons for arguing for a liberal education in university law schools is that it is in accord with at least the rhetoric of those law schools. It could be argued that this argument is equally applicable to those who have a large part in supplying the financial resources on which the law school depends and who set the political constraints within which the law school operates. How is it possible to argue for a liberal education in the law school if those who direct resources into the law school are opposed to the idea? On this basis the analysis above seems to lead to the inevitable conclusion that, whatever the intellectual and humane attractions of a liberal education, to propose such an idea in present times is futile, given that the political circumstances are wholly unpropitious.

'FITFUL ENTHUSIASM'

British higher education's present situation is, in large part, the result of the last 20 to 30 years of British political history. However, assessing accurately the possible options for future development that that situation leaves open involves looking at that very recent history in the context of the more than 700 years history of European universities.

Minogue has argued that European universities came into being as the result of 'fitful enthusiasms' for education rather than as a

[37] See, eg, *Report of the Committee on Legal Education* (The Ormrod Report) (Cmnd 4595, 1971) and *A Time for Change: Report of the Committee on the Future of Legal Education* (The Marre Committee) (London, General Council of the Bar, 1988).

[38] The most important example of this being *First Report on Legal Education and Training* (London, Lord Chancellor's Advisory Committee on Legal Education and Conduct, 1996) 57.

consequence of sustained, deliberate policy.[39] In the case of the United Kingdom it is certainly true that the needs of universities have rarely if ever occupied the centre-stage of British politics. Until the twentieth century their creation owed more to private endeavour than it did to state activity. State recognition of their existence, even into the twentieth century, has been comparatively rare and sustained state involvement in their workings even rarer.[40] The gradual rise in the number of universities and the number of university students, particularly the expansion that followed the Robbins Report, has changed the degree of involvement.[41] Moreover, the shift from an elite system to a mass system, itself a state decision, has accelerated the rate of that change. Nevertheless the state and the political parties that govern the state remain comparatively uninterested in universities. Education is part of the mainstream political agenda but it is schools not universities that interest the parties.

The peripheral place that universities have in the British political arena is problematic for the universities, explaining in part the poor level of resource that they receive. However, it also justifies caution in accepting the argument that a general political aversion to notions of a liberal education means that those notions are impossible to implement in practice. Politicians propose policies for higher education; they have neither the will nor the means to implement them. The attempt to create a wider managerial group within universities through either the appointment of more people into administrative positions or through the co-option of academics into managerial roles can be seen as a political attempt to circumvent this problem.[42] However, this attempt has been, and can be, only partially successful because on the one hand those managers and administrators can themselves take on the attitudes of academics towards the universities that they work in and because those managers and administrators are themselves, by virtue of

[39] K Minogue, *The Concept of a University* (Weidenfeld and Nicolson, 1973) 11.

[40] B Salter and T Tapper, *The State and Higher Education* (Ilford, The Woburn Press, 1994) 5–11.

[41] A Halsey, *Decline of Donnish Dominion* (Oxford, Clarendon Press, 1992) 4–5; T Becher and M Kogan, *Process and Structure in Higher Education* (2nd edn, London, Routledge, 1992) 33–39.

[42] See M Henkel, *Academic Identities and Policy Change in Higher Education* (London, Jessica Kingsley, 2000) ch 11 for a discussion of the changing nature of the academic as an administrator. See D Braun, 'New Managerialism and the Governance of Universities in a Comparative Perspective' in D Braun and F Merrien (eds), *Towards a New Model of Governance for Universities* (London, Jessica Kingsley, 1997) for a discussion of broader changes in administration.

the fact they are not academics, in only slightly a better position than politicians to implement policies about academic practices. In the end academic practices are a matter for the academics who are practising.[43] Moreover, the position for the politicians is complicated by the fact that, in terms of public rhetoric, both the two main parties largely accept the rhetoric of liberal educational goals. The arguments in the previous section of this chapter show that the rhetoric that is used conceals other educational objectives and that those objectives lie in a different direction to the ideal of a liberal education. There is still, however, the perceived political necessity to use the rhetoric of an attachment to liberal education.[44] This puts the parties in a similar position to a recalcitrant, totalitarian political state forced to use the language of human rights to justify its actions even though its desires run along very different lines. The language of the political parties, their rhetorical acceptance of liberal education, can be used against them so that liberal education can be maintained and even enhanced in the universities. Equally, it is important to remember that for some politicians support for notions of a liberal education is much more than a matter of rhetoric. When the Conservative Party published its 1985 Green Paper Robert Rhodes James, who had been appointed to liaise between the Conservative Government and the universities, resigned his job commenting that '[t]he DES does not understand the universities. The Green Paper was not only illiterate but innumerate.'[45] It would be foolish to think that wide support for the universities is now to be found on either side of the House of Commons; it would be equally foolish to think that there is no support at all.

In past decades and centuries the establishment of liberal education in the universities has usually been in the context of a political climate that was hostile or indifferent to those ideas. If liberal education in law schools is to be enhanced it will once again happen in the context of hostility or indifference. Whilst it would be a mistake to ignore this fact it would also be a mistake to be overly concerned about it. Tritely, politics may be the art of the possible; it need not be seen, however, as just being the art of the easy.

[43] To a greater or lesser degree this is the case in all occupations. Holdaway, for example, makes the point that in the hierarchical world of the police constable workplace culture matters more than law or force orders in determining how a constable behaves on a day-to-day basis (S Holdaway, *Inside the British Police* (Oxford, Basil Blackwell,1983)).

[44] M Trow, 'American Perspectives on British Higher Education Under Thatcher and Major' (1998) 24 *Oxford Review of Education* 111 at 116.

[45] M Halcrow, *Keith Joseph* (London, Macmillan, 1989) 185.

PLURALISTIC GOALS AND THE LIBERAL LAW SCHOOL

There are some who, when contemplating the business of the law school, would entirely reject the notion of the university law school as a purveyor of liberal education or who would allocate only the most minimal space for the pursuit of liberal educational goals in the law school and, in so doing, would make effective implementation of a policy of liberal education impossible.[46] The arguments against these positions, setting out the importance of a liberal education in a university, have been set out in Chapter 2 above. There is, however, a third position which would argue for a liberal education but would genuinely seek to combine that liberal education with other educational ends, allowing the university and its law school both to be liberal and to be other things as well. This position raises arguments about the business of the university and its law school that are different in kind from those that have previously been addressed in either this or the previous chapters of this book. However, it is necessary to assess the value of this third suggestion about the proper business of the university and its law school in the context of Pelikan's notion of the 'busy-ness' of the university; it is important that these potential goals should be assessed in the light of the human and financial resources that are available to law schools and universities at the beginning of the twenty-first century.

In the United Kingdom perhaps the most detailed account of the pluralistic law school is that that has been put forward by Twining.[47] Twining's pluralistic vision of the law school, which he has sometimes referred to as the 'International Legal Center model' of a law school, involves the law school making a direct contribution to legal education and the development of knowledge about law at a number of different

[46] This seems to be the position taken by Brayne (H Brayne, 'A Case for Getting Law Students Engaged in the Real Thing: The Challenge to the Saber-Tooth Curriculum' (2000) 34 *The Law Teacher* 17).

[47] Twining does not limit his account to the work of United Kingdom law schools. Indeed he has noted that the only law school in the world that seeks to adhere to the vision of the law school that he prefers is the National Law School of Bangladore (W Twining, *Law in Context* (Oxford, Clarendon Press, 1997) 303). He has also written about legal education in the USA (see, eg, W Twining, 'Rethinking Law Schools' (1996) 21 *Law and Social Inquiry* 1007). However, since the focus of this book is on university legal education in the United Kingdom (though I equally see the arguments as applying to university law schools throughout the world) I will focus on those arguments which Twining has couched largely in the United Kingdom context.

levels or points within society.[48] In *Blackstone's Tower* Twining wrote:

> [t]he most ambitious version [of this model of a law school] . . . is set out in a report by the International Legal Center (I.L.C.) on *Legal Education in a Changing World*, which states:
>
> > 'Law schools, perceived as multipurpose centers, can develop human resources and idealism needed to strengthen legal systems; they can develop research and intellectual direction; they can address problems in fields ranging from land reform to criminal justice; they can foster the development of indigenous languages as vehicles for the administration of law; they can assist institutions involved in training paraprofessionals; they can help to provide materials and encouragement for civic education about law in schools and more intelligent treatment of law in the media; they can organize advanced specialized legal education for professionals who must acquire particular kinds of skills and expertise.'
>
> This [is a] vision of law schools as multi-purpose centres of learning [that might] be grandly labeled the law school as the legal system's, as opposed to the legal profession's, House of Intellect.[49]

This model of the law school, even in its attenuated forms, involves law schools providing not just undergraduate and postgraduate teaching, but also engaging in Continuing Professional Development work for barristers and solicitors and for others engaged in legal work.[50] Moreover, the model envisages the law school's engagement in activities other than undergraduate teaching as being a significant part of its activities rather than it being an occasional or peripheral feature of the law school's role.[51]

Twining's concept of the role of the law school is based on the assumption that '[t]he primary mission of a university is the advancement, stimulation and dissemination of learning.'[52] The significance of this assumption, for those interested in the pursuit of the goals of a liberal education, is enhanced by the fact that:

[48] For an outline of Twining's idea of the proper purposes of the university law school see, eg, W Twining, *Blackstone's Tower: The English Law School* (London, Stevens and Sons/Sweet and Maxwell, 1994) 51–58, ch 15 and W Twining, 'Thinking About Law Schools: Rutland Reviewed' (1998) 25 *Journal of Law and Society* 1.

[49] Twining (1994), above n 48, at 54.

[50] See, eg, Twining (1998), above n 48, at 11–13.

[51] Thus, eg, Twining has suggested that 60 per cent of the teaching resources of a law school should be allocated to non-undergraduate teaching (Twining (1998), above n 48, at 8).

[52] Twining (1997), above n 47, at 254.

> this idea of the university as a House of Intellect is unequivocal in its rejection of strong analogies with factories or emporia or evangelical churches or ideological seminaries.[53]

Thus, notions that are central to the concept of a liberal education, form part of the core of Twining's model yet, at the same time, it incorporates, as being important elements of the law school's work, matters that are, at best, peripheral to traditional conceptions of a liberal education.[54] The model thus raises two problems for those interested in the pursuit of a liberal education. First, it is possible for these different objectives to be followed at the same time? Is there any synergy between them? If there is no synergy can they be pursued together because they are independently important and do not conflict? Secondly, pragmatically, given the very limited resources of United Kingdom law schools, is there sufficient human and financial capital to follow Twining's preferred route? There are a number of reasons why the second, more mundane question should, in this instance, have priority over the first, intellectually more interesting question. Twining himself implicitly recognises the importance of the second question by, for example, suggesting that 'the post-graduate and the "outreach" programme [should be] . . . self-financing.'[55] Equally, logically, if the university literally does not have the resources to do something, there is no profit in considering the desirability of that particular thing. Finally, the more mundane question raises issues which are central to recent suggestions about universities as a whole which would seek to combine more traditional and liberal notions of the business of the university with new ideas about how universities should be run and what missions they should pursue. Before assessing Twining's pluralistic view of the university law school it is therefore necessary to turn back to a broader consideration of how a university could look in the twenty-first century.

[53] Twining, *ibid*. It is tempered, however, by the fact that learning is seen as being compatible with 'both theoretical studies and such aspects of professional training that can appropriately be carried out in institutions with this kind of mission' (Twining, *ibid*).

[54] Such as, eg, professional training.

[55] Twining (1998), above n 48, at 12 and by suggesting that there should be a move away from 'dependency on public funding and the vagaries' of government policy (Twining, *ibid*).

ENTREPRENEURIAL UNIVERSITIES

Chapter 2 above argued the merits of the traditional conception of the university in Western culture, the liberal university. Others have suggested that we need to turn to new concepts of the university in order for it to retain a valuable role in society. In his book *Creating Entrepreneurial Universities*, a case-study of five European universities, Clark, for example, has stated that modern universities:

> face an overload of demands; they are equipped with an undersupply of response capabilities. In a demand-response equation of environment-university relationships they may be seen as falling so badly out of balance that if they remain in traditional form they move into a nearly permanent stage of disequilibrium.[56]

Clark argues that the increase in demands on universities has taken four different forms. First, given a move from elite to mass (and perhaps to universal) higher education '[m]ore students, and more different types of students, seek and obtain access.'[57] Secondly, '[m]ore segments of the labor force demand university graduates trained for highly specialized occupations.'[58] Thirdly, '[p]atrons old and new expect more of higher education.'[59] Finally, '*knowledge outruns resources*.'[60] Basing his observations on the five universities that he studied, Clark argues that universities can and should respond in an entrepreneurial way to these problems. The entrepreneurial response, as Clark analyses it, involves creating a core decision-making group within the university, enhancing peripheries within the university to engage in new activities, creating a diversified, discretionary funding base for the university and stimulating the heartland of the university to engage in enterprising action.[61] Linking each of these individual elements of the entrepreneurial response is the belief that:

> [s]uccessful entrepreneurial beliefs, stressing a will to change, can in time spread to much and even all of an institution, becoming a new *culture*.[62]

[56] B Clark, 'Creating Entrepreneurial Universities: Organizational Pathways of Transformation' (Oxford, IAU Press, 1998) 129.
[57] Clark, *ibid*.
[58] Clark, *ibid*, at 130.
[59] Clark, *ibid*.
[60] Clark, *ibid* (emphasis in original).
[61] Clark, *ibid*, at 137–42.
[62] Clark, *ibid*, at 143.

In other words, taken to its fullest extent, the change to an entrepreneurial university involves not just a change in administrative structures, departmental designations or even sources of funding but, rather, a change to Trow's 'private life' of the university.

The apparent advantages of the entrepreneurial university are manifest. Seeking diversified funding not only brings additional funding to the university but also offers the university greater autonomy because the university is no longer dependent, wholly or mainly, on one source of finance, giving the supplier of that source (typically the state) the de facto power to control the university. However, what is less clear is what the entrepreneurial university is seeking to do with, or what the entrepreneurial university is willing to do for, this diversified funding. What business is the entrepreneurial university in? Clark writes that universities:

> [f]acing complexity and uncertainty . . . will have to assert themselves in new ways at the environment-university interface. *But they will still have to be universities, dominated as ever by educational values in the activities of research, teaching, and study.*[63]

Elsewhere he argues that, in the entrepreneurial university, it is important that 'the administrative backbone fuse . . . new managerial values with traditional academic ones' and that:

> [a]s new patrons contribute [to the university], their expectations of what they should get in return readily intrude to become new constraints. Universities then need greater self-consciousness on where they draw the line between what they are willing to do and not do to meet those demands.[64]

Finally, he notes that for some parts of the university, he instances the humanities, '[d]eliberate effort . . . to go out and raise funds by offering new services may seem particularly out of place, even demeaning.'[65] That Clark envisages the university remaining an academic (and arguably a liberal) institution and not a shopping mall, offering to ever-changing customers a variety of attractive but perhaps worthless goods, is clear. How he sees the university establishing what the academic limits to entrepreneurial activity are is more opaque. In the liberal model of education, education is always transformative and newly

[63] Clark,'Creating Entrepreneurial Universities: Organizational Pathways of Transformation' (Oxford, IAU Press, 1998) at 126 (emphasis added).

[64] Clark, *ibid*, at 137 and 140.

[65] Clark, *ibid*, at 141.

acquired knowledge sometimes unwelcome and often unsettling to those to whom it is transmitted. Whether this is compatible with the concept of entrepreneurialism is uncertain. Trying to sell a customer something that they do not want does not seem to be a sensible goal for the entrepreneur, yet providing unwanted goods is in many ways the key business of the university.

Clark's use of the word 'patrons' above may be instructive. Entrepreneurialism normally calls to mind the notion of seeking new and varied customers for goods and services that one wishes to sell. But customers have wishes and the vendor must accede or appear to accede to these wishes; unwelcome knowledge and unexpected transformations seems to be unlikely to be the things that large numbers of customers will readily seek. A patron is, however, something very different from a customer. Dictionaries ascribe a number of different definitions to the word patron. One may certainly work for patron but one does not simply provide a patron with goods or services at whatever is the market rate, as in the case of the relationship between vendor and customer. Instead, according to the Oxford English Dictionary, the patron is variously expected to advance the interests of the person, institution or cause they protect, to act as an advocate for them and to provide influential support for them. A patron may receive a return because they are a patron but what they receive is a matter of frequent negotiation and renegotiation; the often stormy relationship between Michaelangelo and Pope Julius II offers an excellent example of the position of the patron.[66] The state has long acted as a patron for United Kingdom universities and still continues to do so. In part Clark's argument is a suggestion that universities look for alternative patrons with greater vigour than they have in the past. Whether or not there are sufficient patrons, as opposed to customers, available for the entrepreneurial university so that it can be both entrepreneurial and a university is a moot point. In part, however, Clark's argument is also that universities should look for more customers for its services.[67] Whether a widespread search for customers can sit easily with the academic role is even more debateable.

[66] G Vasari, 'Life of Michaelangelo Buonarroti' in G Vasari, *Lives of the Artists* (Harmondsworth, Penguin Books, 1971) 342–62.
[67] Clark, above n 56, at 17.

ENTREPRENEURIAL UNIVERSITIES, PLURALISTIC LAW SCHOOLS AND A LIBERAL EDUCATION

Both Clark and Twining offer visions that involve a traditional, academic and liberal approach to what the university should do infused with new ideas about what else the university can do as well. Whether these visions are seen to be attractive depends in the first analysis on an empirical question. Can universities and their law schools perform the multiplicity of tasks that both writers suggest? And, if the answer to the first question is yes, more specifically, how many universities and how many law schools can manage these tasks?

Two of the universities that Clark studied are United Kingdom universities, Strathclyde and Warwick.[68] Both are thriving institutions; both have academics whose work, by even the purest of standards, must be accounted the pursuit of knowledge for knowledge's sake. Yet, that which we know about these institutions does not provide us with an answer to the first question above. Clark's argument is made not when we see that an institution thrives; it is made only when the institution thrives as a university. PriceWaterhouseCoopers thrives and in some ways it is in the business of knowledge production but it is not a university. It is not enough that academic work is done in both Strathclyde and Warwick; what is important is the balance between that academic work and the entrepreneurial effort that is made to sustain the institution. Does the effort outweigh the work? Does the effort mean that work that could be academic is not academic? Does the effort mean that individuals who could be academics become entrepreneurs? And if the answer to either of the latter two questions is yes, then the question becomes what proportion of work and what proportion of individuals within the institution?[69] Here there is simply not the research evidence, looking at the work of the two institutions, from which one might seek an answer.[70] Even if one can say that these

[68] The other three were the University of Twente in the Netherlands, Chalmers University of Technology in Sweden and the University of Joensuu in Finland (Clark, *ibid*, at xiv).

[69] One could, of course, raise a whole series of questions about what one might mean by the term 'academic.' Here, however, I am simply taking Clark on his own terms. As we have seen above he retains in his account of the entrepreneurial university the notion that it should be academic.

[70] Clark's account is of how universities become entrepreneurial rather than a detailed account of what each of his five sample universities are doing in each of their various

universities have managed to successfully continue to be academic and even liberal in their aims whilst being entrepreneurial this does not necessarily mean that there is the market for all universities to follow their example.

The same questions and the same answers can be asked and given with respect to Twining's suggestion about the role of university law schools. Can law schools get sufficient revenue from non-undergraduate activities to support such work and, if individual law schools can be successful in doing this, can law schools taken as a whole be successful in this way? Law schools unlike businesses are tied by their geography. They cannot relocate when better opportunities in terms of potential customers are to be found elsewhere. Their location may mean that they have too few customers or too many competitors to be financially successful in such markets. Equally, as with the entrepreneurial university, will the effort outweigh the advantage; to what degree will it still permit the law school to be a place where liberal educational goals are pursued? Here the answer is even more difficult to arrive at than is the case in the instance of Clark's entrepreneurial university because, as Twining observes, no United Kingdom law school has, as yet, set out to follow his model.[71]

Even if the pragmatic, financial questions above can be answered in the affirmative, even if it is possible to pursue goals other than liberal educational goals, either because those other ends will provide resources for the university or because they are seen as being valuable in themselves, and still preserve an appropriate space for liberal educational ends within the university and its law school, the second question about the compatibility of the two kinds of objectives remains. Plainly one can pursue more than one objective even when those objectives have nothing in common. In law schools many people seek both to be academics with all that that entails and, for example, parents with all that that entails. But to do one thing is difficult and to do two things, if they are different, is more difficult and the more things one seeks to

areas of activity. 'Warwick University Ltd,' with its account of a university that had 'a peculiarly subordinate relationship with industry,' might seem to be a work that provides a negative answer to the question in relation to Warwick (E Thompson (ed), *Warwick University Ltd* (Harmondsworth, Penguin Books, 1970) 16). However, this collection of essays is more a polemic than a piece of scholarship and one might therefore view the objectivity of its account of the University of Warwick with some suspicion. In any event the book describes the university at a stage in its history prior to the period of entrepreneurial culture (Clark, above n 56, at 14).

[71] W Twining, *Law in Context* (Oxford, Clarendon Press, 1997) 303.

do the more difficult it becomes. To add to the combination of personal and academic objectives that individuals already have, a range of wildly different academic objectives, may not in itself be conducive to the most effective pursuit of liberal educational goals.

Reaction to ideas such as those put forward by Twining and Clark must both be provisional and cautious. One cannot foreclose the possibility that either or both offer means by which the university and its law school can both enhance its ability to follow liberal educational goals and other objectives that are not in themselves objectionable and are in some cases desirable. There is not enough empirical evidence to justify either assenting to these ideas or rejecting them. Both approaches offer opportunities to the university and the law school and in this they are unlike the programmes of the major political parties in the United Kingdom. However, the approaches also pose potential problems.

THE CORE BUSINESS OF THE LAW SCHOOL

In Chapter 2 above I argued that the idea of a liberal education offered the most compelling account of what a university law school should be about. If a liberal education can be combined with other things or if other things can be used to enable the law school to retains its agenda of working according to the notions of liberal education then all well and good. However, in times of scarcity a company normally focuses on its core business. In the case of the university law school this core business is liberal education. In the face of the competing demands that Clark notes, and in the face of the alternative ends that politicians suggest, it is necessary that a university, and therefore its law school, 'becomes more willing to assert to the outside world that it is different, even distinctive'; that there are demands that its members are capable of meeting but will not meet because they do not fall within the liberal educational objectives of the university.[72] Were resources greater then universities and their law schools might be in a position to look more enthusiastically at work that does not come within their core business.

[72] Clark, above n 56, 147.

4

The Path Less Trodden: The Liberal Curriculum

THE GOALS OF THE CURRICULUM

IN TEACHING, FOR any curriculum, liberal or otherwise, clarity of aim in the curriculum is a prerequisite to success.[1] Thus it is necessary to translate the general principles that lie behind a liberal education, as outlined in Chapter 2 above, into specific goals for the liberal curriculum in the university law school, if that curriculum is going to be an effective means of education.[2]

Because of the historical connection between British university law schools and entry into the legal professions, law school curricula have traditionally seen their goals in terms of subject coverage. The need to teach whatever subjects have constituted the 'core' curriculum for professional purposes has largely driven the law school, dominating decisions as to what should be offered in the curriculum.[3] 'Core' subjects have largely been found in the first two years of the degree and

[1] I Sneddon and J Kremer 'Introduction: Dealing with Change' in I Sneddon and J Kremer (eds), *An Enterprising Curriculum* (Belfast, HMSO, 1994) 3.

[2] This chapter does not examine the literature that analyses the way in which law is best taught, learnt and assessed. This is not because I do not believe in the importance of this literature. On the contrary I accept that the mechanics of teaching have been given too little attention in the law school. Moreover, I believe that academics within law schools have failed to make the necessary connections between what they are doing as teachers and the literature that looks at educational theory and practice. (On this see further F Cownie, 'Searching for Theory in Teaching Law' in F Cownie (ed), *The Law School: Global Issues, Local Questions* (Aldershot, Ashgate, 1999) and J Webb, 'Why Theory Matters' in J Webb and C Maughan (eds), *Teaching Lawyers' Skills* (London, Butterworths, 1996).) However, these are things that concern not just the law school that follows a liberal curriculum but any law school concerned with teaching. They are thus not germane to this chapter or indeed this book.

[3] The legal profession's view as to what constitutes those subjects that have to be studied if a law graduate is to be exempted from Part I of professional qualifying examinations, the Joint Announcement on Qualifying Law Degrees, has varied over the years. The most recent formulation is to be found at http://www.lawzone.co.uk/barcouncil/resources/download/ja.pdf

other subjects in the curriculum have mainly built on those early subjects.[4] Such coherence as curricula have possessed has often come from this perceived need to allow students to secure a place within the legal professions by providing this core to legal learning. Some academics have argued that the subjects that form the focus for the concerns of the legal professions also constitute a 'natural core' to legal learning. Thus, for example, Birks has written that '[a] sound case can be made for the view that the present six [core] subjects . . . are genuinely foundational to the western legal tradition.'[5]

In contrast to the view that there is a necessary subject-focus to legal learning which is dictated by either the demands of the legal professions or by some 'natural' centre, the fact that a liberal education can be found in any of the various disciplines of the social sciences and humanities within the university suggests that, providing inquiry touches in part or whole on the human world, the focus of that inquiry is of no great import in the liberal curriculum. The liberal law curriculum therefore has, in terms of subject coverage, no core content; there is no list of legal material that must be studied if the student is to be considered educated in a liberal manner. Land law can serve as well as legal history, commercial law as well as critical legal studies, as a basis for a liberal education in the law school.[6] What matters is not the subject studied but the attitudes of those who are teaching and studying the subject.

The goal of the liberal law curriculum is not to see that students have acquired particular factual information but, rather, to allow them to understand the structures and values that permeate and underpin law. It is thus not what is studied but the manner in which something is stud-

[4] Harris and Jones' 1996 survey of university law schools concluded that 'seven out of the ten most common options . . . concern the study of areas of law linked far more explicitly to professional legal practice than to the academic study of law in its own right' and that 'a number of essentially "academic" subjects . . . are now offered by less than 30% of law schools' (P Harris and M Jones, 'A Survey of Law Schools in the United Kingdom, 1996' (1997) 31 *The Law Teacher* 38 at 52).

[5] P Birks, 'A Decade of Turmoil in Legal Education' in P Birks, *Examining the Law Syllabus: Beyond the Core* (Oxford, Oxford University Press, 1993) 10). Birks' essay was written before the 'core' expanded to include European Community law.

[6] Of course some areas of law have historically received a treatment that has concerned itself more with the technical aspects of the subject than with any deeper enquiry. But no area of law *has* to be treated in this way. Thus, for example, compare most standard land law textbooks with R Warrington 'Land Law and Legal Education: Is There Any Justice or Morality in Blackacre?' (1984) 18 *The Law Teacher* 77 or contrast standard equity textbooks with H Lima and S Scott-Hunt, *Feminist Perspectives on Equity and Trusts* (London, Cavenish, 2001).

ied that matters. Nevertheless, the fact that virtually anything in law can be seen as being the proper subject of a liberal education in law does not mean that the curriculum can properly be a *smorgasbord*, offering an eclectic and unconnected mix of subjects, dependent for their place in the course solely on the variant whims of the disparate staff in the individual law school that is teaching the student.

GIVING STRUCTURE TO CURIOSITY

The liberal curriculum responds to the inalienable curiosity that is at the heart of human nature. However, in responding to that curiosity, if it is to be something other than entertainment, the curriculum has to build on the curiosity, doing more than provide a momentary feeling of satiety for students. The curriculum should be a pedagogic device that has a clear sense of purpose and direction. Yet, at the same time, if a curriculum is to be liberal, it should not attempt to determine, except in the very broadest terms, what the students will become or what they will take out of the law school.[7] It should be a construct that is designed to introduce the student to the wide variety of conversations that is going on within law at any one moment, so that they can explore law from a range of different stances. If the curriculum is effective it affords the student, in so far as is possible, the opportunity to pursue their own individually chosen future ends, unhampered by an inability to enter

[7] It will be a curriculum about law, even if that is understood in very broad terms and because of that will determine to some extent what students can take out of it. It is a university curriculum and to that extent this also determines what students can take out of it. However, outside these necessary limitations the curriculum should be seen as an opportunity for students rather than something that is imposed on them. This requirement immediately puts the liberal curriculum in conflict with some forms of modern educational thinking and some forms of audit. Thus, eg, there is an increasing literature concerned with the importance of developing a curriculum that contains 'learning outcomes' for students (see, eg, S Otter, *Learning Outcomes in Higher Education* (London, Unit for the Devlopment of Adult Continuing Education (UDACE), 1992)). The Benchmark standard for law is couched in terms of learning outcomes (http://www.qaa.ac.uk/crntwork/benchmark/law.pd). However, there is also a literature that examines the deleterious effects of learning outcomes, focusing on their tendency to attempt to predetermine (the outcomes of the course) what students will take out of their time in higher education (see, eg, J Allan, 'Learning Outcomes in Higher Education' (1996) 21 *Studies in Higher Education* 93; K Eccleston, 'Empowering or Ensnaring?: The Implications of Outcome-based Assessment in Higher Education' (1999) 53 *Higher Education Quarterly* 29; A Bradney, 'Benchmarking: A Pedagogically Valuable Process? An Alternative View' (1997) 2 *Web Journal of Current Legal Issues* (http://www.wbbjcli.ncl.ac.uk).

into a particular argument because of their unfamiliarity with the terms of the debate. Thus, by definition, the liberal curriculum is pluralistic. If the curriculum fails to be pluralistic it seeks to impose values on students, attempting to make student see law from a single or a very limited number of stances. A liberal curriculum cannot forbid debate, by saying to students this one thing is what the study of law is like, although individual courses (and still more individual teachers) within the curriculum may assert the priority of their truth (and assert it as a foundational truth if they so choose), providing they do not do so by denying the right of other courses (and other teachers) to speak on equal terms.[8] The essence of the liberal curriculum in a university law school is that it seeks to introduce students to the intellectual excitement that was outlined in the first chapter of this book.

Pluralism and variety in a curriculum will take different forms in different law schools. No curriculum, in the very short period of time allowed for undergraduate university study in the United Kingdom, can seek to address all the various areas of law and approaches to studying those areas of law that are currently the focus of research and scholarship. Every undergraduate law degree is little more than an introduction to the study of law. The smaller the law school the more difficult it will be to give students a meaningful indication of the full range of study available to them. The smaller the number of faculty staff the smaller is likely to be the range of knowledge amongst that staff. Perhaps more importantly, the smaller the number of staff the smaller is likely to be the range of approaches to the study of law found amongst those staff. This is not to say that a small law school cannot offer a liberal education but, for the student, all other things being equal, the larger the law school, the better the opportunities that it can afford.[9] The need for variety does not forbid some element of focus in the law school's curriculum, achieved either by courses that progres-

[8] It is easier to describe the importance of this balance than it is to maintain it in practice. The balance that is sought is best seen in an example. In an age when traditional, descriptive doctrinal law, which in research terms tended to mean the multiplication of case notes and in pedagogic terms the inculcation of legal rules, has increasingly lost favour in the law school, this kind of doctrinal lawyer's protestation that, this is what the study of law is like, still has a place within the curriculum (as has the response, this is what intellectual suicide is like).

[9] Size in itself is not enough. A very large law school could contain staff who all had very similar intellectual interests. Such a law school would have no more to offer a student than a very small law school. Law schools are used to looking for subject coverage when appointing staff. A liberal law school also has to be alive to the need for intellectual width in its staff.

sively build through the years of study or by courses that repeatedly address particular areas of law or approaches to study, nor does the need for variety suggest that the mix on offer will be the same in all law schools. On the contrary the law school's curriculum must reflect the interests and approaches of the particular group of scholars who are teaching within it.[10] Thus no law school will straightforwardly replicate another.[11] But, for the liberal curriculum, any focus that there is should not be achieved at the expense of giving students some appreciation of the whole of the story that is law as we currently understand it.

SENSIBILITY, INTELLIGENCE AND A TECHNICAL EDUCATION

In writing a curriculum for the liberal law school it is important to remember the two-fold character of a liberal education that was identified in Chapter 2 above. In his discussion of the university Leavis wrote that '[t]he problem [for liberal education] is to produce specialists who are in touch with a humane centre.'[12] Both being a specialist and being in touch with 'the humane centre' are important for Leavis' thesis; both the knowledge of detailed technical information and an awareness of the structures and values that permeate and connect that information are necessary; neither can be dispensed with. Later in the same book Leavis argued that:

> [t]he essential discipline of an English School is the literary-critical . . . It trains, in a way no other discipline can, intelligence and sensibility together, cultivating a sensitiveness and precision of response and a delicate integrity of intelligence—intelligence that integrates as well as analyses and must have pertinacity and staying power as well as delicacy.[13]

[10] The majority of English university law schools that were graded 'Excellent' in the 1994 Teaching Quality Assessment exercise were praised for their research-led teaching (A Bradney, 'The Quality of Teaching Quality Assessment in English Law Schools' (1996) 30 *The Law Teacher* 150 at 161). This reflects a wider literature in higher education which argues that the highest quality of teaching is found in those staff who draw on their own research knowledge (see, eg, R André and P Frost (eds), *Researchers Hooked on Teaching* (London, Sage Publications, 1997)).

[11] There can be no blue-print for a liberal curriculum in the university law school because each curriculum must reflect the local circumstances of each law school and must change as those circumstances change.

[12] F Leavis, *Education and the University* (2nd edn, London, Chatto and Windus, 1948) 28.

[13] Leavis, *ibid*, at 34.

Again both sensibility and intelligence are important for Leavis. Newman similarly saw both that the function of the university was to educate 'the intellect to reason well in all matters, to reach out towards the truth, and to grasp it' and that '[i]t requires a great deal of reading, or a wide range of information, to warrant us putting forward our opinions on any serious subjects.'[14] A liberal education thus involves a search for structures and seeks to inculcate in a student an awareness of the all-pervasive nature of values and questions about values in the world that surrounds them. This is the most characteristic and the most important element of a liberal education. It is not, however, the totality of a liberal education and is not in itself sufficient for there to be a liberal education at a level appropriate to a university. A liberal education also involves the inculcation of matters that are wholly technical and, at university level, it involves a mastery of depth and detail.[15] If these latter things are not found then the awareness of structures, the knowledge of values and questions regarding values must itself necessarily be found only at a shallow level. The world, or at least some part of the world, must be known, in an empirical sense, at a rich and deep level, if the fact and significance of the penetration of structures and values in that world is to be fully understood. If the world is only known superficially then the knowledge of structures and values must itself be superficial. In this sense a liberal education does not reject but instead emphasises the importance of factual learning. However, both that technical understanding of detail and the knowledge of structure and values need to be acquired by the student at the same time. Technical information is not acquired, absorbed and later used as the source for liberal inquiry nor is it acquired for its own ends. Instead the value of the technical detail is seen to lie largely in the way that it can be used to understand structures and values rather than as having value in itself. Therefore, in writing a curriculum for a liberal university law school, the task is to produce a structure that will give students the opportunity to acquire both an awareness of the great range of conversations about law that are now going on within the academic world

[14] J Newman, *The Idea of a University* (New York, Holt, Rinehart and Winston, 1960) 95 and 97.

[15] Thus, in the context of the law school, there needs to be 'knowledge of a substantial body of law' (Birks, above n 5). However, that body of law need not be law conceived of in terms of legal rules. Law seen as legal theory or law seen as empirical studies of law in practice are but two examples of those things that can fit the term 'knowledge of a substantial body of law' as well as and indeed instead of a knowledge of cases and statutes.

and, at the same time, to be able to participate fluently in at least some of those conversations.

From the perspective of the liberal curriculum, the precise choice of subject-matter for technical enquiry is of little importance.[16] The choice made can be the law reports and statutes that have long held the affection of the law school but equally, it can be statistical analyses of dispute resolution, ethnographic accounts of pluralistic legal systems, conceptual interrogations of the relationship between gender and state law or a host of other material that relates to law. What matters is not so much what is chosen but the rigour with which the material is examined. A course that focuses on cases but does little more than superficially describe a small number of judgments fails in exactly the same way that a course that looks at ethnographic accounts of law but does no more than produce a tourist guide to law in far away places fails.

LOVE THY NEIGHBOUR

One example will suffice to illustrate the way in which a liberal education can change the direction of that which is done in the curriculum whilst at the same time continuing a tradition of law being a technical training.[17]

In *Donoghue v Stevenson* Lord Atkin famously said that:

> [t]he rule that you are to love your neighbour becomes in law: You must not injure your neighbour, and the lawyers' question: Who is my neighbour? receives a restricted reply. You must take reasonable care to avoid acts or omissions which you can reasonably foresee would be likely to injure your neighbour. Who then, in law, is my neighbour? The answer seems to be persons who are so closely and directly affected by my act that I ought reasonably to have them in contemplation as being so affected when I am directing my mind to the acts or omissions which are called in question.[18]

[16] Of course the precise focus of study might be important for other purposes. Thus, eg, if the law degree is seen as being part of a process of professional training as well as a liberal education it will become vital that students spend time studying the effects of gender difference given both the fact that professional lawyers will have both male and female clients and given the prevailing climate of sexual inequality in the legal professions (see further F Cownie and A Bradney, *English Legal System in Context* (2nd edn, London, Butterworths, 2000) 148–52 and 155–56).

[17] My thanks are due to the Reverend Dr Ian McIntosh who read an earlier version of this section and drew my attention to some of the references. Any errors in analysis that remain are, of course, my own.

[18] *Donoghue v Stevenson* [1932] AC 562 at 580.

In learning the law of tort, even if a student acquires no other knowledge, they will still be able to recite the neighbour principle and may even be able to quote or paraphrase the passage above.[19] Atkin's description of the neighbour principle is quoted in textbooks and forms the basis for all the subsequent discussion of the law of negligence that will be found there.[20] Moreover, if the student is diligent, they will read other cases that will also cite Atkin's principle and, as with textbooks, sometimes even quote Atkin's words. Learning this passage is for the student the beginning of an acquisition of a technical mastery of an intricate area of the law. Learning other cases that cite the passage is further technical learning. It can be an example of mastering detail and exploring the law in depth; a beginning of becoming a specialist in law. Looking at the self-same passage can, however, also be the start of a liberal education in law; the start of an education in sensibility. What matters is what the student is expected to see in the passage.

At a purely technical level the neighbour principle is the starting point for a process of inquiry which asks, when will I be regarded, in law, as being negligent; when will I have to pay damages for harm that I do to another? The answer to this question requires the student to acquire a detailed, technical knowledge of the law partially because, in the view of many commentators and judges, the law in this area lacks coherent principle.[21] Individual rules relating to particular areas of human conduct need to be learnt in a manner which almost amounts to learning a catechism if one is to understand the law of negligence in a manner that will enable one to predict who will be found negligent. If

[19] It has been said that '[i]f one were to ask a recent graduate of an English, Canadian, Australian or New Zealand law school what was the most important decision in all of the common law, he or she would likely and without hesitation say *Donoghue v Stevenson*'. (J Smith, *Liability in Negligence* (London, Sweet and Maxwell, 1984) 15). Similarly, in his biography of Lord Atkin, Lewis describes the neighbour principle as being 'the most quoted metaphor' in English law (G Lewis,' (London, Butterworths, 1983) 61).

[20] See, eg, R Heuston and R Buckley (eds), *Salmond and Heuston on the Law of Torts* (21st edn, London, Sweet and Maxwell, 1996) 199 and M Jones, *Textbook on Torts* (7th edn, London, Blackstone Press, 2000) 32.

[21] See, eg, Conaghan and Mansell's comment about the 'extraordinary emptiness' of the neighbour principle (J Conaghan and W Mansell, *The Wrongs of Tort* (London, Pluto Press, 1993) 12) and Lord Pearson's assertion that 'it is true that the Donaghue v Stevenson principle . . . is a basic and general but not universal principle and does not in law apply to all the situations which are covered by the wide words of the passage. To some extent the decision in this case must [therefore] be a matter of impression and instinctive judgement as to what is fair and just.' (*Dorset Yacht Co v Home Office* [1970] AC 1004 at 1054).

a great mass of detail is not learnt, that which the student does know is so trivialised as almost to amount to ignorance. It is not just that the student with limited learning knows only a small number of areas in which the neighbour principle has been applied but, rather, that, in knowing only a small number of areas, they will never know whether what they have learnt will be applicable to new instances that are put before them. Consideration of the neighbour principle can, therefore, result in a sophisticated knowledge of detail that will enable a student to understand how the minutia of the law can determine the outcome of individual cases. However, analysis of the neighbour principle can also serve a quite different end.

Cane notes that the principle 'love thy neighbour' is a 'religious injunction.'[22] It is this juxtaposition in Atkin's judgment of an ancient religious precept and a new legal principle that gives rise to an analysis that can serve as a part of a liberal education.[23]

The starting point for Atkin's arguments lies outside the law in a theology and a code of morals that Atkin, in 1932, might have expected his readers to be both familiar with and broadly to accept.[24] Atkin's use of the reference is thus not merely felicitous; he intends his judgment's connection between Christian imagery and legal argument to be persuasive, resulting in assent to his position.[25] Atkin observes that '[t]he liability for negligence . . . is no doubt based upon a general public sentiment of moral wrongdoing for which the offender must pay.'[26] Loosely connecting his arguments about legal principle with long-standing Christian notions of right conduct is one way in which Atkin seeks to situate his judgment in the mainstream of 'general public sentiment.' In noting this fact, the student immediately begins to be alerted

[22] P Cane, *The Anatomy of Tort Law* (Oxford, Hart Publishing, 1997) 64.

[23] The arguments to be found here are a development of ideas I first put forward in A Bradney, 'Liberalising Legal Education' in F Cownie (ed), *The Law Schoo:l Global Issues, Local Question* (Aldershot, Dartmouth, 1999).

[24] On the position of organised Christianity in Great Britain at this time see J Wolffe, *God and Great Britain: Religion and National Life in Britain and Ireland 1843–1945* (London, Routledge, 1992) 70–72.

[25] It has been argued that 'Lord Atkin's passing analogy to Christian theology [was] probably added as a mere rhetorical flourish or by way of literary license' (Smith, above n 19, at 20; J Smith and P Burns, 'Donghue v Stevenson: The Not So Golden Anniversary' (1983) 46 *Modern Law Review* 147). This, of course, is speculative but even if it is true it has no effect on the argument here. Lord Atkin saw the connection between Christian theology and his annunciation of a new legal principle as being persuasive; how important he thought that persuasive force for the purposes of his judgment is irrelevant for my purposes here.

[26] *Donoghue v Stevenson* [1932] AC 562 at 580.

to the way in which values and questions about values permeate the law.[27] Atkin's argument about the neighbour principle is not merely a technical application of legal rules but is, instead, the result of a particular moral view of the world (though that moral view is much more complex than a superficial reading of his words would suggest) that both accepts the Christian message and allows it to be 'restricted' in law.[28] Moreover, a closer comparative examination of both the passage in Atkin's judgment and the relevant verses in the *New Testament* shows the way in which religious values are manipulated by Atkin in order to reach a result which is both put forward as being in accord with the Christian message and yet directly contradicts those precepts.[29]

The starting point for Atkin's arguments is the Christian teaching to be found in the parable of the Good Samaritan.[30] In Luke's gospel this parable is the answer given to the lawyer's question, put to Christ, 'who is my neighbour?'[31] The instruction to 'love thy neighbour as thyself' is found in Leviticus.[32] However, at the time of Christ, '[the rabbis] regarded neighbour as a term of limited liability and endlessly debated what classes of men were excluded by it from the scope of the commandment.'[33] Thus, for example, in Jewish teaching at the time the duty to love thy neighbour was thought to extend to fellow citizens but not to non-Israelites.[34] The lawyer therefore seeks from Christ a definitive, doctrinal answer to a longstanding, doctrinal question. The answer that Christ gives to this question does not, however, just extend the notion of a neighbour beyond its then traditional bounds. Rather,

[27] In an increasingly secular age students are unlikely to see the connection between religious and legal argument for themselves. Atkin himself was clear that, 'as far as the law is concerned, it is perpetually laying before the student standards of conduct which are standards of conduct which it is desirable to have maintained in the social state' (Lord Atkin, 'Law as an Educational Subject' (1932) *Journal of the Society of Public Teachers of Law* 27 at 30).

[28] Atkin was a dedicated member of the Church of Wales (Lewis, above n 19, at 20).

[29] The values that are implicit in Atkin's judgment have received relatively little attention in law schools. For one recent reading, however, see Z Bankowski, *Living Lawfully: Love in Law and Law in Love* (Dordrecht, Kluwer Academic Publishers, 2001) 71–72 and 99–100.

[30] Luke 10:25–37.

[31] Luke 10:25.

[32] Leviticus 19:18.

[33] G C Baird, *Saint Luke* (Harmondsworth, Penguin Books, 1963) 148. See similarly J Ford, *My Enemy is My Guest* (Maryknoll, New York, Orbis Books, 1984) 92.

[34] A Leaney, *A Commentary on the Gospel According to St Luke* (2nd edn, London, Adam and Charles Black, 1966) 182.

by arguing that we have a duty to love even those who are strangers and even enemies (as was then the case in the relationship between Samaritans and Jews), by setting no boundaries on this duty of love, Christ implicitly argues that the question to be put should not be 'who is my neighbour?' but, instead, 'to whom can I be a neighbour?'[35] It provides not the doctrinal answer sought by the lawyer but, instead, the suggestion that seeking to base one's behaviour on such doctrinal precepts is, in itself, an error. 'The conversation between Jesus and the lawyer perfectly illustrates the difference between the ethics of law and the ethics of love.'[36]

Atkin, in his use of the lawyer's question, observes that the law gives 'a restricted reply' to the question, 'who is my neighbour?' The word 'restriction' suggests limitation or constraint. A restricted observance of a code of manners or morals is still an observance; it is merely not full adherence to the code. By using the word 'restricted' Atkin thus links the law's answer to the question, 'who is my neighbour?', to Christianity's answer to the same question, suggesting that the law is operating on the same moral plane as Christianity. In fact the relationship between the two answers to the question is very different to the one that Atkin describes.

Several judgments subsequent to *Donoghue v Stevenson* have observed that an application of Atkin's neighbour principle to those involved in the parable of the Good Samaritan would lead to both the priest and the Levite escaping liability for their actions.[37] Neither the priest nor the Levite are neighbours to the injured man in English law; there is no general legal duty to aid the afflicted.[38] Christianity might judge their actions harshly; English law does not. The answer that English law gives to the question, who is my neighbour, is therefore not a 'restricted' one. English law rejects the notion of unlimited love. The English law's answer to the question is, instead, very different from the Christian message, building on quite separate images of how humanity

[35] Caird, above n 33, at 148. On the longstanding enmity between Jews and Samaritans at the time of the parable see Ford, above n 33, at 80–90.

[36] Caird, above n 33, at 147.

[37] Per Lord Diplock in *Dorset Yacht Co v Home Office* [1940] AC 1004 at 1060 and per Windeyer in *Hargrave v Goldman* (1963) 110 CLR at 66.

[38] This point was noted very soon after Atkin gave judgment (P Winfield, 'Duty in Tortious Negligence' (1934) 34 *Columbia Law Review* 41 at 60). It has continued to be a principle of the law of negligence even in the modern era (see, eg, Smith, above n 19, at 16).

does and should interact.[39] English law seeks to work in the same way that Jewish law had worked at the time that the lawyer questioned Christ, limiting liability by limiting the notion of who qualifies as being my neighbour.[40] Atkin's answer, and thus English law, is couched in precisely the same form of argument that Christ sought to reject. In turn Atkin's image of humanity and the way that it behaves can be related to ideas of humanity as economic actors that are themselves far removed from the theology of the *New Testament*.[41]

Focusing, in the manner above, on the way in which values permeate and are manipulated in Atkin's judgment is not intended to inculcate into the student any particular response to the judgment. It is the observing of the permeation and manipulation of values that is vital to the educational process. On closer examination of the passage where Atkin argues for the neighbour principle students might accept his position, arguing for example that the Christian message of unlimited love is untenable in a modern or post-modern society where people frequently meet each other only fleetingly as strangers.[42] Equally they might reject Atkin's ethics, seeing them as a counsel of moral despair or failure, in favour of the Christian or some other message.[43] A student might see the manner of Atkin's argument as being a cynical abuse of the likely faith of readers of the judgment or, equally, an appropriate way to lead people to a conclusion that is necessary for the effective and efficient operation of law in the modern era. What, in this sense, the student makes of the passage is irrelevant. A liberal education involves inculcating in students an awareness of the pervasive nature of values not leading them to adherence to a particular set of values. The important point is that they see Atkin's judgment in *Donoghue v Stevenson* as both technical information and also something that is much more than this.

[39] Commentators on *Donoghue v Stevenson* have often taken Atkin's dictum at his own estimation. Thus Lewis writes of the 'moral basis of responsibility, related to but narrower than Christian morality, which made so memorable his great statement' (Lewis, above n 19, at 58). In fact the only relationship between the English legal and the Christian approaches is one of antithesis.

[40] Thus, eg, I might not be proximate enough to somebody to be their neighbour (R Heuston and R Buckley, *Salmond and Heuston on the Law of Torts* (21st edn, London, Sweet and Maxwell, 1996) 203).

[41] For an examination of this economic view see R Bowles, *Law and Economy* (Oxford, Martin Robertson, 1982) 112–18.

[42] A Giddens, *Consequences of Modernity* (Stanford, Stanford University Press, 1990) 80.

[43] The 'Meditations' of Marcus Aurelius are as much a rejection of the modern law of negligence's view of how to live in the world as is Christianity.

A liberal education involves constant attention to both the acquisition of technical information so as to make the student a specialist and to questions of values so as to train their sensibility. What distinguishes a liberal education from a technical education is not observing the fact that the priest and the Levite escape censure under English law; a number of doctrinal accounts of the law of negligence have done this.[44] What makes a liberal education different is the fact that this point is seen as being not just worthy of a passing paragraph or sentence but as deserving sustained interrogation. Moreover, in looking at negligence, a liberal education means not just spending time analysing Atkin's observations in the manner above but also looking at succeeding judgments in order to see similar points recurring in the way that judges construct their arguments. There is in this sense nothing special about Lord Atkin's annunciation of the neighbour principle. It is precisely the essence of a liberal education that the interplay of values found in his words are part of the normal woof and weft of the law; that understanding the law means understanding this continual interplay in all the judgments that are read.

If the process above is to be followed, if students are to understand not just the new rules that are to be found in judgments but are also to see the complex processes that create those new rules, it necessarily follows that students will learn less technical information. Time in a curriculum is finite. If the students are to both acquire a technical learning and an awareness of values and structures they will have to learn less technical information than they would have done if they had just focused on that. Yet, in drawing the balance between learning technical information and learning about values and structures, it is necessary to remember the importance of producing the specialist as well as the importance of producing the educated person. Focusing solely on technical information produces graduates who are nothing more than semi-intelligent dictionaries. However, ignoring the importance of acquiring technical information produces shallow thinkers whose knowledge of the empirical world is based on the random accidents of their upbringing, an upbringing that, no matter what their class, gender, cultural or other background, is necessarily limited and limiting.[45]

[44] See, eg, W Prosser, *The Law of Torts* (4th edn, St Paul Minnesota, West Publishing Co, 1991) 344 and Jones, above n 20, at 49.

[45] On the background of students see further A Bradney, 'An Educational Ambition for "Law and Literature" ' (2000) 7 *International Journal of the Legal Professions* 343 at 346–48.

In Atkin's discussion of the neighbour principle the values and structures that underlie the doctrine are ethical in their nature. This will not always be the case. It is vital that the fact that a liberal education is an education in values should not be interpreted as a proposition that a liberal education is an education about ethics. Values are more wide-ranging than this. Indeed ethics are not the only set of values that underpin Atkin's pronouncement. As I have noted above economic ideas are also inherent in his arguments and discussion of these ideas is also important in the pursuit of a liberal education. In other instances, however, the discussion of completely different value structures may be important in gaining an understanding of the complexity of the law. Thus, for example, in analysing the English law of divorce modern textbooks have noted that the establishment of a 'special procedure' to facilitate divorce and the withdrawal of legal aid to fund litigation has meant the almost total demise of contested divorce cases.[46] Divorce law, though not the ancillary matters relating to children and property that are attendant on divorce, is now bureaucracy. This has meant that divorce is no longer regarded as an important area of study.[47] However, consideration of the structures of a legal regime that lacks any of the expected features of contest and yet is a ubiquitous feature of modern life is as useful a pedagogic device in furthering a student's liberal education in law as is inquiry into the ethical contortions inherent in Lord Atkin's use of Christian theology. In this instance the normal interplay between substantive and procedural rules that constitutes law has become in effect pure procedure and a very different image of law obtains to that which normally prevails in the law school curriculum. Once again values and structures that permeate and underpin law are revealed by detailed study of something that might otherwise be considered irrelevant or marginal to the law school's curriculum.

THE LIBERAL CURRICULA AND DOCTRINAL LAW

The pursuit of doctrinal law, understood as an interest in the content of legal rules rather than their nature or effect, has had rather a bad

[46] See, eg, N Lowe and G Douglas, *Bromley's Family Law* (9th edn, London, Butterworths, 1998) 231.

[47] Lowe and Douglas describe the procedure as being 'the most fundamental, yet relatively unremarked-upon change in divorce since the introduction of judicial divorce in 1857' (Lowe and Douglas, *ibid*).

press in British law schools during the last few decades. Most of the new developments in the law school have been concerned not with doctrinal law but with analyses that take legal rules as their starting point and seek to trace their interaction with other features in society or analyses that eschew the study of particular rules altogether in favour of more abstract studies relating to the theory of law. Nevertheless doctrinal law remains part of the work done by the academic legal community though, for some, it creates a 'cramping . . . spirit that encourages scholars and jurists to maintain legal study as an inward-looking and self-contained discipline.'[48] In this context it is necessary to ask whether doctrinal accounts of the law are compatible with a liberal pedagogic agenda.

The discussion of the neighbour principle in the preceding section of this chapter shows that analysis of judgments can be part of a liberal education in law. However, that analysis was, in the strictest terms, not a doctrinal analysis of law but an analysis of the doctrine of law; it focused on the minutia of judicial reasoning but not so as to explicate the meaning of that reasoning but so as to critique its manner and form. The question is thus, not can a liberal curriculum include study of legal rules but can a liberal curriculum include study of legal rules that is solely focused on the meaning of those rules?

Criticism of doctrinal law generally takes one of two forms. First, doctrinal law can be seen as being a low-level attempt to describe legal rules in simple language. This kind of analysis can be seen in some case-notes that are no more than an attempt to précis a lengthy judgment or some textbooks that are intended to present accessible accounts of the law to students or to practising lawyers. Such work exists in profusion and plainly is used in teaching in many law schools (and is also used by students in their learning even when lecturers do not refer to such material themselves). The criticism of this kind of work is that it brings clarity to that which is complex simply by ignoring the complexity. It is not an account of legal rules. It is a narcotic that dulls the user's sense of the reality of the legal world. Doctrine here is deception. Those schooled in this manner know the law in the same sense that people who have eaten tins of Heinz baked beans and sausages could claim to know what it is to eat cassoulet. As such this type of doctrinal law has no place in the liberal law school which is attempting to facilitate a

48 A Hutchinson, 'Casaubon's Ghosts: the Haunting of Legal Scholarship' (2001) 21 *Legal Studies* 65 at 66.

student's acquisition of an understanding of the richness of legal worlds. Indeed, notwithstanding its pervasiveness and commercial profitability, such work has, in general, no place in the courses in any kind of university law school.[49]

Doctrinal law need not be mere description of wraiths. In line with Goff's much quoted argument, it can be the attempt to discern the line of principle that underlies the particularities of individual judgments.[50] The criticism of this form of doctrinal analysis is that such principle does not exist or exists so rarely and so fleetingly as to not properly be thought of as being something that can be studied as the structure of English law.[51] To advance such criticism of this kind of doctrinal law is not necessarily to impugn the integrity, dedication or intelligence of those that espouse this form of study; it is merely to observe that phrenology was once regarded as a legitimate area of inquiry and that the search for the Holy Grail proved to be fruitless. Can such doctrinal inquiry find a place in the curriculum of the law school? More particularly, if one is critical of doctrinal law in the manner suggested, can one still see a value in teaching doctrinal law in the liberal law school? Here the purpose of the liberal law curriculum becomes vital. The curriculum is there to facilitate the study of individual students. It does not represent the truth as the law school understands it. It is there to enable the students to pursue their own best ends in learning law by taking part in as many conversations about law as they are able to do, so that they can come to their own view as to the truth about law (if, indeed, they come to think there is any truth about law). As an individual scholar one may conclude that the study of doctrinal law, even in the sense that Goff understands it, is something that is incapable of producing anything of lasting value.[52] However, one cannot deny that there are serious writers who see great merit in such work. It is for the student to decide which view they take. There is an ongoing conversation about doctrinal law. The study of doctrinal law is therefore properly part of the liberal law school's curriculum.[53] But the study of

[49] The one exception to this is those introductory skills courses that make no attempt to inquire into law but instead introduce students to some of the ways by which they can make that inquiry. Here simplified accounts of the law can be used so as to focus on the skills necessary in inquiry rather than the substance of the inquiry.

[50] Lord Goff, 'The Search for Principle' (1983) LXIX *Proceedings of the British Academy* 169.

[51] See generally P Goodrich, *Reading the Law* (Oxford, Basil Blackwell, 1986).

[52] That is my conclusion about the pure pursuit of doctrinal law.

[53] This does not mean that the only way of studying doctrinal law is by providing courses that are themselves doctrinal accounts of some area of law. One may analyse

doctrinal law can never in itself be a liberal education. Even if one accepts the validity of doctrinal law it is only one perspective about law and is, at that, a very narrow perspective. Doctrinal law, understood in Goff's sense, is one voice in the conversations that there are about law but the plurality of the liberal law school will always demand that the curriculum contains more than just doctrinal law.

VOCATIONAL GOALS AND LIBERAL CURRICULA

The description of the curriculum above, whilst allowing for many different types of curricula, does forbid the construction of some kinds of course. Most obviously, curricula which are intended to send the student down some predetermined path, fitting them to a fixed occupation, are, by definition, not liberal and not suitable for undergraduate students in the university law school. Such curricula attempt to respond not to human curiosity but to the personnel needs of occupations that seek to improve their profit margins by passing their training costs onto the public purse. The intention in such curricula is not to provide an education for a citizen or human being but to train an employee suitable for the present purposes of the employer in question.[54] From the perspective of the theory of liberal education the objection to such curricula remains the same as it was in Newman's day when, in his lectures on the concept of the university, he quoted Dr Copelston on vocational education:

> the more the powers of each individual are concentrated in one employment, the greater the skill and quickness will he naturally display in performing it. But, whilst he thus contributes more effectually to the accumulation of national wealth, he becomes himself more and more degraded as a rational being. In proportion as his sphere of action is narrowed his mental powers and habits become contracted; and he resembles a subordinate part of some powerful machinery, useful in its place, but insignificant and worthless out of it.[55]

doctrinal law without actually practising it. Still less does it mean that it would be legitimate to insist that someone taught from the perspective of doctrinal law despite their own individual beliefs because of the approach's importance for the liberal law school's curriculum. Academics should not lie and they should not be asked to lie.

[54] This suitability being measured not only in terms of the technical skills or the knowledge that the student has but also in terms of their attitudes. Thus the courses constitute an attempt to mould the values of students so as to make them malleable employees.

[55] J Newman, *The Idea of a University* (New York, Holt, Rinehart and Winston, 1960) 127.

The comparatively high earnings that those engaged in the law often enjoy should not blind us to its routinised and alienated nature. In most cases it is in the end work; labour carried out for reward so that life can be lived elsewhere. To educate people to do this is to educate them only partially; to say that this vocational education is the highest form of education available, and thus to imply that work should be their highest goal, is not to educate them at all.

Even when they are viewed on their own terms, vocational curricula for university law schools have become problematic in modern times. Increasingly fractured legal professions struggle to find any common core in what they do that can be said to be suitable to serve as a focus for undergraduate education.[56] Here the traditional split between the work of barristers and solicitors is not so important as the varied and ever more specialised nature of the work of individual solicitors and barristers.

In recent years the long acknowledged differences between various types of lawyers have increased and groups that were once seen as being united on some levels have proved to be fissile. Thus, for example, the division between solicitors working in the largest London firms and other solicitors has taken on a new and more urgent tone in an era when, in 1999, the group of the largest London firms now have in excess of 80 partners each and a median figure for gross fee earnings of £85,599,000 per firm per year whilst, at the other end of the spectrum, the median figure for gross fee earnings for sole practitioners was only £97,000.[57] Moreover, within those London firms, jobs are more and more focused on particular areas of legal work, 'in the Energy Group, but only on gas projects (and then only off-shore gas),' so that to say that one works as a solicitor in a top London firm says very little about

[56] Different groups of solicitors are now unable to agree about even the desirable content of vocational content of courses that students are to take after graduation, resulting in specialist vocational courses for particular types of solicitor being set up (L Hickman, 'Legal Education' (2001) 98 No 3 *Law Society Gazette* 18).

[57] *Trends in the Solicitors' Profession: Annual Statistical Report 1999* (London, The Law Society, 2000) 47. Firms with more than 80 partners at this time constituted 0.3 per cent of all firms of solicitors but employed 17.5 per cent of all solicitors. By contrast sole practitioners constituted 42.5 per cent of all firms but provided employment for only 9.0 per cent of all solicitors (*ibid* at 32). Ten years ago Law Society figures categorised the largest firms as being those with five or more partners. In Greater London these firms had gross fees of £87,000 per partner with sole practitioners in the same area having gross fees of £65,000 (*Annual Statistical Report 1989* (London, The Law Society, 1989) 21). (On the nature of work in large law firms seer Lee, *Firm Views: Work of and Work in the Largest Law Firms* (London, The Law Society, 1999).)

the precise nature of your work and to say that this disparate group of workers and, for example, sole practitioners in the provinces are all solicitors indicates little more than a formal as opposed to substantive similarity in the work that they do.[58]

In the face of such chaos it is difficult to see what vocational curricula at undergraduate level should seek to address. Talk of transferable skills, when it addresses the wide range of potential occupations that constitute the reality of the modern world of legal practice, soon becomes so vague in its content as to leave one wondering what curricula could not be said to address, at least in an implicit manner, such increasingly, loosely defined skills.[59] Alternatively, if varied curricula are created at undergraduate level, seeking to service individually the multiplicity of law jobs that are now to be found in the legal professions, students will be required to make career choices before most of them have any substantial degree of information about the consequences of those choices.[60] Equally, even if were possible to write such curricula, the only thing we now know about the future work of those in legal practice is that it will be different from the present manner of working in ways that we cannot yet imagine. Thus, the more closely vocational curricula fit students to the present ways in which the legal professions work, the more closely they fit them to a way of work that will necessarily be outmoded and the more certainly they ensure the

[58] R Lee, ' "Up or Out"—Means or Ends? Staff Retention in Large Firms' in P Thomas (ed), *Discriminating Lawyers* (London, Cavendish Publishing, 2000) 185. This is not to say there are not unifying cultural elements for such workers. Thus, for example, for those in large firms the corporate hierarchy which they work in remains the same whatever the precise nature of their work (Lee, above n 57, passim). However, even if the subject-matter of the work done is ignored, this very corporate hierarchy serves to distinguish the working lives of 'solicitors' in large London firms from the working lives of 'solicitors' in much smaller firms and 'solicitors' who are sole practitioners.

[59] Vocational courses have a raison d'être only if they are tightly tied to a particular occupation. Once they become generic in their nature, losing their focus on a particular job, it becomes possible to argue that '[t]he skills identified for the work-place are the critical and imaginative skills . . . cherished by the liberal education tradition' (J Bell and J Johnstone, *General Transferable Skills in the Law Curriculum* (London, DFEE, 1998) 10). If this is so, what need is there for a vocational course? Academic courses will do all that is necessary.

[60] A 1998 survey of trainee solicitors showed that 39 per cent of them wanted to leave the profession (*The Lawyer*, 19 May 1998). Requiring students to make earlier choices as to careers than they have to at present, deciding at 17 when they apply to law school that they wish to become a City solicitor or a legal aid practitioner or whatever, will almost necessarily increase those drop-out rates. If students can take what they have learnt on the vocational courses into other occupations then such drop-out rates need not be seen as wastage.

redundancy of their own graduates.[61] Universities in general and law schools in particular can then address this failing in their vocational courses by providing short training courses for graduates which teach them new skills; this activity being either an entrepreneurial reaction to the knowledge market or the cynical creation of planned obsolescence in the product (the graduating student) created by the law school or both.

Liberal curricula in law schools seek to avoid the pitfalls and limitations of vocational curricula by attempting a much larger task. Students who have the ability to pursue conversations about law in a variety of ways have, by definition, the intellectual tools as well as the flexibility in their approach that will allow them to address themselves to a wide range of tasks, adapting what they know to new conditions. On one view the purpose of the liberal curriculum can be seen as being to enable students to understand what kind of questions can be asked about law and what kind of arguments can be used in trying to answer those questions. Students who graduate from such a course are thus in a better position, at least in the long run, to adapt to new demands, building on the varied languages that they have learnt in the law school. More importantly from the vocational viewpoint, they are not only in a better position to respond to the varied technical demands of being a lawyer but also to appreciate the professional responsibilities that such work involves.[62] More importantly from the educational viewpoint, the material that they have learnt will not just help them in doing their job but also in choosing what job they wish to do and in the myriad other decisions that they will have to make as a member of the society in which they live.

[61] Vocational curricula are not necessarily linked to the traditional legal professions. Law graduates have always found employment in jobs other than that of barrister or solicitor (J Wilson, 'A Survey of Legal Education in the United Kingdom' (1996) 9 *Journal of the Society of Public Teachers of Law* 1 at 55). This phenomenon has increased over the decades (J Wilson, 'A Third Survey of University Legal Education' (1993) 13 *Legal Studies* 143 at 173–74). However, the arguments above apply equally to attempts to fit the curricula of the law school to these other occupations.

[62] Nicolson and Webb ascribe the failure of lawyers to live up to their own rhetoric of professional responsibility in part to what they see being as the prevailing dominance of legal formalism and the black-letter tradition in the teaching of law (D Nicolson and J Webb,' (Oxford, Oxford University Press, 1999) 66–70).

5

Conversations: Research in the Liberal Law School

DOUBTS AND HESITATIONS

CURRENT ACADEMIC ATTITUDES towards research are complex, reflecting, in different combinations, both what individual academics do feel and what they think that they should feel about the balance between research and teaching.

Conventional analyses of modern academic identity see that identity in terms of a tripartite division between teaching, research and either management or administration.[1] These three roles are not, however, regarded as being of equal importance. 'A common theme of recent literature about the nature of academic work and careers is the dominant role of research and the low priority given to teaching.'[2] Research is the major thing that academics are publicly valued for by other academics. 'In the world of scholarship we are what we write.'[3] Research, or the promise of being able to produce research, is the way that academic jobs can be secured and subsequent promotion ensured.[4] However, research is not just of importance to academics because of instrumental, career-oriented reasons. Frequently, it is something that they do

[1] See, eg, M Henkel, *Academic Identities and Policy Change in Higher Education* (London, Jessica Kingsley Publishers, 2000). The distinction between conceptualising one part of academic identity as being either management or administration is an important one, reflecting deep-rooted differences in perceptions about the nature of the university (see further Chapter 6 below).

[2] S Court, 'Negotiating the Research Imperative: The Views of UK Academics on Career Opportunities' (1999) 53 *Higher Education Quarterly* 65. This is not just a recent phenomenon. Halsey observed the shift to a research orientation in universities in the 1970s (A Halsey, *Decline of Donnish Dominion* (Oxford, Clarendon Press, 1992) 184–85). It is noteworthy that the third part of the academic role, administration, is entirely ignored. See further Chapter 6 below.

[3] D Kennedy, *Academic Duty* (Cambridge, Harvard University Press, 1997) 186.

[4] See, eg, T Becher and P Trowler, *Academic Tribes and Territories* (2nd edn, Buckingham, SRHE and Open University Press, 2001) 136–40.

primarily because of the enjoyment that they derive from the activity.[5] There is thus, in the pursuit of research, a synergy between enjoyment and career, between Frost's 'avocation and vocation.'[6] Moreover, if the two come into conflict, it is the thing that is interesting, research, not the career, which can carry the day. Thus, for example, such is their focus on research that, in the modern climate, academics sometimes prefer to retire from their university, exchanging a full salary for a much lower pension, in order to better be able to pursue their research.[7] Equally, Henkel, in her survey of academic life, notes cases off individuals knowingly making choices in their research focus that involve 'career deterrents.'[8] Finally, research is something that some academics will continue to do, even when it is apparent that no one wishes to read or even publish their work and even when their career is not in issue. Thus Professor George Zeyer, Emeritus Professor of Central European History, in Amis' novel *Ending Up*, comes to think, after some years of retirement, 'that no editor or publisher was interested in any article or book he might produce; nevertheless he would continue to write.'[9] Research is what differentiates academic life from

[5] In research done for the Dearing Committee 51 per cent of respondents to a study said that the most important reason for them doing research was because they enjoyed it (National Committee of Inquiry into Higher Education, Report 3, *Academic Staff in Higher Education: their Experience and Expectations* (London, National Committee of Inquiry into Higher Education, 1997) Table 3.3). See also Becher and Trowler, above n 4, at 148.

[6] 'But yield who they will to their separation,/My object in living is to unite/My avocation and my vocation/As my two eyes make one in sight./Only where love and need are one,/And the work is play for mortal stakes ,/Is the deed ever really done/For heaven and the future's sakes.' R Frost, 'Two Tramps in Mud Time.' On this see further Chapter 8 below.

[7] A Halsey, *Decline of Donnish Dominion* (Oxford, Clarendon Press, 1992) 175. The practice of academics registering time as holiday with their departments in order better to be able to pursue research, which is now found in both old and new universities, is illustrative of the attachment that academics have to research, the increasing pressure on academic lives produced by increased teaching and administrative loads and increased bureaucratic pressures which lead to the view that academics should record their holidays. Even academics who retire at the usual age will often continue to research. In Day, Langham and Pearson's survey of American legal academic 30.22 per cent said that they intended to continue writing in retirement whilst McMorrow and Baldwin's survey of retired American legal academics found that 23.08 per cent reported that they spent a great deal of time researching and writing and 39.42 per cent reported that they spent some time researching and writing (D Day, T Langham and S Pearson, 'Senior Law Faculty Attitudes Toward Retirement' (1991) 41 *Journal of Legal Education* 397 at 405; J McMorrow and A Baldwin, 'Life After Law School: On Being a Retired Law Professor' (1991) 41 *Journal of Legal Education* 407 at 416).

[8] Henkel, above n 1, at 196.

[9] K Amis, *Ending Up* (London, Jonathan Cape, 1974) 167.

almost every other area of paid employment because it is something where '*the activity itself, not its exchange value, is . . . [the] primary goal.*'[10]

Whilst academics might have a high regard for research, prizing it more than other things, there is, within the university, a feeling that research is not what the university is valued for in the world outside the academy. Thus, for example, Kennedy asserts, '[o]f the many expectations that society has of the modern university, the most important is that it will teach well.'[11] There is a perception amongst academics that, for people outside the university, '[academic] writing is just an ego-trip'; that what academics value most, the outside world values least, if at all.[12] Perhaps because of these perceptions about the general public's view of research, and perhaps because of the difficulties that there are in articulating what research is and why it is important, some academics argue that:

> it is a great privilege to be able to it. The kind of research we do here is parasitic on the public purse and if we are educating the younger generation, we are giving a little bit in return.[13]

The idea that it is a privilege to do what one is employed to do, a privilege that demands a penalty in the form of the duty to teach, and even more the idea that research in universities is 'parasitic on the public purse,' even though research-quality is one of the things that universities are now audited for and even though British universities are manifestly hugely under-funded, attests to both the pleasure that

[10] A Gorz, *Critique of Economic Reason* (London, Verso, 1989) 137–38 (emphasis in original). The difference between academic work and most other forms of work is not simply the fact that academics enjoy their work. There are some other sites of work where this is true (as, eg, in the case of McDowell's study of merchant banking (L McDowell, *Capital Culture: Gender at Work in the City* (Oxford, Blackwell Publishers, 1997)). However, even in the case of these sites, the work is done for economic reasons. Once they reach pensionable age, or once they have accumulated sufficient wealth, most workers will not continue with their occupation or with any part of it, even if they have enjoyed their working life. Many academics continue to be fascinated by their subject long after its pursuit has ceased to be of economic advantage.

[11] Kennedy, above n 3, at 59.

[12] C Evans, *English People* (Buckingham, Open University Press, 1993) 111. The experience is not new nor is it limited to the situation in the United Kingdom. Weber in his 1919 essay, 'Science as a Vocation,' writes of the way in which a passion for research is 'ridiculed by every outsider' (M Weber, 'Science as a Vocation' in H Gerth and C Wright Mills (eds), *From Max Weber: Essays in Sociology* (London, Routledge, 1970) 135).

[13] Henkel, above n 1, at 184. Whilst attempting to describe what research is, Ball comments '[r]esearch seems to fragment as one approaches it' (C Ball, 'The Problem of Research' (1989) 43 *Higher Education Quarterly* 205 at 206).

academics find in research and the guilt that that pleasure sometimes causes them.[14]

Nonetheless, notwithstanding all of the above, it is also necessary to note that for some people, albeit a minority, research is a dispensable part of the university's activities. No one would envisage a university without teaching. No one could envisage a university without either management or administration. Some, however, can picture a university without research or a university where that which goes on under the name of research bears little relationship to traditional notions of that activity. Thus, for example, the attempt to recast universities as active agents in encouraging economic growth, sometimes at a very local level, often involves both a focus on universities as teaching institutions and a conception of research that is far-removed from the developmental pattern of most British universities.[15] It is not just that some people do not value the research that is being done in universities. Rather, they think that universities can continue to be universities without that research being carried out.

More deeply than doubts about how much the world at large values the university's research activities and whether or not it wants universities to engage in research, there are also debates within and outside the university about what constitutes research.[16] Whether applied work can be research, whether writing textbooks can be research and whether, if something is to be research, it must be published, either at all or to the world at large, as opposed to being a purely private activity or something done just for a commercial or state sponsor are but some of the questions that have been, and continue to be, asked about the nature of research.[17]

[14] It is also, of course, a view that, whilst commonly held, is wholly incapable of rational defence.

[15] See, eg, M Binks, 'The Changing Relationship Between Higher Education and Small and Medium Sized Enterprises' in H Gray (ed), *Universities and the Creation of Wealth* (Buckingham, Society for Research into Higher Education and Open University Press, 1999) and D Fraser, 'Universities and Communities: Cases from North-East England' in Gray (ed), *ibid*. For universities without research see C Ball, 'The Problem of Research' (1989) 43 *Higher Education Quarterly* 205.

[16] Those in the academy outside the law school have long been rather suspicious about the nature of the research done by academic lawyers. Commenting on the propensity of legal academics to produce textbooks and to be esteemed for doing so, Samuelson, an economist, noted dryly, '[w]hen I became a successful textbook writer, I had to live dowr that by producing more and better scientific research' (P Samuelson, 'The Convergence (the Law School and the University' (1975) 43 *The American Scholar* 256 at 260).

[17] A recent example of such debate on the nature of research is to be found in the pr - nouncements of the law panel for the 2001 Research Assessment Exercise. The par l

Plainly, conceptualising the nature of research is difficult. Even the seemingly simplest and most basic propositions are, on closer analysis, difficult. Thus, for example, we may wish to argue that writing is not in itself necessarily research (or, at least, is not necessarily university research), since journalism is one thing and scholarly writing another, but drawing the lines that demarcate that writing which is and that which is not research, or that writing that is research which is the university's business, is a fraught process.[18] And, for those in universities, inherent in attempts to articulate a clear conception of research, there is often the anxiety that few outside the academy care what research is or care about it.

UNIVERSITY LAW SCHOOLS AND RESEARCH

The ambivalence and uncertainty that is found when universities reflect on their research role is also a feature of the culture of their law schools. Whether legal academics should research and what can constitute that research are and always have been deeply contested questions.

A superficial examination of the literature would suggest that the notion of the importance of research to the academic identity is deeply embedded in the history of British university law schools. For example, Holdsworth, in his 1924 presidential address to the Society of Public Teachers of Law, at that time the only body representing those working in British university law schools, argued that:

accepted that work done for private or public bodies that was never published to a wider audience could constitute research for the purposes of the exercise (*Assessment Panels' Criteria and Working Methods*, RAE Circular 5/99, http://www.rae.ac.uk/Pubs/, para 3.28.9). Student textbooks and works for practitioners were accepted as being research provided they contained 'significant scholarly material' (para 3.28.11). Whether a new edition could be said to be research depended on 'the extent to which the edition has been revised' (para 3.28.12). Whilst determinant for the purposes of the exercise such observations do not, of course, foreclose further debate. In particular the suggestion that work that was disclosed only to those bodies that had commissioned it could properly, in the university context, be called research seems to be unlikely to receive wide support. The expansion of knowledge for humanity seems rather clearly to be one thing and market research or product development another.

[18] As with almost anything else one might say about research, even distinguishing research and journalism would be unacceptable for some (see, eg, S Lee, *Judging Judges* (London, Faber and Faber, 1988) 9–10).

> [a]ll Public Teachers of Law, and more especially those who devote their whole time to teaching law, should undertake some piece of research . . . [T]he Public Teacher should be a researcher into some branch of law.[19]

Holdsworth's view that research was intrinsic to the work of the law school was neither iconoclastic nor idiosyncratic at this time. In the decades leading up to the Second World War many other contributors to the *Journal of the Society of Public Teachers of Law* took a similar view. Winfield, writing a few years later, suggested that '[n]o teacher worth the name can afford to neglect this [research], for it is part of his equipment for his profession.'[20] De Zuluetta worried that:

> our methods of recruitment secure able men and efficient teachers, [but] they do not give sufficient weight to research. Young men have too little incentive to embark on it as affording a gateway to a career as a scholar.[21]

Given these and other similar statements in the literature, acknowledgement of the value of, even the necessity for, research being done by all academics within the university law school has, it seems, a long history within British universities. Yet closer examination of these early arguments about the role of research within the law school discloses ambivalence about precisely how important research is for the life of the legal academic and a connected degree of uncertainty about what constitutes research.

RESEARCH AND TEACHING IN LAW SCHOOLS

During the first half of the twentieth century most writers from British university law schools argued that research was important because, if it was done, it would improve teaching in the law school. Those working in university law schools were 'Public Teachers of Law,' not simply academics. Research was necessary because it helped them in their role as teacher. Thus Winfield asserts that '[t]eaching is almost certain to be devoid of inspiration' unless the teacher is also a researcher.[22] Smith, in an earlier article, had observed that, 'research should never be entirely

[19] W Holdsworth, 'The Vocation of a Public Teacher of Law' (1925) *Journal of the Society of Public Teachers of Law* 1 at 9.

[20] P Winfield, 'Reforms in the Teaching of Law' (1930) *Journal of the Society of Public Teachers of Law* 1 at 1.

[21] F de Zulueta, 'The Recruitment of Public Teachers of Law' (1933) *Journal of the Society of Public Teachers of Law* 1 at 9.

[22] Winfield, above n 20.

divorced from teaching.'[23] The definition given to research is affected by this perceived relationship to teaching. Winfield notes that by research he means 'independent investigation of any subject whether the conclusions arrived at are published to the world or not.'[24] Others outside the law school have commented on the beneficial effect that research has on teaching. Jaspers, for example, in his essay on the nature of the university, suggested that 'teaching vitally needs the substance that only research can give it.'[25] What is unusual in the British academic legal literature is the degree to which research is linked to teaching. Blackstone, in his eighteenth century discussion of the place of law in British universities, had devoted no time to considering the role of research by the legal academic.[26] Dicey in his nineteenth century reflections on the same topic merely noted that there was no opposition between teaching and research because 'easy and lucid lectures are the fruit of hard reading and long if not painful meditation.'[27] Early twentieth century discussion concedes a role for research in the university law school but only as an ancillary to teaching, which is regarded as being central to the academic function: research is less important than teaching and the reason for doing research is so that teaching can be improved. Thus, because of this, although Holdsworth asserted that legal academics have to carry out research, he devoted only one page of his address to discussing the research role whilst four pages are given over to discussing teaching.[28] Moreover, the rhetorical support for the importance of research was not entirely matched by the reality of everyday life at this time. Whilst some academics of the time plainly did pursue an active research career, Holdsworth's monumental history of English law being one result, others seem, at best, to have preferred

[23] H Smith, 'The Imperial School of Law' (1927) *Journal of the Society of Public Teachers of Law* 12 at 14.

[24] Winfield, above n 20.

[25] K Jaspers, *The Idea of the University* (London, Peter Owen, 1960) 58. However, it is also important to note that some outside the law school have seen precisely the reverse role between teaching and research. Veblen once wrote that 'the work of teaching belongs properly within the university only because and in so far as it incites and facilitates the university man's work of inquiry' (T Veblen, *The Higher Learning in America* (New York, August Kelley, Bookseller, 1965) 17).

[26] W Blackstone, 'On the Study of Law' in W Blackstone, *Commentaries on the Law of England* vol 1 (London, T Cadell, 1825).

[27] A Dicey, *Can English Law be Taught in the Universities?* (London, Macmillan and Co, 1883) 25.

[28] The fact that the literature constantly refers to teachers of law rather than to legal academics or some similar usage is in itself significant.

Winfield's notion 'independent investigation' unaccompanied by publication.

From the above it is clear that, historically, British university law schools have not adhered to the view that research is something that is to be carried on independently of teaching because research is, in itself, part of the role of the university. This limited acceptance of the importance of research in the law school finds its counterpart in modern-day views about research within law schools. Publisher's catalogues, the contents pages of journals and the annual reports and mission statements of many law schools attest to both the quantity of research done in British university law schools and to the importance, at least at the rhetorical level, that the law schools attach to that research. However, whilst all British university law schools teach not every British law school has entered every Research Assessment Exercise.[29] Not all academic staff in those law schools that have entered such exercises have been listed by their departments as being research active.[30] The importance of these facts can, of course, be over-estimated. They do not necessarily mean that departments or individuals who have not been entered for the Research Assessment Exercises were not in fact research active. The Research Assessment Exercises have been accompanied by complaints about the definition of research used for the purpose of measuring research quality.[31] Some law schools may simply have felt that the research that was being done in their department would not be properly recognised by the exercise or that this was true for the research of at least some individuals within the school. However, given the numbers of staff and departments who were not entered in the exercises, it is difficult to resist the suggestion that there are some academics in law schools who do not see research as being a necessary feature of their work.[32] Moreover, perhaps more surpris-

[29] Only 60 law schools, for example, entered the most recent 2001 Research Assessment Exercise (http://www.rae.ac.uk/); 64 institutions entered the previous 1996 exercise (http://www.niss.ac.uk/).

[30] By comparison only a miniscule number of academic staff in British law schools do no teaching though some may, because of their research commitments, have only limited teaching duties, there being some speculation that there is a developing divide between those who do research and those who do teaching (T Murphy, 'Postmodernism: Legal Theory, Legal Education and the Future' (2000) 7 *International Journal of the Legal Profession* 358 at 370).

[31] See, eg, P Leighton, 'Government and Education News' (1997) 31 *The Law Teacher* 127 at 128–29 and P Leighton, 'Government and Education News' (2000) 34 *The Law Teacher* 77 at 81.

[32] This suggestion is supported by the interview data collected by Cownie for her analysis of the attitude of legal academics towards their working lives (see further

ingly, such attitudes seem to be spread throughout British university law schools. Some law schools that would consider themselves highly prestigious failed to enter all of their academic staff in both the 1996 and the 2001 Research Assessment Exercises.[33] As recently as 2001, Becher and Trowler noted that, in law, 'it is possible to become an eminent academic consultant without having had to write a great deal.'[34] Even more surprisingly, given the strong connection between research and academic identity suggested at the beginning of this chapter, closer examination shows that academics in law schools are not the only ones who sometimes seems reluctant to link research unequivocally with the academic role.

RELUCTANT RESEARCHERS

There are a number of voices who would see research as either not being part of the role of all academics or of all universities.[35] These voices reflect the views of, amongst others, that minority, but

F Cownie, *Legal Academics: Culture and Identities* (Oxford, Hart Publishing, forthcoming).

[33] See http://www.niss.ac.uk/ and http://www.rae.ac.uk/

[34] T Becher and P Trowler, *Academic Tribes and Territories* (2nd edn, Milton Keynes, SRHE and Open University Press, 2001) 76. This having been said, it is also worth noting that the rate of research in British university law schools is comparable with other jurisdictions. The 2001 Research Assessment Exercise in the United Kingdom saw approximately 60 per cent of full-time legal academics entered. (This percentage is arrived at by comparing the total number of full-time academics recorded in the 1996 Harris and Jones survey with the number of legal academics entered for the 2001 Research Assessment (P Harris and M Jones, 'A Survey of Law Schools in the United Kingdom, 1996' (1997) 31 *The Law Teacher* 38 at 82; http://www.rae.ac.uk/).) Swygert and Gozansky's 1985 survey of 'senior law faculty' in the USA found that 44.21 per cent had failed to publish within the 3three-year period of the study (M Swygert and N Gozansky, 'Senior Law Faculty Publication Study: Comparisons of Law School Productivity' (1985) 35 *Journal of Legal Education* 373 at 393). Postelwaite's later study of 'senior professors' in law schools in the USA found that on the whole they publish their work in fora other than elite academic journals (P Postewaite, 'Life After Tenure: Where Have All the Articles Gone?' (1998) 48 *Journal of Legal Education* 558 at 567).

[35] Thus, eg, research done for the Dearing Committee found that 'some individuals and institutions . . . continue to assert the primacy of teaching' when considering the university mission (National Committee of Inquiry into Higher Education, Report 3, *Academic Staff in Higher Education: their Experience and Expectations* (London, National Committee of Inquiry into Higher Education, 1997) para 3.1). Henkel's study of academic identity noted a small percentage of respondents in each discipline studied who saw themselves as being either wholly or mainly teachers (M Henkel, *Academic Identities and Policy Change in Higher Education* (London, Jessica Kingsley Publishers, 2000) 182).

nonetheless sizeable, part of the academic community who never publish research.[36] Moreover, there is a further group of commentators who would want to look closely at the definition of research, seeing it as having in the present era a very different function to that which has historically been ascribed to it.[37] Finally, policy proposals, suggesting changes to British higher education, do not always see an inevitable link between universities and research. Thus, for example, although the 1997 Dearing Committee report on higher education noted a 'near-universal rejection of the idea that some institutions of higher education should be 'teaching' only institutions' it also thought that it was inevitable that 'some parts of higher education will receive only limited amounts of research funding, or none at all.'[38] Dearing went on to argue that, for some staff, research should be regarded as being a 'private activity' and that some departments, particularly those in post-1992 universities, that are primarily engaged in this kind of research should not be entered in the Research Assessment Exercises.[39] The Dearing Report failed to specify the precise nature of this 'private research.' On the one hand the Report said that such research should be 'in support of . . . teaching.'[40] At the same time Dearing noted that:

[36] Even as late as 1989 Halsey found 27 per cent of the academics he surveyed in the then polytechnic sector and 3 per cent of the academics in the university sector had not published a single paper (A Halsey, *Decline of Donnish Dominion* (Oxford, Clarendon Press, 1992) 187). In some instances the failure to produce research results not from a principled belief in the importance of other activities in the university such as teaching or administration but, rather, because of a principled belief in the importance of doing as little work as possible. As Davies observes of universities '[o]f course . . . we have our scoundrels and our thieves' (R Davies, *The Rebel Angels* (Harmondsworth, Penguin Books, 1983) 192). However, it would plainly be wrong to assert all academics who fail to produce research are simply dilatory in their behaviour; some take a different view about the proper nature of academic life to that which is taken by the majority.

[37] Thus, eg, Gibbons asserts approvingly that '[r]esearch [in universities] is nowadays oriented to socio-economic need. And the process of orientation has not been imposed by industry alone but by government with the support of industry'. (M Gibbons, 'The Industrial-Academic Research Agenda' in T Whiston and R Geiger (eds), *Research and Higher Education* (Buckingham, Society for Research into Higher Education and the Open University Press, 1992) 94.

[38] *The National Committee of Inquiry into Higher Education* (The Dearing Report) (London, National Committee of Inquiry into Higher Education, 1997) para 11.60 and para 11.59.

[39] Dearing Report, *ibid*, at paras 11.61–11.65.

[40] *Ibid*, at para 11.64.

> [f]or the majority of respondents [to the Committee] such an institution [ie a teaching only institution] would simply not be a 'university' in any legitimate sense of that term.[41]

Dearing did not contest, still less contradict, this view about the use of the term university, which leaves the status and purpose of 'private research' unclear.[42]

The existence of critics who question the place of research in the university, academics who value research but whose consequent guilt about doing that research needs to be assuaged with vigorous doses of teaching, academics who do no research but wish to retain the title of university lecturer and others who see research as merely being an adjunct to teaching underscores the necessity for analysing the nature and role of research in the university. No case needs to be made for the place of teaching in the liberal law school; the only questions to be raised relate to the manner and content of the teaching. However, if research is to be part of the life of the liberal law school there needs to be a clear understanding of why that is so and what can be done in the name of research.

NEWMAN AND RESEARCH IN THE LIBERAL UNIVERSITY

At first sight research appears to have little to do with the agenda for a liberal education at university. Thus, for example, in the preface to his lectures on the university Newman seemed to exclude research from the liberal university's role:

> [The University] is a place of *teaching* universal *knowledge*. This implies that its object is, on the one hand, intellectual, not moral; and on the other, that it is the diffusion and extension of knowledge rather than the advancement. If its object were scientific and philosophical discovery, I do not see why a University should have students.[43]

[41] *Ibid*, at para 11.60. (In the light of arguments in this chapter above it is noteworthy that, for a minority of respondents, the notion of a 'teaching only' university was a legitimate use of the term 'university.')

[42] The tendency in the Dearing Report to put forward competing propositions without taking side with one or other of them or seriously analysing them has been widely noted (see, eg, G Williams, 'Editorial' (1998) 52 *Higher Education Quarterly* 1).

[43] J Newman, *The Idea of a University* (New York, Holt, Rinehart and Winston, 1960) xxxvii.

Some writers have fastened on this statement as support for the notion that research is not in fact vital to the university function.[44] In fact Newman's attitude towards research in the university was more equivocal than this bald statement would seem to suggest. Ker has pointed to the element of hyperbole that is found in Newman's writings.[45] Nevertheless, there is, in Newman's lectures, a certain ambivalence towards the idea of research in the university that is not be found when the place of teaching is being discussed. Whilst, on closer examination, Newman may be seen to permit the pursuit of research in the university he does comparatively little to promote it; he certainly does not put it at the centre of the university's work. However, deeper interrogation of the basic concepts that support liberal educational theories produced by Newman and others both show why research is vital to the liberal law school and indicate what forms that research can take.

THE INEVITABILITY OF CURIOSITY; THE INEVITABILITY OF RESEARCH

In Chapter 2 above we saw that, from propositions about human nature, theorists of liberal education have developed arguments about the importance of education being conducted simply for its own sake. The appropriate nature of learning in the law school is shaped by these propositions. One can equally argue that these and other similar propositions about human nature lead to the conclusion that as human beings we are always involved in inquiry; that, thus, we are always involved in research; that these propositions indicate why and how research in the law school should be carried out.

As human beings we all have no choice but to seek to make sense of the world around us; we have no choice but to act and, in acting, to make choices about how we act. We are reasoning beings even if we abandon reason.[46] These things follow straightforwardly from the fact of our humanity.[47] This insight into human nature has recurred through history, being characterised in various different ways.

[44] See, eg, P Scott, *The Crisis of the University* (Beckenham, Croom Helm, 1984) 3.

[45] I Ker, *The Achievement of John Henry Newman* (London, Collins, 1991) 3.

[46] We may also be in addition things other than reasoning beings.

[47] They may also follow for animals other than human beings (see, eg, F de Waal, *The Ape and the Sushi Master* (London, Allen Lane, Penguin Press, (2001) and F de Waal, *Chimpanzee Politics: Sex and Power Amongst Apes* (rev edn, Baltimore, John Hopkins University Press, 2000)). This, however, is not germane to the arguments in this book.

Aristotle, for example, wrote that 'all men possess by nature a craving for knowledge,' Descartes that 'the capacity to judge correctly and distinguish true from false . . . is naturally equal in all men' and Sartre described the human species as being 'condemned forever to be free.'[48] The observation continues to be repeated to the present day, still serving as a stimulus to further thought. In a recent book Steiner writes '[m]ore than *homo sapiens*, we are *homo quaerens*, the animal that asks and asks.'[49]

Despite their differences one thing that unites these very disparate sources is the realisation that the world is not simply given to us. We cannot simply see the world. We cannot just be in the world. We must act in it. We have no choice but to seek to understand it. Data does not come to us ready processed. We must select, categorise and connect. And the 'must' here is a literal must. It is not that this is desirable or that it is something that the educated, the civilized, the articulate or the privileged can aspire to. It is something that must be done as much by someone born in poverty in an urban slum as by someone born to wealth. It must be done even when one is unconscious of doing it.[50] This necessity comes with being born and the only alternative is a permanent, if usually short-lived, vegetative state. Cicero, one of the writers frequently used as a source by those concerned with the nature of liberal education, argued that once:

> our minds are no sooner free from the thoughts and engagements of necessary business . . . we presently long to be either seeing, or hearing, or learning of something.[51]

In fact the argument goes back further than this. It is only by first learning something that we can provide what Cicero calls 'the necessaries and conveniences of life'; first we must learn what it is that is necessary, first we must learn what it is that is convenient, then we must learn how to provide it.[52] We need knowledge in order to secure food and shelter just as much as we need knowledge for anything else. What

[48] Quoted in AE Housman, 'Introductory Lecture' in AE Housman, *Selected Prose* (Cambridge, Cambridge University Press, 1961) 16; R Descartes, *Discourse on Method* (Harmondsworth, Penguin Books, 1968) 27; JP Sartre, *The Age of Reason* (London, Hamish Hamilton, 1947) 290.

[49] G Steiner, *Grammars of Creation* (London, Faber and Faber, 2000) 16. See also M Polanyi, *Personal Knowledge* (London, Routledge and Kegan Paul, 1958).

[50] Though, if done unconsciously, it is more likely to be done badly.

[51] Cicero, *The Offices* (London, Dent, 1909) 6–7.

[52] Cicero, *ibid*, at 6.

changes is not whether or not we are engaged in learning but what that learning is about; what changes is what we choose as the subject for our research and how we conduct that research. Because human beings are reasoning beings, human beings are researching beings. By being reasoning beings and by being researching beings as fully as possible, human beings put themselves into the best position to be able to 'call their minds their own.'[53]

Research, understood in this way, is both personal and need not be novel. It is an individual search that may (usually will) reveal to me, at least at on one level, only what (many) others already knew. Some approaches to research in universities in the arguments above seem to partially reflect this conception of research. Research, understood in this way, is of course necessary to any university academic. How can they teach unless they have first researched something to teach?[54] Such research may properly be called, in Dearing's phrase, 'private activity' because it arises out of what the individual needs for their own purposes.[55] It is an individual activity done purely so that they can better pursue their own ends.[56] Such an argument quickly leads to the conclusion that research is an inevitable part of the university's role (if that role is to include teaching) and an inevitable part of the academic's role (if that role includes teaching). However, the view of human nature that lies at the base of the concept of a liberal education can prompt even deeper analysis than this, showing that the inevitability of research in universities goes beyond these private activities to the production of research for general consumption.

[53] M Nussbaum, *Cultivating Humanity: A Classical Defense of Reform in Liberal Education* (Cambridge, Harvard University Press, 1997) 293.

[54] Those who do this may not view this activity as research (see further, F Cownie, *Legal Academics: Culture and Identities* (Oxford, Hart Publishing, forthcoming)). Equally they may do it very badly, producing ideas on which they base their teaching which are wholly or partially fallacious. However, neither what they see themselves as doing nor their ability as regards that activity alter the nature of it.

[55] This type of research corresponds with what some commentators have called 'scholarship' (see, eg, C Ball, 'Teaching and Research' in T Whiston and R Geiger (eds), *Research and Higher Education* (Buckingham, SRHE and Open University Press, 1992) at 134. I have avoided this term because it is usually intended to emphasise the difference between the activity that goes under the head of scholarship and the activity that these authors would accept as being research. I, on the other hand, wish to emphasise the similarity and the continuity that exists between various activities, including some that would not normally be thought of under the heading of research.

[56] These ends, teaching, are public activity but the research that was done in order to allow the teaching remains private and the end is not better served if it is anything other than private.

SYSTEMATISING CURIOSITY

Research in one sense is an ordinary and everyday matter, being not particular to the university or its law school but, rather, simply a necessary feature of the way humans live, and have always lived, their lives. But, just as teaching at university is both a response to human curiosity and more than simply a response to human curiosity, itself an inevitable feature of the way that human beings live, involving instead a structuring of learning that is intended to facilitate the possibility of progress and advancement on the part of the student, so research at university level seeks to systematise the human need to inquire so that what is sought becomes not just new to the seeker but to the world at large.

The process whereby the systematisation of research in the university occurs can be misunderstood. Some writers prefer to distinguish the previous, private type of research discussed in this chapter from what they call 'fundamental research.'[57] The use of this terminology can lead to a notion that research in this larger sense involves some almost superhuman effort to produce an idea that will count as being both new and true and thus an advance in human knowledge. Research, on this view, is a matter that is far-removed from the mundane world and those who inhabit that world. It is the product of genius, or something approaching genius, and those who do not have such genius either cannot produce research or can only produce research of such mediocre quality that is unworthy of the attention of others.[58] This then allows either for the proposition that academics should only be employed by universities if they have the requisite genius or, more commonly, that academics can be divided in to those who both research and teach and those who only teach.[59]

The notion that the systematised research that is the proper function of the university is distant from the ordinary research of everyday life is a partial truth even if the idea that it is the product of genius or even something wholly removed from ordinary experience is wrong.

[57] See, eg, Ball, above n 55.

[58] Something of this view about research might lie behind the views of those who complain about the increased quantity of academic publications. Of course, this argument raises the question of what one might mean by genius. On this question see M Garber, *Academic Instincts* (Princeton, Princeton University Press, 2001) 79–85.

[59] This division being drawn sometimes by those who would regard themselves as solely being capable of teaching.

Research in the university is often arcane, abstruse and difficult, venturing far beyond the reaches of the quotidian lives of most people. It is concerned with minute questions, precise and obscure terminology and results that sometimes seem to generate only ever-more minute questions and ever-more difficult terminology. At its best it is, and ought to be, very different from ordinary, everyday experience. But, at the same time, even in its most arcane moments, research is nothing more than a personal report of phenomena in the world around the researcher that they felt to be of interest.[60] What differentiates research at university level from research done in the course of everyday life, or even research purely in preparation for teaching, is the degree of focus and concentration that is inherent in university research and that is required before this personal report can be made.[61] The familiar dictums that speak of the necessity of doubting everything and always verifying one's sources say most of that which needs to be said about the nature of this kind of research. To know something, to be able to know what to say about that thing and to know how to say it all become, under the weight of these injunctions, when one realises they demand precisely what they say, difficult, and even almost impossible, matters. And the result is ever-more minute questions (as one tries to break down into manageable intellectual portions what it is that is known and not known), ever-more difficult language (as one attempts to be precise in what one says) and ever-more intricate and abstract inquiries (as one follows the interconnections of the matters that are being examined).

If the rules of scholarship are followed, which include the necessity of considering the reports of others before one produces one's own account, personal observation then becomes, of necessity, novel observation. As I seek to trace what I see, to justify what I say, and to view the world as clearly as I can, so my report becomes both personal and new. The highest level of university research is, on this view, produced not because of genius but because of persistence and endurance. Evans writes about research that needs 'patience and exactness' and argues that:

[60] Larkin's observation that 'once you have walked the length of your mind, what/You command is clear as a lading-list./Anything else must not, for you, be thought/To exist' is an apt description of this facet of the nature of what research is to the individual who is engaged in it (P Larkin, 'Continuing to Live').

[61] Thus, Weber argues '[t]he dilettante [in ideas] differs from the expert . . . only in that he lacks a firm and reliable work procedure' (M Weber, 'Science as a Vocation' in H Gerth and C Wright Mills (eds), *From Max Weber: Essays in Sociology* (London, Routledge, 1970) 136).

> it is perhaps this sheer habit of hard work, this taking for granted that one is seeking to find out something new, to which the university teacher ought automatically to expose his students.[62]

Persistence and patience in producing research is something that can be asked of anyone who claims the intelligence necessary to teach at university level and the argument that it is possible to be a good university teacher but not be capable of publishing research becomes impossible to sustain.

In the liberal law school, teaching asks the student to consider questions and issues that are set for them and to report their views. The limited tenure of the student in the law school, as well as their apprentice status, means that their views are relatively under-developed in scholarly terms. Research in the liberal law school makes the same demands of the academic as are made of the student except that the academic sets their own questions and their permanent residence in the law school allows for a more developed answer. In both the case of teaching or learning and that of research a liberal education involves no more and no less than the concentration of curiosity. Academics, on one level, must inquire into issues because they cannot teach unless they do so. On another level they must continue that inquiry until they are satisfied with their personal answers for the same reason that they demand that their students continue their inquiry until they are sure of their answers.[63] And they must publish the results of their inquiry as an act of reciprocity because they rely on the work of others who have published; because not to do so is to listen to and benefit from a conversation without contributing to it.[64]

[62] G Evans, *Calling Academia to Account* (Buckingham, SRHE and Open University Press, 1999) 11.

[63] Finite time and resource issues mean that there must be some selection in what it is that one chooses to make the subject of one's research. The duty to pursue research is derived from the basic principles of a liberal education; the question of what that research is can, from the perspective of a philosophy of liberal education, be a matter of politics, religion, pragmatics or whim as the individual wishes.

[64] And because publication provides a structure and prompt to inquiry. Without publisher's deadlines inquiry can be put off or ideas can endlessly be tinkered with even though the minor changes made involve no great improvement and may even serve to damage the work when taken as a whole. Balzac's short story, 'The Unknown Masterpiece,' in which a painter of great talent endlessly repaints what is to be his master-work until, when it is finished, it is revealed to be 'nothing . . . but colors piled upon one another in confusion' is pertinent here (H de Balzac, *The Unknown Masterpiece* (London, Caxton Publishing House, undated) 42).

WRITING, TEACHING AND RESEARCH

In her book *Academic Instincts* Garber argues that the difference between journalistic writing and scholarly writing is not that:

> journalists write in a style that is simple and clear (though some do) and that scholars write in a style that is complex and difficult (though some do) . . . The difference is rather that the journalist of ideas attempts to explain and describe them, while the scholar attempts to think through them, to enter into and advance an ongoing intellectual discussion. Every scholarly move is part of a dialogue.[65]

Garber's distinction is helpful in identifying what is and what is not writing that can constitute research in the context of the university law school.[66]

Much writing produced within the law school is not, and is not intended to be, research. Using Garber's work, writing that is intended to do no more than explain and describe ideas cannot, by definition, be regarded as being research. Thus writing that simply tries to explain ideas for students or simply tries to explain material for solicitors or barristers cannot be research.[67] In both cases the writing is a form of teaching. It may well have merit as a pedagogic device, it may well be an appropriate thing for an academic to do as part of their job, but it has no merit as research.[68] However, this does not mean that something that is categorised as a practitioner or student textbook cannot, because of this, be research. In both cases, works of this kind can attempt to explain ideas to their expected audiences and also advance

[65] Garber, above n 58, at 34.

[66] Research can, of course, be published other than by the written word. Most obviously, conference papers constitute a way of disseminating research. Similarly, video-conferences, video-tapes and other forms can be used to put research findings before the world at large. However, the written word continues to be the mechanism that allows for the most precise form of expression and thus constitutes the best way in which research can be published.

[67] The notion that description is a synonym for research is still plainly to be found within the law school. One instance of it occurring is when the asinine question, 'have they written a big book,' is asked when someone's employment or promotion is being considered. It is noticeable that law textbooks often tend to grow in size as they go into successive editions. This presumably reflects the author's view that length and merit are to be equated (see further A Bradney, 'University Legal Education in the Twenty-First Century' in J Grant, R Jagtenberg and K Nijkerk (eds), *Legal Education: 2000* (Aldershot, Avebury, 2000) 267 and 277–78).

[68] Of course, it may have required considerable research in the first sense described above, to write it.

debate about the matter that is the subject of the textbook. If the textbook is of this kind then it is, at least in its first edition, research.[69] Teaching that is in accord with the theory of liberal education, described in the previous chapter, will try to engage a student in a conversation and not simply describe or explain. Thus a textbook that follows a theory of liberal education will always tend to be both a teaching tool and a work of research. However, it is evident that not all textbooks are written with a theory of liberal education in mind but are, instead, merely intended to supply accessible quantities of information that can be assimilated by the reader.

THE PLURALISTIC NATURE OF RESEARCH IN THE LAW SCHOOL

Because research is personal, because research should be the individual's own account of that which they have taken for their subject, research in the liberal law school should be pluralistic in the sense that it should reflect the individual interests, beliefs and enthusiasms of those in the law school. Given the need for diversity in staff in the law school if students are to be afforded an appropriate opportunity to look at the range of legal scholarship available, the research that the law school produces should be similarly diverse.

The notion of a liberal education does not give priority to any particular method of research. What makes something research is the intention that lies behind it, not the particular method chosen. Thus, for example, doctrinal research, the attempt to discern the principles that lie underneath the mass of cases without resort to other scholarship outside those cases, now seems to many in the law school to be akin to astrology or phrenology in the likelihood of it achieving any plausible conclusions because, like astrology and phrenology, the rules of this particular science seem to have very little relationship to reality.[70] But both astrology and phrenology have in their time been seen as

[69] New editions are research to the extent that they try to bring new ideas into the conversation. When new editions simply put new facts into old arguments they cannot, on this argument, be thought of as being research or, at most, they cannot be regarded as being research of any significant degree of quality.

[70] R Goff, 'The Search for Principle' (1983) *Proceedings of the British Academy* 169 at 171. Goff's analysis is an amplification of Dicey's argument that '[b]y adequate study and careful thought whole departments of law can . . . be reduced to order and exhibited under the form of a few principles which sum up the effect of a hundred cases' (A Dicey, *Can English Law be Taught at the Universities?* (London, Macmillan and Co, 1883) 20).

productive areas of research.[71] They were abandoned as areas of research only when all scholars, not just the majority of scholars, accepted their lack of validity.[72] Writing about cases or statutes is not research when it simply describes them but doctrinal research, seen as a search for underlying principle, remains research that fits within the liberal agenda just as much as any newer, more fashionable approach to research within the law school. Work that can broadly be called social-legal now dominates the research horizons of the law school.[73] However, the mere fact that work is socio-legal does not mean that it fits within the scope of the liberal agenda for research within the law school or that it can properly be accounted research at all. Socio-legal work can be description just as much as writing about cases and statutes. Tired and tiresome writing about, for example, the minutiae of behaviour of actors in the legal field that simply describes and rehearses that behaviour, without in any way trying to analyse it, fails to be research for just the same reason that a meticulous rehearsal of the reasoning in the latest House of Lords case fails to be research; both may be used by others in their research but both, in themselves, fail to add anything to the conversations that constitute research.

Law schools should be marked by the diversity of their approach in research; by the fact that some scholars can see no value in the research that others are doing within the same department. This does not mean that the merits of different research methods should not be vigorously

[71] D de Guistino, *Conquest of the Mind: Phrenology and Victorian Social Thought* (London, Croom Helm, 1975). In India astrology is currently seen as being a valid subject for research. In 2001 the University Grants Commission decided that there was 'an urgent need to rejuvenate the science of Vedic Astrology in India' and agreed in principle to approve the setting up of a number of new departments of Vedic Astrology in Indian Universities. (http://www.education.nic.in/htmlweb/astrologycurriculum.htm#circular).

[72] A modern-day chemist who insisted they wished to continue the search for the Philosopher's Stone would make for an interesting debate about the proper limits of academic freedom.

[73] On the increasing dominance of socio-legal studies see further A Bradney, 'Law as a Parasitic Discipline' (1998) 25 *Journal of Law and Society* 241. By 'socio-legal' I mean work that includes the use of ideas and methods that are taken 'from other disciplines primarily but not exclusively from within the social science and humanities fields' (S Wheeler, 'Company Law' in P Thomas (ed), *Socio-Legal Studies* (Aldershot, Dartmouth, 1997) 285). 'Socio-legal' can be given a much more restricted meaning, pertaining only to that work 'embracing contributions from a range of social sciences' (D Campbell, 'Socio-Legal Analysis of Contract Law' in Thomas, *ibid*, 247). This latter approach would, for example, exclude from the ambit of socio-legal studies work in the law school that builds on literary analysis. Whilst this definition is much more precise and intellectually coherent than the one that I am using it fails to reflect the range of material that is currently being published under the heading of socio-legal research.

debated. Such debate should also be the mark of the law school and each scholar must constantly reappraise their chosen methods and be willing to defend their validity. Conversations should include conversations about what we are doing and how we are proceeding as well as conversations about our results and conclusions. However, in the end, as in teaching, the choice of method and subject is a purely personal one, protected by the concept of academic freedom:

> In the long run we have to persuade the community at large to make an act of faith in what the academic is doing, since only the scholar can make the judgement as to the 'worth-whileness' of what he chooses.[74]

Birks, amongst others, has argued that if research done in the law school 'is ever useless to judges and practising lawyers we will have come adrift from our foundations.'[75] This argument is not consistent with the approach of a liberal law school.[76] Research in the liberal law school is to be done for no other purpose than the exploration of new ideas. The law school does not exist to service the needs of the legal professions or anyone else. If it is to act in a manner that is consistent with the principles of liberal education it is not a 'House of Intellect for the Legal Profession,' it is simply a 'House of Intellect.'[77] The fact that research proves to be of benefit to those outside the university does not mean that it should not be done in the law school. Indeed, in the end humanity always benefits from new ideas because, thereby, it knows the world more thoroughly. However, utility does not validate research in the university law school not does the degree of direct utility increase the importance of research. Ideas are important but there is

[74] M Evans, 'The Crisis in Higher Education' (Milton Keynes, SRHE and Open University Press, 1988) 52. The issues of academic freedom and accountability that this proposition raises are explored in Chapter 7 below.

[75] P Birks, 'Editor's Preface' in P Birks (ed), *Pressing Problems in the Law*, vol 2, *What Are Law Schools For?* (Oxford, Oxford University Press, 1996) ix. Birks goes on to write '[a] law school which professed to have no interest in the decisions of courts or which boldly announced that its research and publications bore no relation to the activities of the courts would be a contradiction in terms' (Birks, *ibid*). If by 'courts' Birks means state courts this argument is patently inaccurate. There is principle nothing wrong with a law school limiting its research to those forms of law that do not have courts (for examples of such work see B Malinowski, *Crime and Custom in Savage Society* (London, Routledge and Kegan Paul, 1926) and A Bradney and F Cownie, *Living Without Law: An Ethnography of Quaker Decision-Making, Dispute Avoidance and Dispute Resolution* (Aldershot, Ashgate, 2000)).

[76] Elsewhere Birks has endorsed the notion of a liberal education in law. See, eg, P Brirks, 'The Academic and the Practioner' (1998) 18 *Legal Studies* 397 at 406.

[77] For a contrary argument see N Savage and G Watts, 'A House of Intellect for the Professions' in Birks (ed), above n 75.

no ranking in their importance.[78] If my research pleases me, or at least does not entirely displease me, and if I attempt to live by the rules of scholarship, it needs no further warrant.[79]

RESEARCH INTO WHAT?

As commonplace in the literature about recent changes in higher education as observations about the priority that the academy now gives to research over teaching are analyses of the increasing constraints for the researcher; constraints that influence, and even in some instances determine, the nature and direction of their research.[80]

Historically, the greatest constraint to research in British university law schools came about because of the self-imposed censorship that formed part of the culture of the law schools. Research in law schools during much of the first three-quarters of the twentieth century consisted largely of doctrinal analysis, legal history or jurisprudence with

[78] Since we must select those who are to be employed within the academy and if we are to have hierarchies in our employment we must make judgements about the quality of research. Those who do 'good' research will be employed and those who do 'good' research will be promoted. But any academic, no matter how little time they have been in post, knows that their judgements about such matters are sometimes opposed vehemently by others who they respect and that in other cases the majority opinion, whether positive or negative, about the quality of some research is the reverse of their own. We know that some good researchers will not be employed and some bad researchers will be promoted and we know that this would happen even if we personally were given the right to make all the decisions about these matters. In some instances we must make judgements about the quality of research but we should not let that lead us to forget that our judgements are always uncertain. We have the authority, and even the duty, to criticise another's research. We do not have the right to prevent it being done.

[79] Edwards much quoted comment that ' "[p]ersonal fascination" is not a sufficient justification for scholarship, of any kind' is wholly wrong (H Edwards, 'The Growing Disjunction Between Legal Education and the Legal Professsion' (1992) *Michigan Law Review* 34 at 56). Only if it is personally fascinating is research validated. Some, perhaps many, legal academics will see import in their research because, as they see it, it has utility for judges or the poor or whatever. It is the fact that they see that research as having importance that justifies it. At the same time as I have completed this book I have also finished a study of the interrelated images of law and family in the television series, 'Buffy the Vampire Slayer.' Such work might be justified by reference to the subversive nature of arguments about law that appear in a series that is watched by millions. However, more importantly, this work is justified by the fact that, for the moment, it has raised questions that I have found more compelling than any others that have occurred to me.

[80] See, eg, G Evans, *Calling Academia to Account* (Buckingham, SRHE and Open University Press, 1999) 55–50 and M Kogan and M Henkel, 'Constraints on the Individual Researcher' in T Whiston and R Geiger (eds), *Research and Higher Education* (Buckingham, Society for Research into Higher Education and Open University Press, 1992).

doctrinal analysis being its dominant concern. Other forms of research into law were left to other parts of the university and, when such research was done, the law school largely ignored it. The twenty-first century sees a very different picture with those in law schools drawing on the rest of the university for methods and concepts as well as for research findings. However, as the law school had become more closely incorporated into the university, so it has found itself subject to constraints that once would not have troubled it.[81]

The last quarter of the twentieth century and the first few years of the twenty-first century have seen a rise in the number of empirical projects in the law school that seek to survey various aspects of legal life. Whilst empirical projects are not unique in raising issues regarding the way in which research can be constrained they do serve to highlight some of the problems that are of general application; it is thus worthwhile considering the rise in the amount of empirical work in the law school at this point.

When pursued on a large scale, empirical projects have considerable funding implications. They cannot be sustained using an individual researcher's own resources or the resources of their department. Those who are interested in such work have thus had to turn to funding councils, government departments, charitable bodies or others to provide support for their work. However, very few if any of these sources offer money simply for high-level research, no matter what its subject-area or methodology. Instead, they have programmes and policies that identify the type of research that they wish to encourage.[82] In itself there can be little that is objectionable in this process. Each body has finite

[81] One thing that has troubled law schools during the last few decades has been the Research Assessment Exercises that have been repeated every four or five years since 1989. Many people in law schools have seen this exercise as directing research down particular paths (see, eg, D Vick, A Murray, G Little and K Campbell, 'The Perceptions of Academic Lawyers Concerning the Effect of the United Kingdom's Research Assessment Exercise' (1998) 25 *Journal of Law and Society* 536 at 556). The Research Assessment Exercises, and their effects, are thus plainly pertinent to the arguments that are raised at this point in this chapter. However, for the purposes of this book I will look at the Research Assessment Exercises in the context of wider attempts to introduce notions of audit into the law school in Chapter 7 below.

[82] Henkel notes of the Economic and Social Research Council, the obvious source of funding for much empirical legal research, 'its funding programmes have been increasingly organized round programmes [and l]ess than 40 per cent of its [the ESRC's] allocations are made in the responsive mode' (M Henkel, *Academic Identities and Policy Change in Higher Education* (London, Jessica Kinglsey Publishers, 2000) 192. There are, of course, policies as to the appropriate nature of an application, even in the case of grants made in 'responsive mode.'

resources and wishes to see those resources used in the way that it thinks most productive. Moreover, many of these bodies, whilst providing funding for research, do not have research-funding as their primary goal, and wish to see research that they finance tied to their larger purposes. In some instances the bodies concerned are simply commercial ventures that are attempting to out-source their research work in the same way, and for the same economic reasons, that they might out-source their IT needs or their catering services.[83] Yet, understandable or not, the result of this process is constraint on research. Large-scale empirical projects that do not fit in with the programmes or purposes of one or other of the potential funding sources will be difficult to carry out. The researcher is then faced with the choice of tailoring their research to a funding body's programme or pursuing research of another form.[84] Problems of this kind are reduced by the existence of multiplicity of funding sources that gives a researcher some room to choose the body that will finance them. At the same time, such problems are enhanced to the degree that funding bodies produce rigid and precise programmes. Equally, such problems are enhanced if the researcher works in a university law school that, on entrepreneurial grounds, sees funded research as being, if not a goal, at least a good.

A particular version of the problems described above is that which has resulted from the attempts of successive governments to push research down paths that they have believed to be most efficacious for the economic development of the United Kingdom. These attempts are especially troubling because they bespeak of an attempt to subvert the whole purpose of the university.[85] A commercial concern that purchases research from the university is merely buying a product. The

[83] Commercial sponsorship of research in law schools has taken two forms in British university law schools. First, there have been those bodies such as the Bar Council or the Law Society that sought tenders for individual research projects. Secondly, there have been those bodies, principally firms of solicitors, which have sponsored posts in law schools. Whilst this might not seem to be a form of research sponsorship it becomes this because when the bodies sponsoring posts dictate the area of law that the person appointed should interested in they also dictate the kind of research that person will produce. Most sponsored posts have unsurprisingly been in broadly commercial areas of law thus shifting the law school's research focus in that direction (see further A Bradney, 'Paying the Piper' (1990) 24 *The Law Teacher* 137; S Bright and M Sunkin, *Commercial Sponsorship of Legal Education* (London, Institute of Advanced Legal Studies, 1991).

[84] C Russell, *Academic Freedom* (London, Routledge, 1993) 77.

[85] The problem is not one unique to the United Kingdom. See, eg, C Polster, 'Dismantling the Liberal University: the State's New Approach to Academic Research' in B Brecher, O Fleischmann and J Halliday, *The University in a Liberal State* (Aldershot, Avebury, 1996) which discusses the very similar Canadian experience in this respect.

university and the researcher can decide whether or not they are in the market to make that product. The relationship between some researchers and some of the larger funding bodies may seem rather akin to that between one of the larger supermarkets and a small farmer but nevertheless the same parallel as in the case of the commercial funding of research can be maintained. One might argue that the recent history of some of the funding bodies comes close to treating research as a product to be bought and sold but still it is for the researcher to decide whether or not they are in the market to sell that product. Government efforts to tell the universities what research they should do are attempts to tell the universities what market they ought to be in when they conduct their research.[86]

Whatever their form, all constraints are problematic for the pursuit of research in the liberal law school. This is not to argue that it is possible to avoid all constraints on research. Even in an ideal world some constraints on research would exist (because, for example, of the finite nature of resources or the psychological or physical frailty of individual researchers). In the present political climate conditions for research are far from ideal and, for the foreseeable future, there are likely to be considerable constraints on research in the law school. However, even an inevitable difficulty must be recognised for what it is, a difficulty, and some difficulties, when seen as such, may, on closer examination, prove to be avoidable. The aim is to try to make sure that research in the liberal law school, like learning, is carried out for its own sake. Attempts to direct research down particular paths or prevent research of a certain form or in certain areas are inimical to the life of the law school. If the liberal law school is to thrive, indeed if the law school is to survive, both the individual academic and the individual law school have to be constantly alert to the need to defend the integrity of their research in the face of pressures from those whose agenda is very far-removed from the philosophy of the law school.

[86] The fact that governments have sought to tie the universities more closely to the economic development of the United Kingdom gives a resonance to the word 'market' in this context. However, it is not the fact that governments have sought to tie the universities to economic development that causes the problem. Rather, it is the fact that universities as a whole have been told that research that relates to economic development is that which should have priority. In the unlikely event that governments told universities that they should link their research to the development of high art in the United Kingdom the problem would be the same. The issue is the failure to respect the autonomy of universities, not the particular way in which that failure manifests itself.

6

A Necessary Evil or Simply Necessary? Administration

A LONG HISTORY OF SILENCE

AT THE BEGINNING of the last chapter I noted that, in most discussions of the nature of the academic job, teaching is seen as coming a poor second to research in terms of the importance that academics attached to it. However, in the analysis of what it means to be an academic, and what it means to be a successful academic, teaching is at least in the race with research, even if it is usually doomed to finish several laps after its more distinguished rival; a third contender that should be in the running, administration, does not even get to the starting line.

All academics will find that administration of some type will be part of their working life. Some academics will not be expected to teach, some will not be expected to do research but every academic will be expected to do some form of administration. This has always been the case. Administration inevitably forms part of academic life, no matter what status the individual academic has.[1] Both teaching and research require work that is not itself teaching or research as a preliminary or a consequence of that primary activity. Non-academics can do some of this preliminary or consequential work but, in the end, some of it will fall on academics. Whether academics should engage in administration is not a matter that is open for discussion; the only things that can be

[1] T Becher and M Kogan, 'Process and Structure in Higher Education' (2nd edn, London, Routledge, 1992) 109. To be precise, Becher and Kogan suggest that this is so for 'nearly every academic.' This is, I think, an example of academic caution becoming academic error. I am unable to conceive of a situation where someone could both be an academic and yet not undertake some element of administration. The administrative activity involved might be limited and related only to their own other academic work but it will always be there. There are, of course, many examples of academics who are kept from serious or complex administrative work because of the havoc they would cause if they did engage in such activity.

debated are the quantity of administration that is undertaken or the form that it takes. Moreover, administration matters:

> The university fulfils its task . . . within an institutional framework. It requires buildings, materials, books and institutes and their orderly administration. Privileges and duties must be distributed among its members.[2]

The way in which these things are done must necessarily, intimately affect the teaching and research that goes on in the university. Yet, despite its pervasive nature and despite its importance, administration is the least discussed and least analysed facet of academic life, not just in the law school but also in the university as a whole.

The first detailed studies of the nature of British university law schools were the three surveys that were carried out under the auspices of what was then the Society of Public Teachers of Law.[3] In each of these three surveys administration receives only a cursory mention.[4] Other surveys of British university law schools have continued in this tradition with no specific attention being given to the administrative responsibilities of academics and the focus instead being on their teaching and research duties.[5] In a similar vein the general literature on British legal education has, from its very beginnings to the present day, almost entirely ignored the subject of administration. Thus, for example, whilst, in the period leading up to the Second World War, the *Journal of the Society of Public Teachers of Law* featured many articles on matters relating to teaching or research in the law school, only Winfield's 1930 article, 'Reforms in the Teaching of Law,' refers to the 'highly necessary' administrative work that academics engage in; even here the reference is in the very briefest of terms.[6] Similarly, in the modern era, study of the volumes of *The Law Teacher* for the last decade

[2] K Jaspers, *The Idea of the University* (London, Peter Owen, 1960) 83.

[3] J Wilson, 'A Survey of Legal Education in the United Kingdom' (1966) *Journal of the Society of Public Teachers of Law* 1; J Wilson, 'A Third Survey of University Legal Education in the United Kingdom' (1993) 13 *Legal Studies* 143; J Wilson and S Marsh, 'A Second Survey of Legal Education in the United Kingdom' (1975) *Journal of the Society of Public Teachers of Law* 239.

[4] Wilson (1966), above n 3, at 33; Wilson (1993), above n 3, at 160; Wilson and Marsh, above n 3, at 272.

[5] See, eg, P Harris and S Bellerby with P Leighton and J Hodgson, *A Survey of Law Teaching 1993* (London, Sweet and Maxwell and the Association of Law Teachers, 1994); P Leighton, T Mortimer and N Whatley, *Today's Law Teachers: Lawyers or Academics?* (London, Cavendish Publishing, 1995) and P Harris and M Jones, 'A Survey of Law Schools in the United Kingdom' (1997) 31 *The Law Teacher* 38.

[6] P Winfield, 'Reforms in the Teaching of Law' (1930) *Journal of the Society of Public Teachers of Law* 1.

discloses the same story. Administration is and always has been the forgotten aspect of the law school's life.[7]

If one turns from the literature on British university law schools to the literature on universities in general a similar picture to that drawn above obtains. Whilst discussion of research and, to a lesser extent, teaching is to be found in this wider literature, both in the form of articles and monographs, analysis of administration is largely absent. It would be wrong to see this absence as simply being accidental. Becher, in his largely positive discussion on the nature of academic life that is based on interviews with academics notes:

> [t]his is not to say that there are no boring or unsatisfactory facets of academic life. The most common candidates were administration, committee work and marking undergraduate essays and exam scripts.[8]

Academics do administration but very few of them will report the same direct pleasure from the activity that they get, in varying degrees, from engaging in teaching and research. '[T]he average faculty member who serves on a committee is surrendering time to some purpose that holds no special interest or reward for him or her.'[9] Even those few academics who do have a liking for administration are aware of their atypical nature. Thus, in Henkel's study of academic identity, one respondent observes: '[i]t may seem an odd thing to say but I prefer administration . . . [though] administration is certainly thought to be the province of both fools and the inadequate.'[10] Research done for the Dearing Committee's report on higher education found that 'across the board' academic staff wanted to cut the time that they spent on

[7] My own writing on legal education provides an illustrative example of this phenomenon. In the course of 15 years of writing about the law school, during which I have produced some 25 books, articles and essays, I have only once turned to administration as a focus for my analysis. Even this example was something better described as journalism rather than scholarship (T Bradney, 'Reasons to be Cheerful' (1999) *SPTL Reporter* (Spring) 1).

[8] Although they are separated by a period of over a decade, both the first and second editions of his book make the same point. See T Becher, *Academic Tribes and Territories* (Stony Stratford, Society for Research into Higher Education and the Open University Press, 1989) 123 and T Becher and P Trowler, *Academic Tribes and Territories* (2nd edn, Buckingham, SRHE and Open University Press, 2001) 148 .

[9] D Kennedy, *Academic Duty* (Cambridge, Harvard University Press, 1997) 141. Writing in the context of the law school, Twining observes 'administration is now equated more with obligation than power' (W Twining, *Blackstone's Tower* (London, Stevens and Sons/Sweet and Maxwell, 1994) 70).

[10] M Henkel, *Academic Identities and Policy Change in Higher Education* (London, Jessica Kingsley, 2000) 240.

administration by one half.[11] On an emotional and psychological level this may provide part of the explanation for the university's silence when it comes to administration. Teaching or research, or teaching and research, is why people become academics, whether in law departments or in other parts of the university. Administration is simply something that comes with that job. It is endured as evil even though it might be seen as a necessary evil. The prospect of analysing it does not excite the imagination in the way that happens when one considers research or teaching.

Despite the manifest similarities between the general literature on the universities and the specific literature on law schools, in the case of this wider literature there is however one significant difference; as one gets closer to the present day so one finds a slight but perceptible rise in the quantity of material that pertains to academic administration.[12] In part this does no more than reflect the fact that there is simply a greater quantity of analysis of the nature of university life the closer one gets to the present day; that an area of study which was once largely just a hobby for a minority has, over the past few decades, become a professional field of research for an increasing number of academics. In part, however, it can also be argued that the increase in the amount of literature on administration is not just quantitative but also proportionate. A possible explanation for this qualitative change in the attention that the academy has paid to the analysis of administration can be gleaned from Halsey's *Decline of Donnish Dominion*. Although Halsey's book, published in 1992, gives over little space to specific discussion of university administration, it does note that, in both universities and polytechnics (as they then were), the quantity of administrative work undertaken by individual academics increased from the mid-seventies onwards.[13] Barnett, in an article published in 1993, makes a similar observation:

[11] *Higher Education in the Learning Society*, Report 3, *Academic Staff in Higher Education: their Experiences and Expectations* (London, National Committee of Inquiry into Higher Education, 1997) 115.

[12] The point should not be exaggerated. Even in the present day there is very little writing on university administration. Moreover, that which there is tends to focus on the work of senior administrative figures such as vice chancellors, deans or heads of department rather than the day-to-day work of ordinary, individual academics engaged in administration.

[13] A Halsey, *Decline of Donnish Dominion* (Oxford, Clarendon Press, 1992) 185. Halsey suggests an increase from 19 per cent of academic time in a university being spent on administration in 1976 to 24 per cent in 1989 with the comparative figures for polytechnics being 25 per cent and 28 per cent (Halsey, *ibid*, 186).

> With the emergence of a mass higher education system, in which universities are being asked to be more effective with relatively fewer resources, the work of running institutions takes on a higher profile. Consequently, the role of management and administration in institutions is becoming increasingly significant.[14]

Administration has increased and continues to increase in quantity in universities and this increase can, in itself, lead to administration taking on a different character. If there is more administration it must be dealt with more efficiently and therefore perhaps differently than before if it is not to encroach unduly on time that could otherwise be devoted to teaching or research. Equally there have been attempts to change the character of university administration, not as a consequence of the increase in its quantity but in response to the pressures to change the nature of the university that have already been referred to in the previous chapters of this book; in this respect there is not just an increase in administration but also an attempt to transform administration into management.[15] A reaction to both these pressures is a greater concern with the nature of university administration; a belated realization that administration, like research and teaching, matters in the life of the university and that thus the analysis of administration also matters.

[14] R Barnett, 'The Idea of Academic Administration' (1993) 27 *Journal of Philosophy of Education* 179. Barnett's article is concerned with a wider idea of administration than Halsey's finding because Barnett is concerned with both the administration that is done by academics and the work of the full-time university administrator. Indeed his article concentrates on the latter figures although his analysis is just as pertinent to the work of academics who are carrying out administration.

[15] Obvious referents for this argument would include the Jarratt Report and the attempt to introduce New Public Management ideals into the university (Committee of Vice-Chancellors and Principals, *Report of the Steering Committee for Efficiency Studies in Universities* (The Jarratt Report) (London, CVCP, 1985); M Kogan and S Hanney, *Reforming Higher Education* (London, Jessica Kingsley Publishers, 2000) 31–33). In addition to the comparison between administration and management the literature in this area sometimes compares the necessary existence of management in the university with the introduction of a managerialist approach to that management (see, eg, Becher and Kogan, above n 1, 181). It is the opposition in the dichotomies that are important rather than the precise terminology used.

EQUAL AND AUTONOMOUS INDIVIDUALS[16]

In Chapter 2 above I argued that, although the subject of university administration receives comparatively little attention in the standard texts on liberal education, there is a clear underlying theme regarding it to be found in these works if they are read closely.[17] Administration is, perhaps, not discussed at length precisely because the basic tenets that relate to it seem to the authors concerned to be both self-evident and uncontroversial. However, as in the case of teaching and research, the general principles that underlie a liberal education need to be translated into specific proposals if the liberal law school is to function properly.

Newman's view of the university as '[a]n assemblage of learned men' provides a good starting point for any discussion about how a liberal law school should be organised.[18] The key to his statement is the idea that a university is an institution that is, in essence, a community of scholars.[19] Academics are not just learned individuals but, rather, derive their status from their association with others who are also academics.[20] Moreover, their relationship with their university is not simply, and indeed is not primarily, a matter that can be described by reference to a contract that makes them an employee of the institution; they are, instead, members of the institution[21]:

> Faculty members think of themselves not as working for the institution, but rather as having responsibility for the institution's work. Because they are responsible for the academic work of the institution, and because that is,

[16] '[A]ccording to Schleirmacher, writing at the beginning of the nineteenth century, the search for truth could only be realised on the basis of free communication between equal and autonomous individuals.' Barnett, above n 14, 180.

[17] The discussion of the nature of administration here should be read in conjunction with the discussion of administration in Chapter 2 above.

[18] J Newman, *The Idea of a University* (New York, Holt, Rinehart and Winston, 1960) 76.

[19] See similarly Jaspers, above n 2, at 88 and G Evans, *Calling Academia to Account* (Buckingham, SRHE and Open University Press, 1999) 67.

[20] Universities are not the only place in which academics come together. Professional associations, conferences, e-mail networks and individual collaborations and friendships are also all ways in which academics come together in a community of scholarship. Academics have overlapping and conflicting loyalties arsing from their membership of a number of different 'assemblages' at the same time. On this phenomenon see, eg, D Crane, *Invisible Colleges* (Chicago, University of Chicago Press, 1972) and C Evans, *English People* (Buckingham, Open University Press, 1993).

[21] G Evans, above n 19, at 90.

> after all, the university's central purpose, their version of 'who owns' (or, often, 'who *is*?') the university makes sense.[22]

Together with students, in many senses academics, thus, are the institution.

Those who come into the law school as academics come in largely as equals and the administrative structure of the law school, and more importantly the administrative ethos of the law school, has to reflect this equality. In traditional terms the law school, if it is to work as a liberal law school, must be collegial in its form.

COLLEGIALITY

The use of the term 'collegial' can easily lead to misunderstandings. In the United Kingdom it is a phrase that, because of its historical usage, carries with it connotations of class and exclusion that would be unacceptable to many working in modern university law schools. It is a term that is closely associated with both the Oxbridge university form and with the atmosphere of wealth and privilege which that particular form implies.[23] This association is unfortunate because it sometimes masks extremely simple propositions about the appropriate nature of university administration that can be derived from an understanding of the concept; propositions that would be acceptable to a very broad range of academic opinion within university law schools including even those who regard Oxbridge colleges as an anathema. At the same time as being unfortunate, the association of collegiality and the Oxbridge university type is inaccurate if it results in the conclusion that collegiality is, first, only to be found universities and, secondly, only to be found in universities in the kind of setting exemplified by Oxbridge.

[22] Kennedy, above n 9, at 119. Kennedy goes on to observe that others might take a different view, arguing that the fiduciary position of the university needs protecting (Kennedy, *ibid*, 120–22). This latter argument is rooted firmly in the particular funding circumstances of the major private universities of the USA.

[23] The notion of the collegium is one that 'has and still has different meanings and relationships to the university' (A Cabal, *The University as an Institution Today* (Ottowa, International Development Research Centre, and Paris, UNESCO, 1993) 42). Thus, eg, in the USA the power that the administration has been able to exercise over the faculty has historically been much greater than that in the United Kingdom (Cabal, *ibid*, 57). In this chapter I will be concerned with the basic concept rather than the precise form that it has historically taken in either the United Kingdom or elsewhere.

Sciulli notes that:

> [t]he collegial form is in evidence, in varying degrees of integrity, within the extant universities, private and public research centres, professional associations, intellectual, literary and artistic networks, courts, legislatures, public boards, and commissions of modern societies.[24]

In a similar vein Walters links weaker forms of this organisational ideal with:

> worker cooperatives, professional and academic organizations, religious sects and cults, legal boards and commissions, industrial democracies, labour unions, social movements, [and] political parties.[25]

Far from being specifically linked solely with universities collegiality is an organisational form and a principle of authority that is found in many different areas of society. It is thus unsurprising that collegiality finds a place in Weber's general typology of forms of authority.[26] Moreover, it is a principle of authority that constantly reinvents itself in new institutional settings. Anarchists and feminists would both perhaps object to having their organisational ideals described as being collegial, noting that collegial universities have frequently excluded non-academic workers and women workers, even if they were women academics, from their collegiality yet, in many ways, both theoretical approaches share with traditional universities the aspiration towards inclusion that is the ethic that lies behind the concept of collegiality.[27]

Walters argues that:

> [c]ollegial structures are those in which there is dominant orientation to a consensus achieved between the members of a body of experts who are theoretically equal in their levels of expertise but who are specialized by area of interest.[28]

These general arguments about the way in which collegiality is expressed find their counterpart in specific statements about liberal education. The community that can be deduced from Newman's vision

[24] D Sciulli, 'Voluntaristic Action as a Distinct Concept: Theoretical Foundations of Societal Constitutionalism' (1986) 51 *American Sociological Review* 743 at 755.

[25] M Walters, 'Alternative Organizational Formations: a NeoWeberian Typology of Polycratic Administrative Systems' (1993) 41 *The Sociological Review* 55 at 59.

[26] See, eg, M Weber, *Economy and Society* (New York, Bedminister Press, 1968) 271–82, 994–98 and 1089–90.

[27] See, eg, C Ward, *Anarchy in Action* (London, Freedom Press, 1973).

[28] M Waters, 'Collegiality, Bureaucratization, and Professionalization: A Weberian Analysis' (1989) 94 *American Journal of Sociology* 945 at 956.

of the university has its own particular form. 'The corporate structure . . . [traditionally] expressed a relationship of equality among its members.'[29] This reflects the unusual nature of the university and its law school. Each member of the law school has their own particular expertise and their own particular site of work. The teaching and the research the individuals do are, in the end, teaching and research that can only be done by them. Others in their departments may work in the same field but each person will call upon a unique range of knowledge that leads them to be the individual academic that they are.[30] Hierarchical forms of authority are counterproductive in such a setting because, on the one hand, they presume a degree of knowledge as to what should be done and how others should perform tasks that simply is not present and because, on the other hand, they stifle the creativity that is the essence of high-quality teaching and researching. Instead, traditionally, in order to preserve the quality of academic work:

> [a]cademic departments consist in part of autocrats who individually run certain operations, even dictatorially, and then come together as equals and part-equals to decide collectively on larger matters.[31]

Notwithstanding this ideal of the collegium, in practice, of course, universities are, and always have been, hierarchies. Kogan and Hanney define the collegium as:

> a group of academics of equal decision-making power acting together to determine standards of entry and accreditation, to share collective resources, and to determine divisions of labour and reward systems.[32]

Using this definition, they go on to observe that '[t]he collegium has hardly ever existed except in mixed or diluted form.'[33] Theoretical equality is belied by the inequalities of ability, achievement, eminence and status.[34] More directly, universities, just as much as supermarkets, rank their employees, even their academic employees, through their

[29] G Evans, above n 19, at 67.

[30] '[T]he basis for autonomy lies in the power of knowledge and the freedom of the thinking spirit' (Cabal, above n 23, at 54).

[31] B Clark, 'Governing the Higher Education System' in M Shattock (ed), *The Structure and Governance of Higher Education* (Guilford, Society for Research into Higher Education, 1983) 22.

[32] Kogan and Hanney, above n 15, at 189.

[33] *Ibid*, at 190.

[34] Thus, eg, Polyani notes 'scientific authority is not distributed evenly throughout the body of scientists; some distinguished members of the profession predominate over others of more junior standing' (M Polyani, 'The Republic of Science' (1962) 1 *Minerva* 54 at 60).

different job titles. However, this official hierarchy in the university is relatively flat with the differences in rank amongst a university's academic members being slight and the consequences that flow from those differences being even slighter.[35] Moreover, this official hierarchy can conflict with the other hierarchies that arise out of the multiple community membership that academics can enter into. A professor may believe that they derive superiority from their title but find that their failure to produce research of an adequate quality, engage in new and innovative teaching or take part in the wider academic life to be found outside their department means that, in other hierarchies of esteem, they are ranked more lowly than some in their department who are lecturers.[36] This phenomenon of multiple hierarchies is of great consequence in an area of work where individuals owe greater allegiance to their discipline than they do to their employer.[37]

COLLEGIALITY AND THE NEW UNIVERSITIES

The degree to which British universities are or ever could be said to be collegial varies depending on a number of different factors. First, as I note below, the aspiration to practice collegiality is one thing and the implementation of such a practice is another. An institution or a law school may have collegiate rules of governance or proclaim a collegiate ethos but the life it lives may be very different. Secondly, the precise degree to which individual universities aspire to be collegial has varied greatly in the past. In this respect the new universities, those institutions that did not have university status prior to 1992, have usually been regarded as neither having a history of a collegial ethos prior to

[35] This argument has to be read in a comparative context. I am arguing that, compared with most other sites of work, when one analyses the position of their academic members, universities are relatively non-hierarchical. Universities of course differ one from another and, as I note below, post-1992 universities in the United Kingdom tend to be more hierarchical than those that are of an earlier foundation. Even in the case of post-1992 universities, however, I would contend that less follows for academics from their position in hierarchical relationships than would be true in many other sites of work. However, I am not arguing that the relatively non-hierarchical structure of the university is unique. For an interesting examination of a collegial organisational form in a firm of lawyers see E Lazega, *The Collegial Phenomenon: The Social Mechanisms of Cooperation Among Peers in a Corporate Law Partnership* (Oxford, Oxford University Press, 2001).

[36] On this phenomenon see further A Bradney and F Cownie, 'Working on a Chain Gang' (1996) II(2) *Contemporary Issues in Law* 15.

[37] On this allegiance to a discipline see Becher and Trowler, above n 8, ch 5.

their acquisition of university status nor as wishing to transform themselves into collegial bodies in the present day. Thus, for example, in his study of academics in departments of English literature, Evans compares a number of different universities in England, Scotland and Wales and the then Polytechnic of North London. Of the latter he notes:

> PNL . . . does not suffer from the confusion between the two organizational modes, collegiality and hierarchy . . . PNL has line management.[38]

Similarly, in Ainley's study of a 'Home Counties' university and an 'Inner City' university, the latter being a post-1992 university, he observes that the Home Counties university 'tends to the collegial Oxbridge model of donnish democracy in comparison with the more centralised hierarchy at Inner City.'[39] In broad terms, to argue for the necessity of a collegial ethos in a liberal university law school is to argue for a form of administration that has historically found favour in only one part of British higher education and which continues to find favour in only one part of British higher education.[40]

COLLEGIALITY AND THE TEA AND COFFEE FUND

Where there is discussion of administration in the university or its law school it usually centres on the way in which decisions are taken. Such discussion is often about the work of people such as vice-chancellors, deans or heads of department, about who gain such positions and about the relationship between them and academics within their institutions.[41] This focus is in some respects understandable. In any

[38] C Evans, above n 20, at 107.

[39] P Ainley, *Degrees of Difference: Higher Education in the 1990s* (London, Lawrence and Wishart, 1994) 84.

[40] The argument that the new universities are hostile to collegial notions can be taken too far. In 1987, two years after the Jarratt Report had argued for the introduction of managerialism into the universities, a similar report for polytechnics argued that 'people work best if they are not only committed to what they are doing but also have control over the resources and activities involved' (Becher and Kogan, above n 1, at 181–82). It would be foolish to argue that the new universities or their law schools are driven by notions of collegiality. It would be equally foolish to argue that aspects of collegiality are entirely absent from their working practices.

[41] See, eg, V Strieb, 'Law Deanships: Must They Be Nasty, Brutish and Short?' (1994) 44 *Journal of Legal Education* 116; R Phillips, 'The Origins and Destinations of Law School Deans' (1988) 38 *Journal of Legal Education* 331; A Thody, 'University Management Observed: a Method of Studying its Unique Nature' (1989) 14 *Studies in*

institution the way in which decisions are taken is an important matter and in some institutions and some law schools will indeed be the most important matter. However, when considering collegiality, to concentrate on decision-making in this manner in many ways represents a misunderstanding of the nature of collegiality in practice.

Collegiality connotes community:

> Given the university's corporate nature, participation is a necessary condition for effective, coordinated action. As the word indicates, participation means to take part in the comanagement of all the diverse university activities. Participation implies sharing, not only distributing duties and responsibilities.[42]

Collegiality implies a set of principles about the way in which an academic ought to engage with other academics. These principles are as important for the person who is in charge of the tea and coffee fund within a department as they are for a dean. Working in a collegial manner implies a constant attempt to take account of other academics' views, it implies an attempt to play a part in the administrative work of the institution and the discipline which equals the effort put in by others, it implies reciprocity in one's behaviour and finally it implies a degree of trust in one's colleagues.[43] The tea and coffee fund can be administered in a dictatorial fashion with no attempt being made to ascertain people's wishes as what should be provided. The same fund can also be administered in a slapdash fashion with tea and coffee often not being replaced when supplies run low; the fund can be run in a way that involves the person responsible for the fund constantly asking others to do the job for them and so on and so forth. If any of these things happen then a slight dent is made in the collegial nature of the institution that is concerned. And, since collegiality involves reciprocity, each slight dent is significant. If one person does not act in a collegial manner why should others behave towards them in a collegial fashion? If a number of people in a law school do not act in a collegial

Higher Education 279 and A Bone and T Bourner, 'Developing University Managers' (1998) 52 *Higher Education Quarterly* 283.

[42] Cabal, above n 23, at 61.

[43] Universities cannot be divided into those that are collegial and those that are not. Even a university that has a managerial ideology may have collegiate aspects to its practices. Thus, in Henkel's study of academic identity, a social sciences dean declares himself to be a middle manager but also says '[y]ou must manage on the basis of trust and not on the basis of control' (M Henkel, *Academic Identities And Policy Change in Higher Education* (London, Jessica Kingsley Publishers, 2000) 239). That which is true of universities is also true of their law schools.

manner why should anyone do so, since to behave collegially when others do not behave in the same way is simply to take on what would otherwise be their work or to accede to wishes of others instead of following one's own interests? Collegiality is an atmosphere that depends on collective endeavour and collective attitude as well as a set of rules about the locus of authority within the law school. Collegiality connotes both the belief that there are no unimportant administrative tasks in the law school, no tasks that can safely be ignored, and the belief that, in the end, no tasks speak of a higher status for those who are doing them.

It is clear that the comparative lack of attention paid to administration does affect the collegial nature of universities and their law schools. It appears to be legitimate for an academic to declare themselves to be a poor administrator in a way that would not be acceptable if they declared themselves to be a poor researcher or a poor teacher. Such self-attribution usually signifies little more than an unwillingness to engage in administration rather than anything else. Administrative tasks demand time and attention. Whilst there might be some administrative tasks within a law school that some individuals could not engage in because they lack the necessary skills or knowledge, a general inability on the part of an academic to do any kind of administration is inconceivable. Thus a professed inability to do administration merely signifies an unwillingness to give the necessary time and attention to the activity.[44] Because administration receives such scant attention in the university an unwillingness to engage in it, or a habit of continually doing it poorly, is not likely to have the same consequences for career or reputation that would follow if there was the same behaviour with respect to research or teaching.[45]

[44] '[W]hen they [academics] undertake administration they frequently fail to give it the time and energy it requires, offering only an impoverished management to others' (J Dearlove, 'The Deadly Dull Issue of University "Administration": Good Governance, Managerialism and Organising Academic Work' (1998) 11 *Higher Education Policy* 59 at 72).

[45] Thus, eg, although Evans' book on academics working in departments of English acknowledges that the job involves being 'a researcher/writer/teacher/administrator,' the section of the book entitled 'Doing the Job' is split into two sections 'Teaching' and 'Research' (C Evans, above n 20, at 80; C Evans, *ibid*, 80–89). Administration is in the job but is not important enough to write about at any length. Wells suggests that this practice in the law school is gendered; women are overloaded with administration whilst 'the "absent-minded" male intellectual is excused from the mundane work of administration' (C Wells, 'Working Out Women in Law Schools' (2001) 21 *Legal Studies* 116 at 124). For evidence of this phenomenon see F Cownie, *Legal Academics: Culture and Identities* (Oxford, Hart Publishing, 2003).

COLLEGIALITY AND GOVERNANCE

Whilst it is a mistake to see collegiality as just being concerned with a narrowly focused notion of governance, collegial governance is nevertheless vital for the functioning of the liberal law school. Recognition of this fact is implicit in much writing about the law school. Thus, for example, in one of Twining's descriptions of the law school at the fictional University of Rutland he observes that '[m]ost of the Faculty office-holders are non-professors.'[46] Whilst he goes on to suggest that this results not from a conscious effort at democracy but from the fact that the professors have largely opted out of administration, he also observes that such offices are not associated by academics in the law school with power.[47] The fact that, at Rutland, power is not seen to lie in such offices is significant, reflecting the collegial nature of the law school.[48]

Collegial governance in the law school involves two things. First, it involves an attempt to govern by consensus, with decisions being taken in an hierarchical fashion in the smallest possible number of cases. Secondly, it involves making sure that decisions infringe on the personal discretion of individual academics to the smallest possible degree. This type of governance 'is represented in concrete practice in the form of numerous university committees which arrive at decisions through discussion and debate.'[49]

One major advantage of collegiality is that it is the type of governance that is least likely to infringe on the academic freedom of those working in the law school, a freedom that is itself basic to the successful operation of the liberal law school. Decisions that are reached by consensus are precisely decisions that are in accord with the wishes of those making them. However, in practice, even the most dedicated attempts to obtain consensus will sometimes fail. Even in Quaker Meetings, where decisions result from an attempt to discern the will of God (a process that to the outsider and to some Quaker insiders seems like an attempt to reach consensus) and where that ethos is a community value that has prevailed over generations, '[t]here must be

[46] Twining, above n 9, at 70.
[47] Twining, *ibid.*
[48] Twining later refers to the 'sense of collegiality' that is part of the law school (Twining, *ibid*, 80).
[49] P Ramsden, *Learning to Lead* (London, Routledge, 1998) 23.

occasions when some people disagree with a decision but are prepared to accept it—[it] shouldn't happen but it does.'[50] Some accounts of the university do not simply note an occasional failure to achieve collegiality but go further and doubt how dedicated the attempt at collegiality has been, even in those departments that have professed the idea to be their working principle. Thus, for example, in her analysis of British university law schools, Wells describes a 'white middle-class, male collegiality' that she sees as a 'masculinist culture' which has been and is disempowering for women academics.[51] Plainly the practice of collegiality has to be disentangled from the principle of collegiality. The principle of collegial governance offers an inclusive vision of the university for all academics. Indeed in relation to women academics, in its stress on the importance of inclusion, it is strikingly similar to the notion of the feminine voice, described by Gilligan, that emphasises the importance of recognising connection when taking moral decisions.[52] This thus suggests that, in principle, collegial governance should be empowering to women. Nonetheless, the historical practice of collegial governance in universities has plainly often been very different to that which one might have expected from an analysis of its principles. That which has been said of American universities is also true of British universities:

> campuses are divided by each of the diversities—race, ethnicity, class, age, sexual orientation, or handicap—insidiously or overtly replicating the social [world] and its hierarchies.[53]

Despite the fact that, traditionally, British universities and their law schools have aspired to an ideal of collegiality their achievements have

[50] A Bradney and F Cownie, *Living Without Law: An Ethnography of Quaker Decision-Making, Dispute Avoidance and Dispute Resolution* (Aldershot, Ashgate, 2000) 148. Quaker decision-making is an extreme version of collegiality.

[51] Wells, above n 45, at 129. Similarly, on the effect of race see P Goodrich and L Mills, 'The Law of White Spaces: Race, Culture and Legal Education' (2001) 51 *Journal of Legal Education* 15.

[52] C Gilligan, *In a Different Voice* (Cambridge, Harvard University Press, 1982); L Morley, *Organising Feminisms: The Micropolitics of the Academy* (London, Macmillan Press, 1999).

[53] N Benkraitiz, 'Working in the Ivory Basement: Subtle Sex Discrimination in Higher Education' in L Collins, J Chrisler and K Quina (eds), *Career Strategies for Women in America* (London, Sage Publications, 1998) 8. There is, of course, a much wider literature that sees British universities as being essentially patriarchal institutions (see, eg, Morley, above n 52). Collegiality and patriarchy are clearly not compatible concepts.

never wholly matched their aspirations.[54] Thus, for example, no-one could seriously doubt that British university law schools are and long have been gendered sites of work, even if the manner in which gender affects work practices is complex, operates differently in different law schools and is a changing phenomenon.[55] Nor is the problem limited to gender. In British law schools, as much as elsewhere in the world-wide academic community, '[t]he realities of hidden hierarchies . . . and autocratic styles of god-professors . . . contrasts with the rhetoric of a community of self-governing scholars.'[56] Nevertheless, despite problems in practice, the power in the principle remains, making its proper implementation even more important for the liberal law school.

Protection of academic freedom is not the only advantageous outcome that follows from the use of collegiality in the institutional structures of the university and its law school. 'Collegiality favours greater thoroughness in the weighing of administrative decisions.'[57] The necessity of inclusion, the structure of committees and other fora for decision-making and, of course, the intellectual quality of those academics engaged in the business of administration all help to ensure that any matter under consideration in a collegial setting is given the

[54] Indeed, it is necessary to be cautious when saying that collegiality has represented an aspiration for universities and their law schools because the institutional structures of these bodies have always shown a mixture of collegial and other managerial forms. See further T Becher and M Kogan, *Process and Structure in Higher Education* (2nd edn, London, Routledge, 1992) 71–74.

[55] See further R Collier, 'Masculinism, Law and Law Teaching' (1991) 19 *International Journal of the Sociology of Law* 427; R Collier, ' "Nutty Professors," "Men in Suits" and "New Entrepreneurs": Corporeality, Subjectivity and Change in the Law School and the Legal Profession' (1998) 7 *Social and Legal Studies* 27; F Cownie, 'Women Legal Academics—A New Research Agenda?' (1998) 25 *Journal of Law and Society* 102; F Cownie, 'Women in the Law School: Shoals of Fish, Starfish or Fish Out of Water' in P Thomas (ed), *Discriminating Lawyers* (London, Cavendish Publishing, 2000); F Cownie, above n 45; C McGlynn, *The Woman Lawyer* (London, Butterworths, 1998) ch 2 and Wells, above n 45. This problem is, of course, not one that is peculiar to British university law schools. See, eg, The Chilly Collective (eds), *Breaking Anonymity: The Chilly Climate for Women Faculty* (Waterloo, Ontario, Wilfrid Laurier Press, 1995) and M Thornton, 'Hegemonic Masculinity and the Academy' (1989) 17 *International Journal of the Sociology of Law* 115.

[56] J Currie and L Vidovich, 'Micro-Economic Reform Through Managerialism in American and Australian Universities' in J Currie and J Newson (eds), *Universities and Globalization* (London, Sage Publications, 1998) 168.

[57] Weber, above n 26, at 277. Not every author has taken this view. Adam Smith argued that collegiality would mean that academics would be 'likely to make common cause, to be all very indulgent to one another, and every man to consent that his neighbour neglect his duty provided he himself is allowed to neglect his own' (A Smith, *An Inquiry into the Nature and Causes of the Wealth of Nations*, vol 2 (Oxford, Clarendon Press, 1976) 761).

closest possible attention.[58] It is, however, precisely this advantage that has, in recent years, given rise to the greatest challenge to the principle of using collegiality in administering British universities.

THE ADVANCE OF MANAGERIALISM?

In his discussion of collegiality Weber noted the advantages that it possessed where thoroughness in making decisions was regarded as being more important than 'precision and rapidity.'[59] The perception that rapidity in decision-making has now become a necessary feature of modern academic life has resulted in doubts being raised about the appropriateness of continuing to use collegiality as the only or even the main way in which the university administers its affairs. Thus, for example, Ramsden asserts that:

> [a] higher education system whose institutions need to search for new funding sources, plan strategically, and compete with each other in a market with manifold clients no longer possesses the homogeneity and stability which can make collegiality an effective form of getting things done.[60]

In the United Kingdom the most important early statement in this regard was the Jarratt Report in 1985.[61] This:

> specified that the vice-chancellors should be chief executives, that there should be a corporate plan in which lay members of council together with the vice-chancellor and his senior management team should lay down the objectives of the university, and that the power of departments should give way to corporate planning.[62]

The Jarratt proposals, if implemented, would have affected much of the university, involving, for example, the suggestion that heads of department should take on the role of middle managers. As such the Report presents in many ways a complete antithesis of collegiality as

[58] Although some would suggest that decision-making in such an environment tends to be conservative and does not allow for the 'generation of creative strategic thinking' (A Wilson, 'The Management of Change in a Large Civic University' in S Weil (ed), *Introducing Change from the Top in Universities and Colleges* (London, Kogan Page, 1994) 98).

[59] Weber, above n 26, at 277.

[60] Ramsden, above n 49, at 23.

[61] Jarratt Report, above n 15.

[62] Becher and Kogan, above n 1, at 68–69.

a picture of the manner in which the university should administer itself.[63]

The idea that universities should take managerialism as an approach to the way in which they organised themselves was part of wider arguments that suggested universities needed to change the way in which they saw their role that have already been explored in Chapter 3 above. When related specifically to administration these wider arguments focused on the degree to which collegial or other forms of governance could be said to be an efficient way of running universities. Thus, for example, the Jarratt Report, itself 'part of a series of efficiency studies conducted throughout government departments,' began with a very early assertion that there was a need for 'increased efficiency.'[64] After 1985 efficiency is a mantra that runs through arguments about administration in the universities.[65]

Notwithstanding the frequency with which the term efficiency has been used in debating the management of universities, it has remained a relatively under-developed concept. The rhetorical force that the concept possesses comes in part from its place in wider political arguments about the performance of public sector institutions. The 1980s and the 1990s were an era when the efficiency or, more commonly, the perceived inefficiency of such institutions became a matter for common comment. The civil service in particular was subject to a series of efficiency scrutinies 'aimed at identifying and eliminating areas of waste, inefficiency, duplication and overlap.'[66] Analysis of the 'efficiency' of the universities was linked in with this process. However, even in the wider context of the search for efficiency in public sector institutions, the notion of efficiency has been relatively under-theorised. Indeed, part of its power lay in the very fact of it being under-theorised. To be efficient or to be more efficient was seen as being a simple unalloyed good, 'a very real and persuasive dream' that did not need further elucidation.[67] Long before the 1980s and 1990s, it had been said that 'to be

[63] Becher and Kogan, above n 1, at 181.

[64] Kogan and Hanney, above n 15, at 150; Jarratt Report, above n 15, at para 2.9. For another example of the use of the term see *The Development of Higher Education into the 1990s* (Cmnd 9524, 1985) paras 7.1–7.5.

[65] It is not the only mantra. Accountability is also a slogan that runs through debate from this time on. See further Chapter 7 below.

[66] L Metcalfe and S Richards, *Improving Public Management* (2nd edn, London, Sage Publications, 1990) 7.

[67] A Hopwood, 'Accounting and the Pursuit of Efficiency' in A Hopwood and C Tomkins, *Issues in Public Sector Accounting* (Oxford, Philip Allan Publishers, 1984) 173.

efficient simply means to take the shortest path, the cheapest means, towards the attainment of the desired goals' and that 'the efficiency criterion is completely [value] neutral.'[68] Thus, an argument against efficiency had the same prospect of success as an argument in favour of sin.[69] And efficiency has meant cost. Simon, in his early 1950s analysis of the matter, had argued that, 'in both commercial and noncommercial organizations . . . the "input" factor can largely be measured in money terms.'[70] Thus, the conclusion that '[s]avings are a good proxy for improved efficiency and effectiveness' was easy to arrive at.[71]

In fact, logically, reducing inputs, producing savings, does not necessarily result in greater efficiency. If there is a loss of output because of the reduction of inputs that exceeds the reduction in inputs the result is not an increase in efficiency but, rather, an increase in inefficiency. However, in the public sector, inputs such as wages or numbers of staff are usually easier to quantify than outputs such as quality of service or justice in provision so the search for efficiency quickly becomes the search for savings[72]:

> In practice, efficiency does not mean the greatest benefit for the cost; it means the greatest *measurable* benefit for the *measurable* cost. In other words, efficiency means *demonstrated* efficiency, *proven* efficiency, above all, *calculated* efficiency. A management obsessed with efficiency is a management obsessed with measurement. The cult of efficiency is the cult of calculation. And therein lies the problem.[73]

Simon himself had noted this problem 40 years or so ago, observing:

> the values which public services seek to realize are seldom expressible in concrete terms . . . [but they] must be stated in tangible and objective terms before results can be observed and measured. A serious dilemma is posed here. The values toward which these services should be directed do not provide sufficiently concrete criteria to be applied to specific decisional problems. However, if the value-indices are employed as criteria in lieu of the

[68] H Simon, *Administrative Behavior* (2nd edn, New York, Macmillan Company, 1957) 14.

[69] Metcalfe and Richards, above n 66, at 29.

[70] Simon, above n 68, at 174.

[71] Metcalfe and Richards, above n 66, at 23.

[72] Metcalfe and Richards, above n 66, at 30–31. In effect efficiency meant little more than tax cuts even if those tax cuts resulted in inefficiency.

[73] (emphasis in original). H Mintzberg, 'A Note on the Dirty Word "Efficiency" ' (1982) 12 *Interfaces* 101 at 102.

values themselves, the 'ends' are likely to be sacrificed for the more tangible means—the substance for the form.[74]

In the United Kingdom, in the public sector from the 1980s onwards, the solution to this dilemma was seen as being to ignore it. As Hopwood comments, '[e]fficiency and value for money, rather than effectiveness, are the focuses for attention.'[75]

In the main, in the universities, the arguments about the inefficiency of collegiality have followed the same pattern as wider arguments about efficiency in the public sector. The contention that collegiality is inefficient seems to have meant no more than that decisions made in a collegial manner tends to take longer to make than decisions that are arrived at using other management models. Time is easily quantifiable. It is thus easy to specify how long it took to change a particular policy. It is harder to quantify how good a particular change in policy was. Collegial decision-making is thus, almost by definition, inefficient. Yet it is evident that in fact the phrase 'quick decisions' and the phrase 'efficient decisions' are far from being synonymous. Decisions are efficient because they produce policies that are effective in maintaining the university and its constituent parts; they are efficient because they best allow the university to pursue effectively the goals that it has set itself. Speed of decision-making is plainly a facet of efficient or effective decision-making but, equally plainly, it is only a facet and not the whole. Quick decisions that are wrong because, for example, they fail to carry with them the community who must implement those decisions are inefficient decisions. Nonetheless, just as the search for savings became a feature in the life of public sector institutions taken as a whole, so the search for rapidity in decision-making became a feature of some analyses of universities.[76] The 1980s, the 1990s and the present day have been times when universities and their law schools have found themselves faced with a welter of demands and documents that they had to respond to and it is understandable that making any response has seemed more efficient than taking the time to make a collegiate response and, in so doing, in the effort to reach consensus, inevitably, in some cases, making no response at all. Nevertheless, despite being understandable, such a response is wrong and in fact the actual attitude in the universities towards collegiality in the modern era has been more subtle than some analyses noted above have recommended.

[74] Simon, above n 66, 176.
[75] Hopwood, aboven 67, at 175.
[76] See, eg, Ramsden, above n 49.

COLLEGIALITY IN THE MODERN UNIVERSITY

Becher and Kogan observe that implementation of the Jarratt Report, with its suggestion of a managerial approach to governance in the universities, has been 'patchy.'[77] The patches where the report have not been implemented are easier to discern than the patches where the report has received unambiguous application. Notwithstanding the rhetorical and political support that it has received, managerialism or the attempt to transform administration into management has had relatively little success to date. In the increasing number of studies of vice-chancellors and similar figures in the university there are very few reports of individuals who simply see themselves as chief executives. Thus, for example, a recent study of vice-chancellors with the apparently unambiguous title *University Leadership: the Role of the Chief Executive* concludes '[t]he meetings culture still prevails in universities.'[78] Similarly in studies of other, more lowly figures, there are few accounts of those who see themselves as being just line-managers. Attitudes towards collegiality and consensus in the modern university are ambivalent and even hesitant but, with few exceptions, it is seen as being a continuing and important feature of academic institutions. In Henkel's analysis of academic identities, she notes that:

> [a] dean of a social sciences faculty in an old university was quite clear that he was a middle manager. He was equally clear that universities must be run by academics: 'You must have people who empathise with the values of people in universities and who know how hard it is to do research—how easy it is to crumple and wither . . . You must manage on the basis of trust and not on the basis of control.'[79]

This is not to argue that the modern university or its law school is governed in a wholly collegial manner. Universities and their law schools continue to reflect different and conflicting concepts of governance with the precise recipe for the mix varying from institution to institution and being dependent in part on the individual attitudes of

[77] Becher and Kogan, above n 1, at 182.

[78] C Bargh, J Bocock, P Scott and D Smith, *University Leadership: the Role of the Chief Executive* (Buckingham, SRHE and Open University Press, 2000) 156. See similarly R Middlehurst, *Leading Academics* (Buckingham, SRHE and Open University Press, 1993).

[79] Henkel, above n 43.

those in the institution (these being attitudes that are in a constant state of flux) and in part on the kind of decision that is being made (the more 'academic' the decision, the more collegial is likely to be the process that makes it). However, the vital word in this observation is 'continue.' In being a mix of governance patterns they remain true to their history. For the liberal law school the mix that attains the highest possible degree of collegiality is the form of governance that will be in keeping with the research and teaching aims of the law school.

COLLEGIALITY AND THE WIDER ACADEMIC LEGAL COMMUNITY

In one respect there has been a radical change in the world that the modern British university law school finds itself inhabiting compared with the world its predecessors lived in. Law schools 40 years ago had comparatively little interaction with each other on either an institutional basis or in terms of the work of individual academics. There were few academic conferences and there were few professional associations or societies that legal academics could belong to. Those associations and societies that did exist were relatively inactive when compared to the same bodies in the present day. In the past two decades there has been a rapid growth in the number of and size of academic conferences and in the scope of the work of professional associations. This change in the nature of the legal academic world has changed what collegiality means for the individual legal academic. Since collegiality springs from the notion of community, and since legal academics inhabit (or should inhabit) a multiple number of communities, their collegiality now needs to be manifested not just in the way in which they work in their individual law schools but in the way in which they work in the outside academic legal community. Recognition of this fact is to be seen in the way in which professional bodies have organised and reorganised themselves in order to reflect the changed nature of the academic legal community, seeking to take account of the diverse backgrounds and attitudes now to be found in law schools.[80] Whether all law schools and whether all legal academics are aware of their changed obligations is more questionable. Individual law schools shelter under the protection afforded by bodies such as the Association of Law Teachers, the Committee of Heads of University Law Schools,

[80] See further Cownie (2000), above n 55, at 67–68.

the Society of Legal Scholars (formerly the Society of Public Teachers of Law) and the Socio-Legal Studies Association. Individual legal scholars take advantage of conferences and seminars. Both law schools and individual academics benefit from the existence of groups and associations such as the Association of Social and Legal Philosophy, the Critical Legal Studies group and the Women Law Teachers Network. In obtaining advantage and benefit law schools and individual academics incur a debt that cannot be paid by simply handing over membership dues or a conference fee. Instead collegiality demands that each academic must take their turn in the organisation of both associations and conferences.

7

A Short History of Madness: Accountability, Audit and Liberal Education

PROMETHEUS BOUND?

UNIVERSITIES AND UNIVERSITY law schools that hold themselves out as pursuing a liberal education make bold claims for themselves, claims that sit uneasily with the prevailing public rhetoric of modern political life. Seeing themselves firmly within a tradition of seers and sages, acknowledging that:

> [i]ntelligent societies have always preserved their wise men in institutions of one kind or another, where their chief business is to be wise, to conserve the fruits of wisdom and to add to them if they can,[1]

and thus acknowledging that they are not historically unique, universities conceived in the liberal tradition, if they are functioning properly, nevertheless make the same declaration that Prometheus made:

> For mortals in their misery hear now. At first
> Mindless, I gave them mind and reason . . .
> In those days they had eyes, but sight was meaningless;
> Heard sounds, but could not listen; all their length of life
> They passed like shapes in dreams, confused and purposeless,
> Of brick-built, sun-warmed houses, or of carpentry,
> They had no notion; lived in holes, like swarms of ants,
> Or deep in sunless caverns; knew no certain way
> To mark off winter, or flowery spring, or fruitful summer;
> Their every act was without knowledge, till I came.

[1] R Davies, *The Rebel Angels* (Harmondsworth, Penguin Books, 1982) 192. Davies goes on to write '[o]f course the pedants and the opportunists get in somehow . . . [and] we have our scoundrels and our thieves' (*ibid*).

> I taught them to determine when stars rise and set—
> A difficult art. Number, the primary science, I
> Invented for them, and how to set down words in writing . . .[2]

Put somewhat differently but no less confidently, the university is seen as being the place where 'the wider society [can] learn how to conduct its debates, practical or theoretical, in a rationally defensible way.'[3] More shortly, universities assert that '[a]ll human skill and science' is their gift.[4] Universities claim, if not sole jurisdiction over knowledge creation and cultural critique, at least a major share in these activities and hegemonic authority in determining whether anything that happens outside the university does in fact constitute knowledge creation or valuable cultural critique.

Recent claims that universities have lost their intellectual dominance over society seem to be, despite their intellectual ingenuity, somewhat at variance with the empirical evidence. There are, of course, sites of knowledge generation and application outside the universities. However, the universities continue to exert a powerful influence in most of these areas and the further such areas are from the possibility of immediate commercial exploitation the more powerful is the influence of the university. One example of the continuing control over knowledge creation exercised by the universities is seen in the phenomenon of the increasing number of articles being published by senior judges. Whilst these articles have just as much a claim to be 'knowledge creation' as articles written by legal academics they can, in large part, make that claim because they have been published in academic journals; their claim to be knowledge creation is authenticated by the fact that they are being published in an academic arena.

Given the width of the jurisdiction that universities assert dominion over, it is not surprising that, in the modern era, political authorities have sought to bind the universities and their law schools, chaining

[2] Aeschylus, *Prometheus Bound* (Harmondsworth, Penguin Books, 1961) 34. '[T]he Aeschylean Prometheus . . . is presented as the saviour of mankind, without whom man would have ceased to exist and with whose help he progresses from mere subsistence to a state of civilization' (D Conacher, *Aeschylus' Prometheus Bound* (Toronto, University of Toronto Press, 1980) 13).

[3] A MacIntyre, *Three Rival Versions of Moral Inquiry* (London, Gerald Duckworth, 1990) 222.

[4] Aeschylus, above n 2, at 35. Such would not have been Newman's view (J Newman, *The Idea of a University* (New York, Holt, Rinehart and Winston, 1960) xxxix–xl). However, the ambitions of the liberal university have grown since his time.

them so as to circumscribe their power.[5] In asserting an academic freedom to pursue their own ends in teaching and research, universities and particularly universities working within the liberal tradition, in effect, deny any final allegiance to the state in which they are located, paying homage instead to a higher duty of critical reflection.[6] Thus Price writes of British universities, '[t]heir accountability has never been to the local community or even to Parliament but rather to international scholarship.'[7] Political institutions, keen to preserve their own jurisdictions, keen to pursue their own ends and keen to develop or preserve a monopoly over power in their countries, are unlikely to view such a position with any degree of favour. More particularly, the oppositional role of the universities, which involves questioning dominant social mores, repeatedly brings them into direct conflict with political power.

When it pursues its oppositional role, the universities' crime is precisely the same crime as that of Prometheus. 'I dared. I saved the human race from being ground to dust, from total death.'[8] Sometimes universities and their law schools commit this crime openly. In providing a place where alternative discourses can be articulated, in putting forward a critique of social hierarchies, in pointing to the ways in which the use of economic and other resources perpetuates and reinforces inequalities within societies and in challenging the virtue of utility, generations of scholars in the universities, working in a range of different theoretical frameworks, have, both in their teaching and in their research, portrayed political and social systems in modern societies as resulting exactly in the human race being 'ground to dust.' For such scholars, Zeus' literal attempt to destroy the human race that Prometheus thwarted, is metaphorically mirrored by modern political

[5] I use the terms 'political authorities' and 'political institutions' rather than 'government' because I am referring not just to the various governments of the day but also to other institutions, bodies and individuals such as all the main political parties and those who have controlled relevant professional and audit bodies.

[6] Of course universities sometimes forget this duty as is seen in the reaction of academics to the revelation that Anthony Blunt had spied for the then Soviet Union. 'Blunt's academic titles, honorary doctorates, fellowships, memberships, editorships [awarded because of his renown as an art historian] began to disappear, hastily and often embarrassedly withdrawn.' (M Carter, *Anthony Blunt: His Lives* (London, Macmillam, 2001) 486). Even in this atmosphere of hysteria there were some encouraging signs. London University's convocation, for example, declined an invitation to 'show the world that academia understood its duty' and voted not to strip Blunt of his emeritus chair (Carter, *ibid*, 487).

[7] C Price, 'Elegant and Democratic Values: How Will the New English Universities Gel?' (1992) 46 *Higher Education Quarterly* 243 at 247.

[8] Aeschylus, above n 2, at 27.

attempts to produce pliable and compliant citizens, ideologically committed to existing social and economic mores. Government has sometimes chided universities because they have not produced 'able, skilled and well-motivated graduates' for industry.[9] Similarly, the legal professions have asserted their need for graduates who are able to fit easily into the milieu of the modern lawyer.[10] For those in the universities who hold to oppositional critiques, a 'well-motivated' employee in most parts of industry or in most parts of the legal professions in the United Kingdom is, by definition, an employee who is ignorant of the socio-economic reality of their circumstances; an employee who does not understand the teaching and the research that the university has provided. Well paid, even extremely well paid, alienated labour is still alienated labour with all the attendant social and personal damage that this brings. The factory worker and the highly paid partner in a large City practice have more in common than they may realise. Government is probably right in believing that there is a degree of ' "anti-business" snobbery' in universities.[11] There is also, however, at a much deeper level, an ethical aversion to the exploitative behaviour that is a characteristic feature of modern industrial societies that reflects both the general left/liberal political sympathies of the majority of academics and the even more prevalent preference amongst academics for a way of life that is very different from that that is enjoyed by most people in British society.[12] This aversion pervades the teaching and research of many in the universities. Just as Prometheus opposed Zeus, so the universities, in their oppositional mode, must oppose forms of political power that seek to dehumanise individuals and theorists of liberal education, with their emphasis on the central importance of educating the whole person and enabling them to take control of their own lives, take their place in such oppositional ranks.

[9] Thus, eg, *The Development of Higher Education into the 1990s* (Cmnd 9524, 1985) para 2.2.

[10] See, eg, A Holroyd, 'Comment' (2001) 98 No 45 *Law Society Gazette* 14.

[11] *The Development of Higher Education into the 1990s*, above n 9, at para 1.6.

[12] Few British academics are willing to support the Conservative Party. In an ICM poll conducted on behalf of the *Times Higher Education Supplement* only 5 per cent of academics said that they intended to vote Conservative in the 2001 general election. In the 1997 and 1992 general elections the percentage willing to vote Conservative had been 8 per cent and 15 per cent respectively (*Times Higher Education Supplement*, 11 May 2001, 1). Even those academics who are willing to support the Conservative Party are, by choosing a way of life that both lies outside the hierarchical structures of modern industry and functions with very different mores, implicitly rejecting the dominant values of that industry.

Sometimes the universities' crimes are more subtle and less obvious than those detailed above. Bloom has argued that, in a democracy, there exists 'the really dangerous form of the tyranny of the majority.'[13] He goes on to argue that this is not the form of tyranny:

> that actively persecutes minorities but the kind that breaks the inner will to resist because there is no qualified source of nonconforming principles and no sense of superior right. The majority is all there is. What the majority decides is the only principle. It is not so much its power that intimidates but its semblance of justice.[14]

In a democracy it is democracy that is the problem.[15] For universities, particularly for universities who aspire to the tradition of liberal education, conforming to the will of the majority in this way is problematic because, as Bloom argues:

> the democratic concentration on the useful, on the solution of what are believed by the populace at large to be the most pressing problems, makes theoretical distance seem not only useless but immoral. When there is poverty, disease and war, who can claim the right to idle in Epicurean gardens, asking questions that have already been answered and keeping a distance when commitment is demanded?[16]

Thus universities, if they are to pursue the goal of liberal education, the pursuit of knowledge for its own sake, have to be oppositional to the proposition that the fact that something is the will of the majority of itself justifies that thing being done. The argument here is not that the concept of democracy does in fact simply mean that the will of the majority should be obeyed and that therefore it is necessary for the universities to oppose democracy. The Human Rights Act 1998, with its basis in an anti-majoritarian conception of fundamental rights, is one good illustration of the complicated nature of the reality of the principles that lie behind modern democracies. Rather, the argument is that, in democracies, the notion that the will of the majority should be

[13] A Bloom, *The Closing of the American Mind* (Harmondsworth, Penguin Books, 1988) 247. Some, probably rightly, have seen Bloom's book as an argument for limiting the kind of people who can properly find a place within the university (see, eg, H Giroux, 'Dreaming about Democracy' in D Gless and B Herrnstein Smith, *The Politics of Liberal Education* (Durham, Duke University Press, 1992) 124). I would want to disentangle and reject this strand of his argument from the argument with which I am concerned here about the proper place of the university in society.

[14] Bloom, above n 13.

[15] Of course, in non-democratic states it is the absence of democracy that is the problem.

[16] Bloom, above n 13, at 250.

obeyed has a strong rhetorical force and it this rhetoric and this insistence on the prosaic that the universities have to confront if they are to survive:

> The university as an institution must compensate for what individuals lack in a democracy and must encourage its members to participate in its spirit. As the repository of the regime's own highest faculty and spirit, it must have a strong sense of its own importance outside the system of individual equality. It must be contemptuous of public opinion because it has within it the source of autonomy—the quest for and even discovery of the truth according to nature.[17]

There is therefore, at a number of different levels, a deep antipathy between the universities and modern day political authorities who are anxious to use the rhetoric of majority opinion for their own purposes and anxious to perpetuate social and political systems that many in the universities would see as being deeply damaging to society.[18]

Aeschylus' play 'Prometheus Bound' is a play that is concerned with

> the conflict between the innovative intellectual . . . and the political authority determined to preserve its rule, unchanged free from question or comment.[19]

The period of the last two decades has, for British universities, been a play with a similar theme. These years have seen a welter of proposals concerned with measuring the performance of the universities. Ostensibly these proposals have been concerned with the efficiency of the universities; in reality they have been more concerned with the nature and direction of the work done in the university. Taken together they constitute a serious potential challenge to the prospects for pursuing a liberal education in the university in general and its law school in particular.

In Chapter 3 above I looked at some of the broader political arguments surrounding the purposes of the university and its law school that have been put forward in recent times. In Chapters 4, 5 and 6 above I looked at what a liberal education could mean for the law school. In this chapter I want to look at the detailed procedures and

[17] Bloom, above n 13, at 254.

[18] Universities are not only oppositional to political authority. They are also supportive of it, offering analyses that will help political authorities better articulate their aims and more efficiently achieve their objectives. Universities are Janus-faced. However, it is the oppositional side of the universities' work that is remembered by political authorities. Prometheus, who advised Zeus in Zeus' battle with Chronos, found the same thing.

[19] J Herrington, *Aeschylus* (New Haven, Yale University Press, 1986) 160.

requirements for measuring the performance of university law schools that have been developed out of broader arguments about the purpose of a university and to ask whether the concept of a liberal education that was developed the last three chapters can be pursued in the age of audit that has arisen in the modern era.

THE MANTRA OF ACCOUNTABILITY

I noted in the last chapter that a requirement for accountability, like the notion of efficiency, has become a mantra that is chanted on as many occasions as possible when discussing the work of universities. Accountability has both been used to justify attempting to chain the university and its law school and has itself formed part of those chains. Thus, for example, the Quality Assurance Agency has sought to justify its intrusive practices in the name of accountability.[20] However, the nature of this accountability has remained relatively under-theorised, even by those who accept its validity. Because of this there is a need to look more closely at the concept when it is used in the context of universities.[21]

HISTORICAL NOTIONS OF THE ACCOUNTABILITY OF THE UNIVERSITY

There is nothing new in the idea that universities and those working in universities should account for themselves nor, in itself, is there

[20] *Memorandum from the Quality Assurance Agency for Higher Education* para 26 in Sixth Report of the Education and Employment Select Committee: Higher Education: Student Retention: Minutes of Evidence, 17 January 2001, HC 124.

[21] To publish an analysis of this process is, it might be argued, in conflict with Oceanus' advice to Prometheus:

> . . . your plight is the inescapable
> Reward, Prometheus, of a too proud-speaking tongue.
> You will not be humble, will not yield to pain;
> You mean to add new sufferings to those you have.
> Come now, accept my guidance: we are ruled by one
> Whole harsh and sole dominion none may call to account.
> Acknowledge this, and cease to kick against the goad.'
> (Aeschylus, above n 2, at 30).

Such an argument has some force; so, too, does the view that 'the official responses of both the appointed leaders and the working members of university communities to their recent external critics . . . [has been] lamentable' (A MacIntyre, *Three Rival Versions of Moral Inquiry* (London, Gerald Duckworth, 1990) 222). Silence in the face of stupidity has not, to date, proved to be an efficacious way of protecting the universities.

anything in the notion of accountability that is problematic for the pursuit of a liberal education. Newman's lectures on the notion of the university, Blackstone's lecture, 'On the Study of Law,' and Dicey's lecture, 'Can English Law be Taught at the Universities?' are all, in one sense, attempts to account for the work of the university or a part of the university.[22] These lectures are more than personal meditations, later published for public perusal. They are all reports on the work that the university should be doing or that it is doing. In this sense academic bodies and individual academics have always held themselves open to the need to account for their behaviour.

When expressed at its most fundamental level, the idea of accountability is not particular to the universities but, rather, pertains to the relationship that any person or institution has with the communities around them. We, as individuals or institutions, are all wholly responsible for our behaviour and must therefore be in a position to account for that behaviour to others who, in turn, must be able to account for their behaviour to us. To argue against such a proposition would be to argue that one can justify, morally, living outside society, in the sense of refusing to participate in that society, whilst still living inside society, in the sense of drawing the benefits that accrue from having others around one. Such an argument would require belief in a form of individualism that allowed one to treat others as simply means rather than as ends in themselves. Accountability is, in this sense, not a demand that comes from particular political authorities at a particular moment in history. Instead, it is something that springs from the very nature of concepts of about participation in society and community.

MODERN DEMANDS FOR ACCOUNTABILITY

Current arguments about the need for universities to be accountable draw their force in part from the very basic, very powerful ethical position outlined above. Such a position, such a demand would be accepted by most people, including most academics working in universities, and is in keeping with the history of the universities. It is this that makes the argument for accountability on the part of the universities seemingly

[22] J Newman, *The Idea of a University* (New York, Holt, Rinehart and Winston, 19060); W Blackstone, 'On the Study of Law' in *Blackstone's Commentaries on the Laws of England*, vol 1 (16th edn, London, T Cadell and J Butterworth and Son, 1825); A Dicey, (London, Macmillan and Co, 1993).

'irresistible.'[23] However, modern demands for accountability go beyond the proposition that an account of the activities of the university should be given and, instead, involve the suggestion that this account should be made against a check-list of desiderata that is externally provided; a demand for accountability thus becomes a denial of autonomy, an argument that is supported by reference to quasi-contractual notions about the rights of those who provide money for the university.

> Not many years ago, any attempt to measure the performance of institutions of higher education would have been regarded with horror in academic circles. Attitudes have changed very rapidly during the 1980s, however, as a result of the government's determination to make the public sector more accountable to the taxpayer. This has inevitably led towards the more careful scrutiny of the way in which the taxpayers' money is being used in order to discover whether the public sector's efficiency could be improved. All parts of the public sector—including higher education—are now expected to monitor and evaluate their activities more carefully than has hitherto been the case.[24]

Recent arguments about the accountability of universities and their law schools have thus been arguments not so much about the fact of them being accountable *for* themselves but, rather, about who they had to account *to* and who determined the measure of the account. In 1988, when new suggestions about the accountability of universities were just beginning to have an effect, Neave asked whether or not 'the purpose of evaluation is to bend recalcitrant academia to what the government deems to be "the new reality." '[25] In the twenty-first century the answer to this question seems plain; evaluation and accountability have largely been an attack on both the autonomy of the universities, demanding that universities subordinate themselves to government, and the philosophy of liberal education, insisting that universities concern themselves not with the pursuit of knowledge but, instead, comply with the perceived training needs of industry.[26]

[23] M Power, *The Audit Society* (Oxford, Oxford University Press, 1999) xv.

[24] J Johnes and J Taylor, *Performance Indicators in Higher Education* (Buckingham, Open University Press, 1990) 1.

[25] G Neave, 'On the Cultivation of Quality, Efficiency and Enterprise: An Overview of Recent Trends in Higher Education in Western Europe, 1986–1988' (1988) 23 *European Journal of Education* 7 at 16.

[26] Thus the annual accounts for the Higher Education Funding Council for England state that Strategic Aim 3 is to 'enhance the relevance of teaching and research to the needs of employers and the economy' with a performance target that '[a]ll institutions be

UNIVERSITY LAW SCHOOLS AND THE LEGAL PROFESSIONS

Because of their relationship with the legal professions, university law schools in England and Wales have long been used to the idea of accounting to those outside the university, according to criteria created for the law schools by those to whom they are doing the accounting.[27]

In 1846 the House of Commons Committee on Legal Education recommended both that the legal professions set up examinations for those seeking professional practising qualifications and that the professions 'admit the certificates of attendance on lectures in the universities, to a certain extent, as exempting from attendance in their own lectures.'[28] Both the Bar and, more hesitantly, the Law Society took up these recommendations. The first examinations for those intending to become solicitors followed an 1860 statute and by 1895, 'the Law Society began excusing law graduates from the intermediate examination in law' that had to be passed before a person could become a solicitor.[29] By 1966 Wilson was observing that, before the Law Society was prepared to grant a law graduate exemption from what had by then become the Part I qualifying examination, it had to be satisfied that 'the syllabus . . . [that the graduate had studied did] not differ too radically from that required for its own examinations.'[30] Thus the universities were required to account to the Law Society for their teaching, showing that they taught the subjects that the Law Society thought appropriate in a way that met with the Society's approval.[31] This practice

implementing their plans for enhancing the employability of their graduates' (Higher Education Funding Council for England, *Annual Accounts for the Year Ended 31 March 2001* http://www.hefce.ac.uk).

[27] The relationship between the law schools in Scotland and those in Northern Ireland and their respective legal professions has been different in detail from that in England and Wales though many of the problems are the same.

[28] House of Commons Committee on Legal Education (1846) Parl Papers x p lxi.

[29] 23 & 24 Victoria c 127; R Abel, *The Legal Profession in England and Wales* (Oxford, Blackwell, 1998) 144. For further details of the historical relationship between the universities and the legal professions see Abel, *ibid*, at 46–49, 143–45 and 280–81; R Cocks, *Foundations of the Modern Bar* (London, Sweet and Maxwell, 1983) and W Holdsworth, *History of English Law*, vol XV (London, Methuen, Sweet and Maxwell, 1965) 237–40.

[30] J Wilson, 'A Survey of Legal Education in the United Kingdom' (1966) *Journal of the Society of Public Teachers of Law* 1 at 78. The General Council of the Bar have acted in a very similar fashion.

[31] The fact that law students have obtained exemption from professional examinations because of their law degree does not fully describe the historical inter-relationship between law schools and the legal professions. Abel, for example, notes of provincial

finds expression in the present day in the Joint Statement issued by the Law Society and the General Council of the Bar.[32] The Joint Statement now lays down a partial curriculum for law schools, detailing not only subjects that must be taught, the seven Foundations of Legal Knowledge, but also skills that must be acquired during their period of study by a law graduate if they are to be exempt from the Common Professional Examination set by the Bar and the Law Society and so achieve practitioner status more quickly than graduates in other disciplines.[33]

Both the Law Society and the Bar can justify the Joint Statement by reference to their need to ensure that those entering into the legal professions are properly qualified. They might then argue that university autonomy is not compromised because there is no requirement that law schools seek qualifying status for their law degrees. However, the existence of the Joint Statement is problematic for the law schools, as at least one of the Law Society's employees has recognised. In an interview that he gave before taking up the post of Director of Legal Education and Training at the Law Society, Roger Smith observed:

> [t]here is a growing tension as HE expands. HE institutions seek more autonomy and the profession may tend to have attitudes that might seem old-fashioned to those involved in the education world.[34]

Recognising the fact that some of their students wish to take advantage of the saving in time and money that obtaining exemption from Common Professional Examination represents, law schools seek qualifying status for their degrees but in so doing their syllabus become constrained by the demands of the Statement. Moreover, the law schools become embroiled in the somewhat mysterious processes that result in the continual writing and rewriting of the Statement. As Leighton has

university law schools in the nineteenth century that 'most of their faculty were practitioners teaching part time to prepare articled clerks for the solicitors' examinations' (Abel, above n 29, at 264). More recently, in the 1980s, many law schools obtained sponsorship for a range of matters, including the provision of academic posts, from firms of solicitors (A Bradney, 'Paying the Piper' (1990) 24 *The Law Teacher* 137). Law schools and the professions have been and continue to be entwined at many different levels of both a formal and informal nature.

32 In full, the 'Joint Statement Issued by the Law Society and the General Council of the Bar on the Completion of the Initial or Academic Stage of Training by Obtaining a Law Degree.'

33 http://www.lawzone.co.uk/barcouncil/index.html. At the time of writing this passage the Statement is the subject of renegotiation.

34 'Roger Smith' (1998) 32 *The Law Teacher* 192.

argued, 'there has never been a clear rationale for precisely why there *are* the Foundation or Core subjects.' Moreover, as she observes:

> [t]here appears to be no forum or opportunity to propose that, say, the law of domestic relations, employment or the law of business associations are far more central to the work of most lawyers or law graduates than, say, public law or equity.[35]

Even academics who believe that the core subjects 'are genuinely foundational to the Western legal tradition' also contend that 'it is now evident that the university law schools are far better placed to say what ought to be learned [for practice].'[36] In principle the writing of a syllabus seems to be plainly a pedagogic matter best left to those who practise education. Nevertheless, in practice the construction of the Joint Statement is a political matter.

Whilst the Joint Statement is drawn up after consultations with a range of academic bodies, and whilst the Statement must be agreed by the Lord Chancellor before it can be brought into force, the responsibility for its contents largely rests with the Law Society and the Bar Council and with their employees.[37] The deliberations of these bodies are private and it is unclear what reasoning lies behind the decisions that they take or, indeed, what qualifications members of these bodies have for making such decisions.[38] The increasingly fractured nature of the legal professions, referred to in Chapter 4 above, makes it is difficult to see what core knowledge or skills all professional lawyers will need. Instead of being grounded in any solid empirical evidence about the nature of legal practice the Joint Statement seems to be based upon very loose propositions about what knowledge or skills lawyers might need; propositions that are put forward in the context of a world where

[35] P Leighton, 'Bench Marking by QAA and Qualifying Degree Standards set out by the Legal Professions of England and Wales' (1999) 33 *The Law Teacher* 218 at 220.

[36] P Birks, 'A Decade of Turmoil' in P Birks (ed), *Examining the Syllabus: Beyond the Core* (Oxford, Oxford University Press, 1993) 10; P Birks, 'Editor's Preface' in P Birks (ed), *Pressing Problems in the Law*, vol 2, *What Are Law Schools For?* (Oxford, Oxford University Press, 1996) xvi. See also P Birks, 'Compulsory Subjects: Will the Seven Foundations Ever Crumble?' (1995) 1 *Web Journal of Current Legal Issues*.

[37] Solicitors' Act 1974, s 2(1).

[38] Becoming a member of these ruling bodies and sub-committees of the Law Society and the General Council of the Bar is a political process. Because of this, there is no necessary reason why any member of these bodies should have any knowledge of either university law schools or the actual needs of the professions as regards the educational background of new entrants. So far as one can judge, decisions as to the content of the Joint Statement seem to rest largely on the anecdotal impressions of those involved in writing the Statement.

increasing specialisation means that, in fact, many or even most lawyers will not use much of what they have been taught.[39] Thus, because the process that leads to the publication of the Joint Statement is certainly not transparent and probably is not rational, law schools are forced to account for their teaching to a standard that is delivered as a ukase.[40] At the same time, by submitting to the Statement, the law schools tacitly underwrite its legitimacy.

The historical relationship between the legal professions and university law schools in England and Wales illustrates the problems that external accountability creates for the pursuit of a liberal education. Until recently the concern of the professions has been focused on the knowledge of legal rules that the law graduate could be expected to have. Latterly this focus has expanded to include skills as well as knowledge. However, whether their concern has been knowledge or skills, the reason for the professions' concern has always been the employability of the graduate; it has always been the question of how quickly the new graduate could start making money.[41] This focus is entirely different from that of the liberal law school concerned to educate citizens. A recent survey found that solicitors regarded autonomy as only the fifteenth most desirable characteristic in a trainee.[42] For the liberal law school the development of an awareness of autonomy is basic to learning. This difference in focus means that law schools are always faced with the possibility of being pushed into putting things into their syllabi which they have little interest in or which they believe to be positively harmful in educational terms. In turn this means that

[39] See further Chapter 4 above. This point has been accepted at least in part by the Law Society (see Holroyd, above n 10).

[40] Most academics would accept that the account has to be given only in relationship to those matters that are covered by the Joint Statement. Brayne, however, has gone further, arguing that once the law schools accept the Joint Statement, '*therefore* the curriculum outcomes purport to relate to the professions' requirements, *therefore* law teachers should be debating how their curriculum and teaching best prepares undergraduate students for legal practice' (H Brayne, 'A Case for Getting Law Students Engaged in the Real Thing: The Challenge to the Saber-Tooth Curriculum' (2000) 34 *The Law Teacher* 17 at 18). It is doubtful that many academics would see any logic in this position, instead preferring the argument that if a law degree has qualifying status the law school is saying no more than it matches the requirements of the Joint Statement. However, if Brayne's argument were accepted, it would considerably extend the degree to which law schools are accountable to the professions.

[41] Holroyd, above n 10.

[42] V Bermingam and J Hodgson, 'Desideratat: What Lawyers Want from their Recruits' (2001) 35 *The Law Teacher* 1 at 22.

they have less space in the syllabus to pursue the kind of ends that they think are appropriate.

The relationship between university law schools and the professions is illustrative of the problems that external accountability brings; poorly reasoned propositions become basis for the content of the syllabus and there is an attempt to make the law school a servant of purely private needs. However, the same relationship is also illustrative of the way in which such problems can be managed, so as to ensure a space for the pursuit of liberal education.

The fact that the legal professions have power to regulate entry into their area of work does not give them carte blanche with respect to decisions that they make about such matters. The powers given to the professions are, in principle, part of a bargain between them and the state.[43] Self-regulation by the professions is regarded as being in the public interest. In accordance with this, with respect to the professions' rules in relation to education, it has been said that, '[a] requirement to have demonstrated basic competence is clearly justified where consumers are not well placed to assess the quality of service.'[44] On this argument, entry rules are not there to serve the profession but, rather, to serve the wider public good.[45] Because of this, any rules that relate to the education of prospective entrants to the legal professions have to be justified by this reference to competence rather than any other reason. In 2001 the Office of Fair Trading, after investigating the then existing entry requirements for both solicitors and barristers, concluded that those rules complied with this requirement.[46] Any future changes to the rules would also have to be justified by reference to this requirement. A Joint Statement that is intended to ensure competence in trainee solicitors and pupil barristers is one thing; a Joint Statement that is intended to ensure that trainees and solicitors are capable of being high fee earners at their point of entry into the legal profession is another. A failure to comply with merely ensuring competence could

[43] For a discussion of the position of the legal professions see F Cownie and A Bradney, *English Legal Sytem in Context* (2nd edn, London, Butterworths, 2000) 142–43.

[44] *Competition in the Professions: A Report by the Director General of Fair Trading* (London, Office of Fair Trading, 2001) 6.

[45] Not every commentator would accept this hypothesis. Abel, for example, describes 'the progressive intensification of Law Society control over supply [of new solicitors] through the multiplication and increase stringency of professional examinations'; for him entry requirements are, at least in part, about market control and attempts by the legal professions to decrease competition (Abel, above n 29, 162).

[46] *Competition in the Professions*, above n 44.

lead to the Joint Statement being referred to the Competition Commission.[47] The professions are thus not unfettered in the range of demands that they can make of law schools.

If the legal professions' lack of autonomy, the requirement to comply with statute, hampers the legal professions to some extent in their negotiations with university law schools so too does the existence of the Common Professional Examination. The Common Professional Examination is a one-year course that is undertaken by those who are not able to obtain the exemption offered by a qualifying university law degree. Since the Law Society and the Bar Council hold out the Common Professional Examination as being part of an educational route that demonstrates competence in a practitioner it follows that the Joint Statement can, in relation to specifically legal skills or knowledge, demand of a three of four year law degree no more than that which can be done in this 12 month course; to ask anything more would be to go beyond the legitimate end of being able to certify competence.[48] Whether or not the Law Society and the Bar Council have restricted themselves to these limits is debatable. The present seven Foundations of Legal Knowledge must, under the rules to be found in the Joint Statement, take no less than one and a half years of study. In addition to this the syllabus of a qualifying law degree must also require some study of the sources, institutions and personnel of the legal system though the Statement does not prescribe how much time must be given over to this study.[49]

[47] Professional rules have been referred to the Monopolies and Mergers Commission, the precursor of the Competition Commission, 14 times (*Competition in the Professions*, above n 44, at 4). Decisions of the professional bodies about the Joint Statement are also potentially susceptible to judicial review. To date the application of judicial review to regulatory bodies such as the Law Society seems to have been limited to their disciplinary functions. See, eg, *R v General Medical Council, ex parte Gee* [1986] 1 WLR 226. However, there seems to be no reason in principle why judicial review should not also be applied to the Law Society's function in regulating law degrees. The courts have been willing to consider the use of judicial review with respect to the General Council of the Bar's exercise of its powers even though there is no statutory basis for these powers. See *R v General Council of the Bar ex parte Percival* [1991] 1 QB 212.

[48] It is, of course, open to the Law Society and Bar to argue that entrants onto the Common Professional Examination course will, by virtue of their being graduates, possess transferable skills that are not specifically legal and that law schools must make sure that their graduates also have these non-legal transferable skills.

[49] http://www.lawzone.co.uk/barcouncil/index.html. In addition the law student must spend a further six months of their course studying law subjects. On the varying length of legal system courses see B Lynch, P Moodie and D Salter, 'The Teaching of Foundation Legal Instruction' (1993) 27 *The Law Teacher* 216 at 219. The Joint Statement does not require the study of legal system to be by way of a separate course.

The constraints on Law Society and Bar Council action noted thus far arise out of the structural relationship between the state, the professional associations and university law schools. In addition the creation of new audit procedures for university law schools has, paradoxically, further fettered the freedom of the Law Society and Bar Council to make demands of law schools.[50] Any arguments about the teaching done in university law schools made by the Law Society and Bar Council have to be either consistent with the position of other bodies that now audit university law schools or the Law Society and Bar Council have to explain and justify any inconsistencies. In an age when the Quality Assurance Agency has concluded that:

> [d]espite some claims to the contrary, our higher education system is among the most coherent and consistent, in terms of academic quality and standards, of any in the world

this is a not inconsiderable difficulty for the legal professions.[51] Thus, for example, although some members of the legal professions have sometimes asserted a lack of quality in the law schools' teaching, such as to justify intrusion and inspection, the Quality Assurance Agency's converse finding, based on the various inspection regimes operated by it and its predecessors, means that the professions would have to provide evidence to justify their assertions if they were to wish to use them as part of a reason for changing the Joint Statement. Moreover, such evidence would have to go beyond the merely anecdotal if it were to outweigh the evidence put forward by the Quality Assurance Agency.[52]

In negotiating the Joint Statement university law schools can bring to bear not only the considerable weight of the fact of a separate academic profession focused on the process of education with some 2,500

[50] Consideration of further audit arrangements has also focused attention on the good faith of professional associations when they debate what universities should be doing. Thus, eg, the Dearing Report stated that '[p]rofessional bodies . . . should be brought into the dialogue [about standards in universities], although there will be need for firm control so that particular interest groups do not place costly and unnecessary requirements on institutions' (National Committee of Inquiry into Higher Education, *Higher Education in the Learning Society* (The Dearing Report) (London, HMSO, 1997) 162).

[51] P Williams, 'Reaping the Benefits' (2001) 9 *Higher Quality* 1 (http://www.qaa.ac.uk).

[52] This not to suggest that the evidence gathered when reviewing teaching has been faultless. The very reverse is the case (see, eg, A Bradney, 'The Quality of Teaching Quality Assessment in English Law Schools' (1996) 30 *The Law Teacher* 150). Nevertheless there is a degree of objectivity and rigour in the analysis and evidence offered by the Quality Assurance Agency that cannot be rebutted by the casual opinions of individual practising lawyers.

members grouped together in 87 law schools but also the logical and political limitations of the position that the legal professions find themselves in.[53] Although the last two decades can be rightly characterised as an era of increasing accountability demands for university law schools, it has also seen law schools react acerbically to what they have regarded as unwarranted intrusions into their autonomy. When, in 1992, Law Society draft proposals sought to replace the 1990 Joint Statement, which had limited descriptions of the content of core courses to six lines or so, 'with two pages of detailed requirements as to course content, coupled with restrictions on methods of assessment and an additional requirement to teach and examine skills' the proposals were attacked as being 'wholly wrong in principle,' 'imping[ing] upon academic freedom' and 'bizarre,' Zander asserting that the proposals should be 'categorically rejected by the academic profession.'[54] Such opposition proved to be successful. Given 'the strength and range of opinion, particularly amongst law teachers' the Law Society decided that 'major changes should be deferred.'[55] Whilst many in university law schools would continue to find the requirements of the Joint Statement irksome, outdated and at times even foolish, there is no doubt that the law schools have, to date, been successful in maintaining for themselves a degree of autonomy that continues to permit the possibility of the pursuit of a liberal education.

THE LAW BENCHMARK

The present Joint Statement is a contemporary example of a form of accountability that law schools have endured for many decades. By comparison the Law Benchmark is a form of accountability that has only been introduced very recently and stems directly from the new audit demands of the present era.[56] The source of audit in these two

[53] These figures being updated versions of those to be found in P Harris and M Jones, 'A Survey of Law Schools in the United Kingdom, 1996' (1997) 31 *The Law Teacher* 38.

[54] A Unger, 'Whose LLB is it Anyway?' *Law Society Gazette*, 9 September 1992; P Birks, 'New Proposals for 1995' (1993) *SPTL Reporter* (Winter) 14; Letter by M Zander, *Law Society Gazette*, 22 October 1992.

[55] 'Law Society's Review of the Academic Stage: Conclusions and Recommendations' (1993) *SPTL Reporter* (Spring) 6l.

[56] The law benchmark discussed here applies to law schools in England, Wales and Northern Ireland ('The Law Benchmark' http://www.qaa.ac.uk/crntwork/benchmark/law.pdf at 1). There is a slightly different benchmark for Scottish law degrees, reflecting their different institutional structure ('The Law Benchmark', *ibid*, at 20).

instances is very different. The Joint Statement reflects the concerns of private bodies, albeit private bodies empowered by the state. The Law Benchmark reflects the concerns of the state, albeit concerns that are mediated through a non-governmental institution. Nevertheless, despite these differences, when one comes to analyse both the problems created for the liberal law school by benchmark standards and the ways in which these problems can be managed, there are a number of similar points to be made when comparing the two forms of audit.

The origins of the Law Benchmark lie in the proposition that, in an age when there are ever-increasing numbers of universities and degree courses, employers and students need more explicit statements of the outcomes that degree syllabi are intended to produce than those that are to be found in the literature published by the universities themselves. Without this information it has been said employers would be unable to determine which graduates would make suitable employees and prospective students would be unable to select appropriate courses.[57] The validity of this contention remains a matter of controversy. Goodlad, for example, has countered this argument with the suggestion that:

> employers must take their own responsibility for selecting the types of employees they want; they really cannot expect universities to do their selecting for them.[58]

From the perspective of the liberal law school, just as particular industries and professions cannot expect the law school to focus on their particular training needs rather than the broader educational agenda of educating citizens, so employers cannot expect university law schools to make sure they get only those graduates who they find to be suitable employees; neither industry nor the professions should attempt to pass the costs of their recruitment practices onto the

[57] M Armstrong, 'Historical and Contextual Perspectives on Benchmarking' in H Smith, M Armstrong and S Brown (eds), *Benchmarking and Threshold Statements in Higher Education* (London, Kogan Page, 1999) 24. For a detailed history of the rise of benchmarking in the context of United Kingdom universities see N Jackson and H Lund, 'Introduction to Benchmarking' in N Jackson and H Lund (eds), *Benchmarking for Higher Education* (Buckingham, SRHE and Open University Press, 2000); H Lund and N Jackson, 'Creating the Conditions for Benchmarking: A Brief History of Performance Assessment in UK HE' in Jackson and Lunds (eds), *ibid* and Armstrong, *ibid*.

[58] S Goodlad, 'Benchmarks and Templates: Some Notes and Queries from a Sceptic' in Smith, Armstrong and Brown (eds), above n 57, at 77–78. See also A Bradney, 'Benchmarking: A Pedagogically Valuable Process? An Alternative View' (1999) (2) *Web Journal of Current Legal Issues*.

universities.[59] Nevertheless, whatever the rational merits of the proposition about the need for more explicit statements of outcomes, the 1997 Dearing Report recommended the creation of benchmark standards across all disciplines that would be supervised by the Quality Assurance Agency.[60] Law was one of the first three benchmark standards to be piloted.[61]

The Law Benchmark 'sets out the minimum achievement which a student should demonstrate before s/he is awarded an honours degree in law.'[62] Historically the requirements laid down by the Law Society and Bar Council have focused on the subject content of the law degree. The Law Benchmark, however, says very little about the subject content of the degree; instead the benchmark specifies skills and competencies that a law degree has to address.[63] This contrast between the two auditing approaches is not coincidental. In principle adherence to the Joint Statement is voluntary; only those law schools seeking exemptions from the Common Professional Examination for their students need concern themselves with it. Adherence to the Law Benchmark, however, is obligatory for all those law schools that want public funding for their students.[64] It is thus easy to see how the Law Benchmark, unlike the Joint Statement, could easily come to be characterised as the equivalent of a compulsory national curriculum for law degrees since it effectively applies to all law degrees at all law schools. For this reason:

> the Law Benchmark is deliberately flexible in setting out what students should learn and how they should learn it. [Because a] national curriculum . . . is not what professionals in higher education wish to see imposed.[65]

[59] The same point applies to prospective students. University law schools produced copious documentation about the degrees that they offered long before the introduction of the Law Benchmark. In addition to this there is a wealth of literature commenting on universities in general and law schools in particular. It is not at all evident that law schools owe prospective students any further duty by way of specifying what will be in their degree programmes.

[60] Dearing Report, above n 50, at 163.

[61] For a description of the process of creating the law benchmark see J Bell, 'Benchmarking in Law' in Smith, Armstrong and Brown (eds), above n 57. At the time of writing 22 benchmarks have been published (http://www.qaa.ac.uk/crntwork/benchmark/benchmarking.htm).

[62] The Law Benchmark, above n 56, at para 1.

[63] The Law Benchmark, above n 56, at paras 14–22.

[64] The Law Benchmark, above n 56, at para 1.1.

[65] J Bell, 'Benchmarking: A Pedagogically Valuable Process?' (1999) (2) *Web Journal of Current Legal Issues*. Opposition to benchmarks becoming the equivalent of a national curriculum is not just to be found in the law school but also in other areas of the academy (see, eg, S Brown, *How Can Threshold Standards Assure and Enhance Quality?* in Smith, Armstrong and Brown (eds), above n 57, at 50).

However, the recognition of the need to inject flexibility into the benchmark signals the difficulty that the benchmark creates for the liberal law school.

If the benchmark is to perform the task set for it, providing a statement of minimum achievement, it must operate as a standard telling the world outside the university what they can expect from someone with a law degree. However, determining the content of this standard is not easy. In the case of the Law Benchmark the setting of the standard involved 'research and discussion . . . supplemented by consultation.'[66] However, the difficulty in setting a standard for syllabi in university law schools is the lack of agreement about the proper content of such syllabi. Anything that can be contested about this content is contested.[67] Thus, notwithstanding the research, discussion and consultation that went on, setting a standard for law in the Law Benchmark necessarily involved *imposing* a standard on law schools and the benchmark thus became the undesired national curriculum, albeit one that takes a limited form.[68]

The degree to which the Law Benchmark that has been imposed on law schools is seen as being problematic for the liberal law school is dependent in large part on the, as yet, unresolved question of precisely how it is going to be implemented. Whilst some aspects of the content of the benchmark are entirely compatible with the work of a liberal law school (for example, the concern with developing in the student autonomy and the ability to learn independently) others are, at best, irrelevant to its aims and some, arguably, are in direct opposition to them. There is, for example, a concern in the benchmark with matters such as the ability to engage in teamworking that seems to relate solely to the perceived employability of a law graduate rather than to any other more important educational objective.[69] Yet, though some parts of the

[66] Bell, above n 65. The Dearing Report had recommended 'that standards should be developed by the academic community itself, through formal groupings for the main areas of study' (Dearing Report, above n 50, at 157).

[67] See further A Bradney, 'The Rise and Rise of Legal Education' (1997) 4 *Web Journal of Current Legal Issues*.

[68] For further analysis of this point see Bradney, above n 53. The two skills in the Law Benchmark that have proved most controversial in the law school have been numeracy and team-working. Whether these skills really are important for the employability of law graduates is open to question. Bermingham and Hodgson's 2001 survey showed that the legal profession regarded team work skills as being the tenth most important matter in a list of 16 skills and attributes that a trainee might have (V Bermingam and J Hodgson, 'Desideratat: What Lawyers Want from their Recruits' (2001) 35 *The Law Teacher* 1 at 22). Numeracy was ranked twelfth in the same listing (Bermingham and Hodgson, *ibid*).

[69] For further analysis of this point see Bradney, above n 58.

benchmark are detrimental to the aims of the liberal law school; others show how a liberal school might be able to manage this form of audit, allowing the pursuance of a liberal educational agenda. First, the benchmark is programme specific and does not necessarily have any impact on the work of any individual academic; law degrees must comply with the benchmark but individual courses within a benchmarked degree need not concern themselves with the directions in the benchmark.[70] Secondly, although the law school must show how it addresses the benchmark it does not need to assess students in each of the skills and competencies that the benchmark refers to; instead evidence that the benchmark standard is being met by students can be provided in a number of different ways including 'assessment on modules, progress files, student records and other processes.'[71] Thirdly, whilst the benchmark does lay down a standard, it does not seek to prescribe the time that the syllabus spends addressing individual matters contained in that standard. Indeed the benchmark goes further than this, explicitly saying that matters in the benchmark may be addressed through the student's involvement in extra-curricular activity.[72] Thus, those matters in the benchmark that the liberal law school finds most problematic can, if the benchmark is interpreted and implemented in a flexible manner, be pushed to the margins of the law school's activities. The benchmark itself says that '[e]xternal examiners and QAA [Quality Assurance Agency] academic reviewers' will need be assured of the 'sufficiency' of the mechanisms that a law school has put in place with respect to the benchmark.[73] Clearly the as yet unresolved question of the attitude of these people to the flexibility of the Law Benchmark will be of paramount importance to the liberal law school.

One further matter about the Law Benchmark may be of assistance to the liberal law school. A plethora of different standards such as, amongst other things, the Joint Statement and the Law Benchmark can be pictured as an ever-increasing number of chains binding the law school to its rock. However, multiple standards can also be seen as being politically advantageous for law schools. A law school with a clear sense of its own educational agenda may, either on its own or with the assistance of the various professional associations for legal

[70] The fact that individual academic freedom in teaching is not affected by the Law Benchmark is worthy of note. However, if every academic in a law school takes advantage of this freedom the law school will be unable to comply with the benchmark.

[71] The Law Benchmark, above n 56, at para 8.

[72] *Ibid*, at para 11.

[73] *Ibid*, at para 11.

academics, be able to play off one standard against another in a manner which ensures that the dictates of the various bodies setting standards are broadly met, whilst also giving the liberal law school the space that is necessary for it to pursue its own goals.

AUDITING TEACHING

In 1993 and 1994 English and Northern Ireland university law schools suffered the most intrusive form of external audit yet to affect them.[74] In the Teaching Quality Assessment (TQA) process of those years all law schools were required to provide a report on their teaching for the Higher Education Funding Council for England (HEFCE) and 34 of those law schools were visited by teams of assessors who questioned students and staff, examined documentation and attended classes.[75] Each law school was publicly graded for teaching quality on a scale that ran from 'Excellent' to 'Unsatisfactory,' individual reports on those law schools that had been visited were published and an overall report on the quality of teaching in English university law schools was also produced.[76] The criteria that determined whether or not teaching was of an appropriate standard were, insofar as they were ever made manifest, set out in a document that was produced by HEFCE with little prior consultation with academics.[77] This was external audit in the most vicious form yet to affect university law schools. Yet, paradoxically, although the TQA process involved an enormous waste of law school resources in responding to the audit demands, an examination of both this process and subsequent attempts to audit teaching in the universities shows the inherent fragility of any attempt to impose a close and detailed audit on university law schools.

In analysing the 1993/94 TQA exercise an important point to bear in mind is the gap between the intention that lay behind the assessment and the reality of that which happened in practice. TQA was not, in the minds of its originators, just about assessing the quality of teaching in university law schools; it was also about who should do that assessing. In the 1991 White Paper, *Higher Education: A New Framework*, the

[74] There were similar separate exercises with respect to Scottish and Welsh law schools.

[75] *Subject Overview Report—Law* (http://www.qaa.ac.uk/revreps/) Annex.

[76] *Ibid.*

[77] HEFCE Circular 3/93. This was later incorporated into HEFCE's *Assessors' Handbook* which was used during assessment visits.

then Conservative government had argued not only for assessment of the quality of university teaching but also for a measure of external involvement by those outside the universities in that assessment.[78] The principle of this kind of external involvement was widely opposed by those in the universities.[79] TQA was, thus, about wider arguments regarding the autonomy of the universities that were examined in Chapter 3 above.

In almost every way the TQA exercise for law was irredeemably flawed. Assessors received little training. When visits were made, different information was collected at different law schools and published reports were not consistent in the information that they contained. Law schools received different gradings without their always being any clear reason why a distinction could be drawn between the quality of their teaching. And the whole exercise expended thousands of hours of staff time.[80] Yet, whilst the whole exercise did relatively little to raise the quality of teaching in university law schools and produced only crude data about the quality of that teaching, it did serve to protect the autonomy of law schools.

Although a number of the assessors came from outside the university sector and most assessment teams contained one such assessor, reflecting the then Government's desire for an external, non-academic aspect to the assessment process, there was no evidence of the use of anything other than academic criteria in the reports that were subsequently produced; one of the most damaging of the original intentions of the exercise was thus subverted. Law schools were criticised in reports for lack of resources or because of the manner of their teaching.[81] But such criticisms reflected longstanding debates about what constituted good teaching rather than any of the new concerns about the employability

[78] Higher Education: A New Framework (Cm 1541, 1991) paras 58 and 68.

[79] M Kogan and S Hanney, *Reforming Higher Education* (London, Jessica Kingsley Publishers, 2000) 105. There had long been an acceptance of audit by a source external to the institution being audited as seen in mechanisms such as external examiner's reports. However, this kind of external audit was still kept within the framework of the academic community.

[80] For a fuller analysis of the Teaching Quality Assessment exercise with respect to law see A Bradney, 'The Quality of Teaching Quality Assessment in English Law Schools' (1996) 30 *The Law Teacher* 150 and R Brownsword, 'Teaching Quality Assessment in Law Schools: A Cause for Concern' (1994) 21 *Journal of Law and Society* 529. For an analysis of the exercise across a range of disciplines see R Barnett *et al*, *Assessment of the Quality of Higher Education* (London, Institute of Education, 1994).

[81] Thus, eg, the overall subject report for law refers to classes where 'teaching did not include any intellectual challenge' (*Subject Overview Report—Law*, above n 75, at para 18).

of graduates that had been raised by the Government. In the eyes of several academics some of the criticisms that were made constituted an attack on academic freedom in attempting to impose a particular style of teaching on law schools.[82] Nevertheless, academic teaching in university law schools was assessed by academic criteria and was, with one exception, pronounced to be 'satisfactory' or 'excellent.' This is not to argue that the teaching audit process was in any way helpful for law schools. Amongst a number of other injurious outcomes the generally good results in audits over a range of disciplines was used as evidence to support the proposition that cuts in state funding were not having a detrimental effect on the universities.[83] However, notwithstanding the obvious damaging effects of this audit process, it was managed in such a way as to reduce the amount of harm that was done and it largely left the law schools free to teach in the manner that they thought best, thus giving the liberal law school the freedom to pursue its pedagogical objectives.

The subsequent history of TQA further underscores the way in which close external auditing can damage the universities and the reason why it proves in the long term to be ineffective. The process of teaching quality audit has been the subject of constant revision and constant complaint from the time of the publication of the reports on law schools until the present day. For most of that time the revisions that have occurred have largely been to matters of detail.[84] Such changes have failed to address the core criticism that they lay behind many of the complaints about the process, the questioning of the legitimacy of detailed, intrusive, external audit of teaching. However, 2001 saw a radical re-examination of the entire nature of teaching quality audit. In February 2001 King's College, London received a critical institutional audit report from the Quality Assurance Agency (QAA), the body which by then had become responsible for administering both teaching audits of specific disciplines within universities and overall institutional audits of individual universities. Rather than giving an

[82] See, eg, W Rogers, 'Quality Assessment: A Personal View' (1994) *SPTL Reporter* (Spring) 31.

[83] See, eg, a statement issued by Graeme Davis, then Chief Executive of HEFCE (*The Times*, 3 March 1995).

[84] Thus, eg, the practice of grading institutions as 'Excellent,' 'Satisfactory' or 'Unsatisfactory' was abandoned in favour of a more complex system that graded on the basis of six components relating to learning and teaching (M Henkel, *Academic Identities and Policy Changes in Higher Education* (London, Jessica Kingsley Publishers, 2000) 80).

undertaking to remedy the matters that had been the subject of censure, King's College simply rejected the QAA report, saying that 'we felt that the auditors didn't understand what we were talking about.'[85] King's College's public attitude reflected a longstanding private disquiet about external auditing procedures that was widely felt in the academic world, particularly in the elite universities.[86] Just as some academics had criticised the TQA process for law schools, arguing that rather than checking teaching quality it had involved imposing particular forms of teaching on law schools, so universities had begun to see external institutional audit as a way of seeking to impose models of governance on institutions that were at variance with the traditions of the university. In March 2001 the London School of Economics decided that it would withdraw from all QAA procedures arguing that, amongst other things, the QAA was trying to impose its own own bureaucratic and pedagogical agenda and that they constituted an impingement on academic freedom.[87] In the same month the Select Committee on Education and Employment recommended that:

> the DfEE and the QAA should agree and publish clear guidelines for the Teaching Quality Assessment which will reduce the burden of paperwork and preparation on both staff and assessors. We recommend that the QAA should consider other forms of inspection—including possibly spot inspection—that might prove less stressful or time-consuming, and should spell out in detail how any lighter touch inspections would operate.[88]

Again in the same month, David Blunkett, the then Secretary of State for Education and Employment, announced that there was to be a 40 per cent reduction in the quantity of the external audit of teaching quality.[89] As a result of this announcement a statement, jointly prepared by the bodies with whom the QAA had a contract to carry out teaching audits, was issued stating that a process of sampling was to be introduced into the teaching quality audit procedures and that, even for those institutions being sampled, the number of reviewer days allocated to the review would be 'well below the current minimum of 19

[85] *Times Higher Education Supplement*, 23 February 2001.

[86] Thus, eg, in the previous year University College, London had only ended a boycott of all QAA procedures when it was promised 'a light touch' in the implementation of such procedures (*Times Higher Education Supplement*, 9 June 2000).

[87] *Times Higher Education Supplement*, 23 March 2001.

[88] *Sixth Report of the Select Committee on Education and Employment* (HC 124, 2001) para 100.

[89] Press notice, 21 March 2001, http://www.dfee.gov.uk/

days.'[90] The Minister's announcement thus meant not only a reduction in the quantity of audit but, because less time was to be given over to each individual audit, also a reduction in the depth of audit. Finally, in July 2001 HEFCE announced that it was 'no longer necessary to maintain comprehensive external review at subject level' and promised 'lightness of touch' in any new regime.[91] Campbell, in his critical account of the assessment of teaching in English departments, had concluded, 'I doubt that TQA will ever return to departments of English; may the earth rest lightly on its grave.'[92] His words have proved to be prophetic for English university law departments. Plans for another round of teaching quality assessment for English law schools in 2002 were abandoned.[93]

The reasons for the demise of the TQA exercise are undoubtedly complex. However, two points are probably of paramount importance. First, close audit demands a heavy use of resources. The more detail that is required the more costly the exercise becomes. The QAA presently have the contract for programme review, the current form that teaching audit takes. In 1999 programme review took up 48 per cent of the expenditure of the QAA; contract income for the QAA rose from £4,185,251 in 1998 to £4,401,685 in 1999 and £5,979,560 in 2000.[94] In addition to these direct costs arising from teaching audit there are also the indirect costs that are incurred by individual departments in preparing for the audit. All of these costs fall, in one way or another, on the public purse. In Chapter 3 above we saw that it is clear that both the main political parties in the United Kingdom would like to see the focus of the universities' work substantially altered yet, at the same time, they are also committed to minimising public spending. How much they are willing to pay for an auditing process that might help to fulfill their goal in refocusing the nature of teaching is an unanswered question. However, the events of 2001 might suggest that the costs of close auditing had grown too great.[95]

[90] 'Quality Assurance in Higher Education: Delivering Lightness of Touch', 27 March 2001, http://www.hefce.ac.uk/, para 11.

[91] HEFCE 01/45, (http://www.hefce.ac.uk/Pubs/hefce/2001/01_45.htm) paras 8 and 9.

[92] G Campbell, 'TQA: The Chair's Report to the Association', 25 May 1995, English Association 1 at 5.

[93] *QAA Progress Report* CL01/02 (http://wwww.qaa.ac.uk/crntwork/newmethod/CL01_02.htm#top).

[94] *QAA Annual Report and Financial Statement 1998–1999* (http://www.qaa.ac.uk/); *QAA Annual Report and Financial Statement 1999–2000* (http://www.qaa.ac.uk/).

[95] The same point about costs for those doing the auditing could, of course, be made with respect to any other intrusive form of audit, whether it stems from government or lawyers' professional bodies.

A second reason for the demise of the close audit of teaching may lie in the fact that, the more detailed an audit is, the more important it becomes to know precisely what the purpose of that audit is. In attempting to supply this precision, the desires of government and the bodies governing practising lawyers regarding the use of audit have been put into conflict with the reality of the nature of audit.

In his book *The Audit Society* Power argued that whilst one can identify 'the most general conceptual ingredients' of audit as being:

> *independence* from the matter being audited; technical work in the form of *evidence* gathering and the examination of documentation; the expression of a *view* based on this evidence; a clearly defined *object* of the audit process

there is, nevertheless, 'no precise agreement about what auditing really is.'[96] Concrete matters such as numbers of staff or numbers of books can be measured and thus audited but, in themselves, such concrete matters constitute neither a measure of teaching quality nor a proxy for a measure of teaching quality. As audit becomes precise it becomes less clear what is being attempted in the audit. The more information that is collected the more insistent becomes the question, what is this information for? What is being gained from all of the millions of pounds that are spent?[97] Audit signals the abandonment of trust and is a search for safety and security but it is less clear, in relation to teaching quality, how either of these two things are to be found through audit. Power went on to suggest that:

> [t]he power of auditing is the vagueness of the idea and to comprehend the audit explosion it matters less what different audit practices 'really are', the endless agony of definitions, than how the idea of audit has assumed such a central role in both public and private sector policy.[98]

Auditing gives the appearance of security but detailed audit highlights the hollowness of that security. There can be no equivalent of company accounts when it comes to auditing teaching quality and the more detailed the audit the greater degree to which this point is emphasised. That which is being sought, an assessment of teaching quality, can only be measured in the crudest of terms and an ever-more urgent demand to provide more information only serves to underscore the fact

[96] M Power, *The Audit Society* (Oxford, Oxford University Press, 1999) 5 and 4.

[97] For further analysis of this point see A Bradney, 'The Quality Assurance Agency and the Politics of Audit' (2001) 98 *Journal of Law and Society* 430.

[98] Power, above n 96, at 7.

that such information does little to assist in the assessment required.[99] Audit fails because, in this context, audit must fail and only bureaucracy remains.

THE RESEARCH ASSESSMENT EXERCISE

The Research Assessment Exercise (RAE) was the first of the modern forms of audit to affect university law schools. In 1985 the then Conservative Government suggested that the quality of research being done in universities should be evaluated on a regular basis.[100] Despite the fact that these suggestions were merely consultative in nature, being contained in a Green Paper, the University Grants Committee almost immediately introduced proposals for research in universities to be evaluated by panels set up by the Committee.[101] Under these proposals individual cost centres (which in most cases in law meant simply individual law schools) within universities had to supply detailed information about research done in the centre in the previous five years. The results of the first exercise were published in 1986. With slight changes in the detail of the format the assessment has subsequently been repeated at regular intervals with the results from the fourth exercise being published in 2001.[102]

For some commentators the introduction of the RAE is a defining event in the history of relations between the state and the universities marking the assertion of state sovereignty over the universities. 'Here then was a dramatic moment in the decline of donnish dominion' comments Halsey.[103] The exercise certainly contained elements that many academics in law schools saw as being contrary to the nature of academic life. During the first exercise John Eekelaar, then chair of the law department at Oxford University, initially declined to indicate which of his department's publications were 'of major significance in the field,' as required under the exercise, because he contended that there were no agreed criteria which would make such an evaluation pos-

[99] This point of course applies to all attempts to audit teaching quality and can also be applied to attempts to audit research quality.

[100] *The Development of Higher Education into the 1990s* (Cmnd 9524, 1985).

[101] A Halsey, *Decline of Donnish Dominion* (Oxford, Clarendon Press, 1992) 189. There is a detailed account of the genesis of the RAE in Kogan and Hanney, above n 79, 96–98.

[102] http://www.rae.ac.uk/

[103] Halsey, above n 101.

sible.[104] Both the first and all subsequent exercises have attracted substantial criticism relating to what has been assessed, who has done the assessing and the measures that have been used in the assessment.[105] Nevertheless, it is possible to argue that the RAE, or rather the RAE as managed by legal academics, is one form of audit that has largely made life easier for the liberal law school rather than harder.

As in the case of teaching audit, the original government paper that resulted in the introduction of research assessment called not just for 'performance indicators' in relation to research but for performance indicators of a particular kind. The Government argued that there was a need to ensure that funds set aside for research in universities were 'effectively deployed.'[106] Crucial here is what was meant by the phrase 'effectively deployed.' The general argument of the paper, which was concerned with higher education in general and not just university research in particular, is set out in its opening paragraphs:

> The Government believes that it is vital for our higher education to contribute more effectively to the improvement of the performance of the economy.[107]

Elsewhere, early in the paper, it was suggested that universities should be:

> concerned with attitudes to the world outside higher education, and in particular to industry and commerce, and to be aware of 'anti-business' snobbery

and that they should 'go out to develop their links with industry and commerce.'[108] In the main the paper was an attempt to redirect the focus of work in universities so that it concentrated more directly on the immediate needs of the economy both in terms of the production of future workers and, in the research context, so that research related to

[104] 'Truth in Assessment' (1993) *SPTL Reporter* (Spring) 4.

[105] See, eg, T Smith, 'The UGC's Research Ranking Exercise' (1987) 41 *Higher Education Quarterly* 303; R Gillet, 'Research Performance Indicators Based on Peer Review: A Critical Analysis' (1989) 43 *Higher Education Quarterly* 20 and M McVicar, 'The 1992/93 Research Assessment Exercise: the View from a Former Polytechnic' (1994) 48 *Higher Education Quarterly* 24. For complaints from within law schools see, eg, P Leighton, 'Government and Education News' (1997) 31 *The Law Teacher* 127 at 128–29 and P Leighton, 'Government and Education News' (2000) 34 *The Law Teacher* 77 at 81.

[106] *The Development of Higher Education into the 1990s* (Cmnd 9524, 1985) para 9.11.

[107] *Ibid*, at para 1.2.

[108] *Ibid*, at para 1.6.

British economic development. Universities were perceived to be too self-absorbed and too little concerned with the interests of the communities in which they were located. In the context of university law schools this argument could easily be translated into a call for a closer connection between the law schools and the legal professions, something that had been and was to continue to be a feature of a variety of official and unofficial reports on the state of university legal education.[109]

The history of research assessment exercises in law to date does not suggest that government aspirations regarding the universities possible closer connection with the outside world have been fulfilled in the law schools. Those who sit on assessment panels are wholly drawn from the academic legal profession.[110] Whilst the final selection of individuals to sit on the panel partly lies in the hands of the Higher Education Funding Council, a body external to the universities, the list of names from whom the selection can be made consists of a combination of past assessors and people nominated by a variety of professional bodies for those working in university law schools.[111] The criteria by which research is to be assessed is first suggested by the Higher Education Funding Council. However, the panel of assessors first examine and amend the criteria, then send it out in draft form for consideration by the academic community and subsequently reconsider it in the light of comments received.[112] The original impetus for the assessment of research may have come from outside the university community but, at least in the case of law, it is now that community who is doing the assessing according to criteria they are largely comfortable with.

[109] See, eg, *Report of the Committee on Legal Education* (The Ormrod Report) (Cmnd 4595, 1971) and *A Time for Change: Report of the Committee on the Future of Legal Education* (The Marre Committee) (London, General Council of the Bar, 1988).

[110] Technically two of the 2001 assessors, Professors H Beale and Professor Thompson, did not work in a university law school at the time of the assessment since they worked as Law Commissioners with, respectively, the English and Scottish Law Commissions. However, in both cases they are seconded to that post from universities and were, both at the date of their nomination and at the date of their appointment, holders of full-time chairs in university law schools.

[111] Both the Law Society and the Law Society of Scotland are bodies who are able to nominate people for membership of the law RAE panel (http://www.niss.ac.uk/education/hefce/rae2001/2_98a.html).

[112] For the draft criteria for law for the 2001 exercise see RAE Circular 4/99 (http://www.rae.ac.uk/Pubs/4_99/byUoA.htm). For the final criteria see RAE Circular 5/99 (http://www.rae.ac.uk/Pubs/5_99/byUoA.htm). A number of matters in the draft were changed including the reference to research into legal education (cf RAE Circular 4/99 para 2.28.23 and RAE Circular 5/99 para 3.28.27).

Moreover the criteria are somewhat removed from the philosophical centre of the Government's 1985 paper. Hicks has observed 'the HEFCE panel [considering research ratings in law] has given the greatest kudos to the journals written by academics for academics.'[113] Work published in practitioner journals is perceived to rank less highly than writing done in academic journals.[114] Writing which is simply the explication of new legal rules or procedures for practising lawyers may well perform the task set out by the Government's 1985 paper but it will score low marks in the Research Assessment Exercise.[115] There is little if anything in the implementation of the Research Assessment Exercise to suggest that the Government's call for a shift in the focus of research has been heeded by those in university law schools. Instead, university law schools have formalised and bureaucratised the academic process of assessing research quality that has long existed in the day-to-day judgements made in matters such as university appointment panels, the refereeing of articles and the establishment and loss of reputation.[116]

For the liberal law school the significance of the RAE lies in the importance that it has given to research. In 2001 60 law schools, including 15 in institutions that historically had not seen themselves as having a research function, entered the exercise.[117] With funding distributions to universities being in part dependant on the RAE gradings received by their departments, universities are pushed by financial imperatives to the notion that academics should be research active or at least to the idea that those academics who are research active are

[113] A Hicks, 'Legal Practice is an Academic Matter' (1995) *SPTL Reporter* (Spring) 6. The criteria for the 2001 RAE said that 'books written for the legal or other professions will be regarded as research output provided that they exhibit significant scholarly material' (*RAE 2001: Panels' Criteria and Working Methods* http://www.rae.ac.uk/ para 3.28.11).

[114] See D Vick, A Murray, G Little and K Campbell, 'The Perceptions of Academic Lawyers Concerning the Effects of the United Kingdom Research Assessment Exercise' (1998) *Journal of Law and Society* 536. Most academics plainly think it unlikely that work could be accessible to the majority of practising lawyers and scholarly (or that it could be sufficiently scholarly so as to be regarded as being of 'international excellence') at the same time.

[115] Work is of 'national excellence' if it 'contributes to knowledge and understanding' (*RAE 2001: Panels' Criteria and Working Methods*, above n 113, at para 3.28.7). This is presumably the best that most practitioner work can expect to be judged as.

[116] This is not just true for law as a discipline. In writing about the RAE Henkel concludes '[i]t had a structure within which academic values and academic control were sustained' (Henkel op cit p 115).

[117] 'RAE 2001: Results' (http://www.rae.ac.uk/).

better academics for the university than those academics who are not.[118] For the liberal law school research and teaching are inseparable. The RAE has added to financial incentives to the intellectual arguments for the importance of research that were developed in Chapter 5 above. Moreover the kind of research that seems to have been favoured by law panels fits easily into the liberal law school's ethos with its emphasis on the production of knowledge. This is not to say that the RAE has proved to be a form of audit that is unproblematic for the liberal law school. Henkel, for example, notes the view that the RAE has tended to make people more competitive and be less willing to do administration.[119] Given the reliance on collegial governance in the liberal law school, if true, this outcome of the RAE is deeply troubling for law schools.[120] Nevertheless, taken overall, thus far the RAE, as managed by the legal academic community, can be said to have been advantageous for the liberal law school.

THE DANGER OF AUDIT

When, because of the content of his teaching, Socrates was charged with crimes against Athens including heresy and corrupting the minds of the young and when the citizens of Athens found him guilty and sentenced him to death, Socrates, despite the entreaties of friends, refused to flee Athens, arguing a duty to obey the laws of the state, took hemlock and died.[121] Modern-day versions of accountability, as for example embodied in the pronouncements of the Quality Assurance Agency, seem weak by comparison to Athenian accountability. Nevertheless the fate of Socrates illustrates the dangers that audit by those outside the university brings for those working in the liberal law school. Since the mission of the liberal law school includes the mundane but also goes beyond it, audit according to quotidian criteria is likely to conflict with the goals that the law school seeks to achieve. For academics in law schools who, as intellectuals, are not 'there to make

[118] On the effects of RAE gradings on university finances see Henkel, above n 84, at 115–16.

[119] Henkel, *ibid*, at 131.

[120] Another suggestion that the RAE results in teaching being devalued is, even if true, less of a problem for the liberal law school given the fact that law schools have historically tended to over-emphasise teaching at the expense of research.

[121] For an account of the trial and Socrates' subsequent death see Plato, *The Last Days of Socrates* (Harmondsworth, Penguin Books, 1959).

his/her audience feel good . . . [but] instead to be embarrassing, contrary, even unpleasant,' accountability and audit are problematic.[122] Yet the lessons of the last two decades is that law schools can, if they make sufficient efforts, manage audit in such a way as to leave themselves the space they need to pursue their own ends.

[122] E Said, *Representations of the Intellectual* (London, Vintage, 1994) 9–10. On this see further L Morley, 'A Comedy of Manners: Quality and Power in Higher Education' in P Trowler (ed), *Higher Education Policy and Institutional Change* (Buckingham, SRHE and Open University Press, 2002).

8

This I Do for Love: Avocation and Vocation in the University Law School

THE INDUSTRIALISATION OF ACADEMIC LIFE

THUS FAR THIS book has been concerned with what can be done in a liberal law school and why law schools should be run according to the principles of liberal education. This final chapter is about what it means to work as an academic in such a law school and how the work that one does there connects with the rest of one's life. I have already touched on some parts of this matter elsewhere in this book, particularly in the discussion of collegiality in the academy in Chapter 6 above. Here, however, I want to change the focus of concern, concentrating not on the law school as whole but, instead, on the individual academics who work in the law school.

In Robert Frost's poem 'Two Tramps in Mud Time,' a meditation on the nature of work, two tramps, 'not long since in the lumber camps,' come across the poem's narrator whilst he is chopping wood:

> Nothing on either side was said.
> They knew they had but to stay their stay
> And all their logic would fill my head:
> As that I had no right to play
> With what was another man's work for gain.
> My right might be love but theirs was need.
> And where the two exist in twain
> Theirs was the better right—agreed.

Yet, having said this, Frost immediately goes on to finish the poem thus:

> But yield who will to their separation,
> My object in living is to unite
> My avocation and my vocation
> As my two eyes make one in sight.

Only where love and need are one,
And the work is play for mortal stakes,
Is the deed ever really done
For Heaven and the future's sakes.

Frost's poem creates a hierarchy of values.[1] Tramps need work to survive and, because of this, their need trumps the right of those who simply love doing the work for its own sake but do not need the work to live. Nonetheless, a better way of life than working to survive is a life where one loves doing what one needs to do to live and where the work is chosen because of that love and not because of the need to survive.[2] At the same time the poem can be read as a protest against the idea that work is to be valued only when it is valorised.[3] At a time when even some in the academy itself are writing:

[1] Both the coherence and the substance of Frost's social philosophy is something that has been the subject of much debate. Here, however, I am concerned only with this individual poem and not with Frost's work taken as a whole. Thus whether or not, as eg Winters argues, Frost's views 'effectually cut Frost off from any really profound understanding of human experience, whether political, moral, metaphysical or religious' is not to the point (Y Winters, 'Robert Frost: or, the Spiritual Drifter as Poet' in J Cox (ed), *Robert Frost: A Collection of Critical Essays* (Eaglewood Cliffs, New Jersey, Prentice-Hall Inc, 1962) 75. All that is relevant for the purposes of this chapter is the power of this particular poem. 'Two Tramps in Mud Time' has itself been the subject of censure. (See, eg, M Cowley, 'The Case Against Mr Frost' in Cox, *ibid*, 41–43 and G Nitchie, 'Human Values in the Poetry of Robert Frost' (North Carolina, Duke University Press, Durham, (1960) 87–89 and 153–55.) The central criticism is, as Cowley puts it, that the poem 'sets before us an ideal, not of charity or brotherhood, but of separateness' (Cowley, *ibid*, at 42). Cowley argues that the poem's narrator should have offered the destitute tramps assistance (Cowley, *ibid*). Such criticisms, notwithstanding the number of times they have been repeated, are invalid because they ignore what the poem is about; it is the narrator, not the tramps nor his relationship with the tramps, who is the focus of the poem. Whether or not the narrator helps the tramps is for another poem; this one is concerned with his thoughts about the core of his being (J Parini, *Robert Frost: A Life* (London, William Hienemann, 1998) 289–90).

[2] 'Better' in the sense that it is a preferable way of life and 'better' in the sense that it springs from (at least in Frost's eyes) a more refined sensibility. The tramps' sensibility is limited. 'Except as a fellow handled an axe,/They had a no way of knowing a fool.' The narrator, by way of contrast, can not only meditate on the merits of their claim to work but also spend three stanzas analysing the precise effects in nature of a season at the point of change. The contrast between two tramps from the lumber camps and the narrator who sees a bluebird, '[h]is song so pitched as not to excite/A single flower as yet to bloom' is a stark one. 'In Frost's mind, perhaps, one of the most absolute dividing walls is the one which separates the men who do their work for play and the men who do their work for love' (J Doyle Jr, *The Poetry of Robert Frost* (Johannesberg, Witwatersand University Press, 1962) 66).

[3] Frost was a poet, a farmer and sometimes an academic who himself struggled to maintain a synergy between all the different aspects of his life (Parini, above n 1, at 289). There are obvious similarities between Frost's position and Cicero's suggestion, much

> [a]cademics may not like it, but teaching has had to be transformed from a pre-Fordist artisan craft process into a Fordist organised mass production operation[4]

both Frost's life and his poem reminds us that there are models of human existence other than the one that divides it into life and work; that it is possible to posit a way of being where each of the different elements are so intertwined as to mean the difference between them is lost; that one does not have to live on a production line.

The model of working life that has now become so prevalent in modern society as to seem almost natural and pre-ordained is in fact the result of a particular moment in history when societies began to industrialise their production processes and separate out sites of consumption and production. As Gorz, following Marx, argues, the task of industrial capitalism was to take the home weaver, for whom weaving was:

> not just a living . . . [but] was a *way of life* governed by traditions which, while they might have been irrational from an economic point of view, were respected by capitalist merchants

and transform them into a factory worker who lived a life ruled by economic reason.[5] The aim was that:

> workers should enter the process of production stripped of their personality and individuality, their personal goals and desires, as simple *labour power*, which was interchangeable and comparable to that of any other workers and which served goals which were not their own and, moreover, meant nothing to them.[6]

Work and life were to be divided; one would work in order to live; one would live one's life outside one's work. In practice, in any area of work, the aim of the industrial revolution is one that has only ever been partially achieved. Even on a genuine production line, a shopfloor culture will enable 'the shopfloor [to wrest] . . . their own space from the

cited by writers on liberal education, that once immediate physical needs are met we naturally turn towards the consideration of knowledge (Cicero, *The Offices* (London, Dent, 1909) 6–7).

[4] J Dearlove, 'The Academic Labour Process: From Collegiality and Professionalism to Managerialism and Proletarianisation?' (1997) 30 *Higher Education Review* 50 at 68.

[5] A Gorz, *Critique of Economic Reason* (London, Verso, 1989) 16 (emphasis in original).

[6] Gorz, *ibid*, at 20 (emphasis in original).

company.'[7] Nonetheless, the transformation that industrialisation brings to people's lives is dramatic:

> The operative is condemned to let his physical and mental powers decay in this utter monotony, it is his mission to be bored every day and all day.[8]

The universities, along with the professional classes, largely escaped this industrial revolution.[9] Their way of life continued to resemble much more that of the home weaver than that of the factory worker on a production line. This is not to say that the conditions of nineteenth and twentieth century universities represent some halcyon idyll. Reflecting their ecclesiastical and monastic ancestry, some universities, rather than encouraging the intertwining of different aspects life, as Frost would want, have officially proscribed academics from having any life outside the university.[10] Yet the collegial tradition constituted a way of organising the university that pre-dated the ethically de-based, hierarchical, organisational forms of the industrial revolution and, for academics, the relationship between what they did as labour and what they valued as people represented at least a partial linking of avocation and vocation.

Whether this will continue to be so in the future is a moot point. What has been variously characterised as the proletarianisation of academic life, the rise of academic capitalism and the growth of entrepreneurialism, put in doubt the way of life traditional for academics and threatens the universities with a belated industrial revolution.[11] In this concluding chapter I will argue that these trends can and should be resisted; that, if the liberal law school is to succeed, academics ought to

[7] S Westwood, *All Day, Every Day: Factory and Family in the Making of Women's Lives* (London, Pluto Press, 1984) 97.

[8] F Engels, *The Condition of the Working Class in England* (London, Panther Books, 1969) 204.

[9] S Slaughter and L Leslie, *Academic Capitalism* (Baltimore, John Hopkins University Press, 1997) 4–5.

[10] Fellows, who could only be men, in Oxford colleges were not allowed to marry until 1869 when this restriction gradually began to be lifted. Some fellowships were still limited to unmarried men in the 1930s (J Dunbabin, 'Finance and Property' in M Brock and M Curthoys (eds), *The History of the University of Oxford*, vol VI, *Nineteenth Century Oxford, Part 1* (Oxford, Clarendon Press, 1997) 413. Even as late as the 1930s '[c]ollege life adjusted only slowly to fellow's marriage . . . Married fellows were treated as honorary bachelors, and felt a strong obligation to dine regularly' (B Harrison, 'College Life, 1918–1939' in B Harrison (ed), *The History of the University of Oxford*, vol VIII, *The Twentieth Century* (Oxford, Clarendon Press, 1994) 86.

[11] See, eg, T Wilson, 'The Proletarianisation of Academic Labour' (1991) *Industrial Relations Journal* 250; Slaughter and Leslie, above n 9, passim and B Clark, *Creating Entrepreneurial Universities* (Oxford, IAU Press, 1998).

continue to live a life without the clear demarcation lines that pervade other areas of working life. Avocation and vocation must be one for academics and academic work must be play for mortal stakes.[12]

THE UNITY OF AVOCATION AND VOCATION

Both pragmatism and principle argue for the unity of avocation and vocation for those working in the law school.[13] The pragmatic arguments are concerned with how law schools are going to continue to attract suitably qualified staff. British university law schools cannot now, and will not in the future, offer financial rewards commensurate with the abilities, responsibilities and effort that they (will) require of their academic staff. Unless they can offer a way of life that is more attractive than that found elsewhere, why should staff not take their talents outside the university and be paid more for doing less? Large law firms can induce hard work from their employees by offering large rewards and the promise of even larger rewards as the hierarchy of the firm is scaled. Law schools can offer only small salaries and, as the differential between professorial and other scales is reduced, only small increases in salary as incentives to do the work that is necessary to succeed.[14] Conditions of service are the only obvious possible market advantage that law schools have over other potential employers when seeking to attract suitable staff. The argument from principle can be put as plainly and more shortly. The unity of avocation and vocation

[12] For a contrary argument that advocates the notion of multiple vocations see G Johnstone, 'Liberal Ideals and Vocational Aims in University Legal Education' [1999] 3 *Web Journal of Current Legal Issues*.

[13] In arguing for the necessity of this unity I am not arguing that academic life cannot continue without this unity. Instead I am arguing that academic life cannot be successful or cannot be as successful if this unity is not found.

[14] Salaries for academics in law schools are, of course, much higher than those enjoyed by most workers in the United Kingdom. In 2000, 50 per cent of all workers earned less than £20,212 whilst 10 per cent earned more than £38,071 (*New Earnings Survey 2000* (London, National Statistics Office, 2000) Table A 1.1). In the same year the starting salary for the Lecturer A grade in old universities was £18,731, for Lecturer B £24,227 and for Senior Lecturer £32,510 with £39,718 being the highest point on the Senior Lecturer scale. But those working in law schools are neither averagely talented nor averagely qualified. The opportunity costs inherent in taking a job in a university law school are unarguable. Participants in the Law Society's cohort survey of law students reported an average starting salary of £21,500 with an average salary after 18 months to three years of service of £30,000 rising to £46,000 for those with City firms (E Duff, M Shiner, A Boon with A Whyte, *Entry into the Legal Professions: The Law Student Chort Study: Year 6* (London, The Law Society, 2000) 43).

involves one focusing on that which one loves and the academic life as lived in a liberal law school means that one constantly engages in that quintessentially human activity, the pursuit of curiosity; if this is, as Steiner suggests, 'the supreme piety of the soul' it thus represents a better way of life than one that either allows one to pursue that which one loves for only part of the time or a way of life that forces one to focus on matters that are of purely instrumental or pragmatic concern.[15]

WORK-LIFE BALANCE

To propose the unity of avocation and vocation for legal academics seems to run counter to two prevailing truths about modern universities and modern society. The first is that modern universities are exploitative in their nature, trading on their academic employees' love of their job; the second is that, in the interests of both the health of workers and the efficient running of businesses, there is a need to ensure that employees enjoy a proper balance between, and therefore separation of, work and life.

Writing about why American post-graduate students might no longer find an academic career attractive, Roberts has speculated that:

> the student finds unattractive the implications of the prioritizing that a successful career in academia often requires. Making certain things one's priorities entails deferring other things, including a varied social life, hobbies, desires to live in a particular place or region, pregnancy or adoption, and sometimes more generally family life.[16]

Noting that academics in the United Kingdom work 15 hours longer a week than other non-manual workers, Wills has, on the basis of survey evidence, argued that long hours of work have begun to cause 'serious social, familial and health difficulties' for academics.[17] More directly, in relation to the law school, Collier has argued that:

[15] G Steiner, *Heidegger* (London, Harvester Press, 1978) 149. See also Hirst: 'the achievement of knowledge is not only the attainment of the good of the mind itself, but also the chief means whereby the good life as a whole is to be found' (P Hirst, 'Liberal Education and the Nature of Knowledge' in P Hirst, *Knowledge and the Curriculum* (London, Routledge and Kegan Paul, 1974) at 30). There are other ways of living a similar kind of life. Frost's pursuit of poetry is an obvious example.

[16] S Roberts, 'Realizing Critical Geographies of the University' (2000) 32 *Antipode* 230 at 239.

[17] J Wills, 'Laboring for Love? A Comment on Academics and their Hours of Work' (1996) 28 *Antipode* 292 at 295 and 296.

> both legal practice and legal academy associate public, visible displays of availability to work long hours with individual's personal commitment to the institution and development of an appropriate 'professional' attitude.[18]

In this context, and given the range of systems that now seek to ensure that academics work in ways that others outside the academy judge to be suitable, suggesting the desirability of the combination of avocation and vocation might seem to be ignoring the fact that the university has turned into a panopticon and that, to use Foucault's terminology, imprisoned academics are being pushed into:

> interiorising [the jailor's gaze] to the point that he [the prisoner] is his own overseer, each individual thus exercising this surveillance over, and against, himself.[19]

From this perspective the concept of the unity of avocation and vocation is no more than a romantic piece of false consciousness, a whimsical affectation that fails to address the less than pleasant realities of everyday academic life:

> Corporate employees are increasingly expected to have their minds and hearts 'on duty' even outside regular working hours. The use of cellular telephones, personal lap computers, modems, fax machines, and airline telephones are extending the available hours of work into leisure and private time, making it possible for the 'knowledge worker' to conduct business not only on the golf course, but from her home or car.[20]

To propose the unity of avocation and vocation might be argued to suggest achieving the same result without the legal academic being aware of the way in which the academy has captured their whole life.

Arguments such as those above take on even greater force in the light of the 'Work-Life Balance Campaign' first launched by the Labour Government in 2000 and research work done in support of that campaign:

> The campaign aims to raise employers' awareness of the business benefits of introducing policies and practices which help employees obtain a better balance between work and the rest of their lives. Central to the campaign is a

[18] R Collier, ' "Nutty Professors," "Men in Suits" and "New Entrepreneurs": Corporality, Subjectivity and Change in the Law School and Legal Practice' (1998) 7 *Social and Legal Studies* 27 at 32.

[19] M Foucault, *Power/Knowledge* (London, Harvester Wheatsheaf, 1980) 155.

[20] C Casey, *Work, Self and Society After Industrialism* (London, Routledge, 1995) 86.

belief—supported by research evidence—that everyone benefits from good practice in work-life balance.[21]

Whilst traditionally arguments in this area have tended to focus on the needs of those caring for children

> [r]ecent evidence suggest that the debate is moving on from 'family friendly' to a wider set of concerns that relate to all aspects of the balance between work and life. Though few employees are likely to achieve a perfect work-life balance, it is apparent that some groups face considerable difficulties achieving a sustainable or desirable one. Lone parents and people with substantial caring responsibilities come immediately to mind, but *there are also groups of employees who whilst having a more privileged position in the labour market have nonetheless achieved a significant degree of imbalance in their lives.* The long hours culture that has according to some evidence developed in many organizations can exact a heavy psychological and physical toll on some people.[22]

Such research seems to be particularly pertinent to universities and their law schools. The Base-Line Study on work-life balance defined 'long hours' as meaning working more than 49 hours per week and 'very long hours' as meaning working more than 60 hours per week.[23] Universities, and presumably their law schools, now aspire to be places where 'people really do want to work a 55-hour week.'[24] Thus many legal academics are certainly part of the 28 per cent of employees who usually work long hours and some at least are part of the 10 per cent who habitually work very long hours.[25] Upon the face of it advocating the combination of avocation and vocation serves only to legitimize a

[21] T Hogarth, C Hasluck and G Pierre with M Winterbotham and D Vivian, *Work-Life Balance 2000: Baseline Study of Work-Life Balance Practices in Great Britain* (Institute for Employment Research and IFF Research, University of Warwick, 2000) 1.

[22] (emphasis added) T Hogarth, C Halsuck and G Pierre with M Winterbotham and D Vivian, *Work-Life Balance 2000: Results from the Baseline Study: Research Report 249* (London, DFEE, 2001) 3.

[23] Hogarth, Halsuck and Pierre with Winterbotham and Vivian, above n 22, at 20.

[24] M Kogan and S Hanney, 'Reforming Higher Education' (London, Jessica Kingsley Publishers, 2000) 194. Actual hours worked will of course vary according to a range of factors such as age, type of university and gender. Women professors have, eg, been reported as working an average of 64.5 hours per week whilst their male counterparts worked an average of 58.6 hours per week (T Becher and P Trowler, *Academic Tribes and Territories* (Buckingham, SRHE and Open University Press, 2001) 150).

[25] Hogarth, Halsuck and Pierre with Winterbotham and Vivian, above n 22, at 48 and 20. It is, however, important to note that whilst this is generally true of those working in British university law schools Cownie's study indicates that not all law schools have a long hours culture (F Cownie, *Legal Academics: Culture and Identities* (Oxford, Hart Publishing, forthcoming).

long hours or very long hours culture in law schools; something that, in other areas of employment, the Government is striving to reverse because of the health risks to employees and consequent inherent inefficiency for industry.

There is much force in both these arguments. Universities and their law schools are sometimes clearly exploitative of their academic employees and some people's health does suffer as a result of this. Equally, law schools are not run more efficiently because some people seem to be physically linked to them by an unbreakable umbilical cord; indeed, the reverse may be the case. Nevertheless, these two modern 'truths,' when applied to university law schools, are in fact a simplistic and superficial analysis of the situation.

The flaws in discussion to date about work-life balance, particularly when it is applied to the circumstances of the liberal law school, become apparent once it central arguments are examined. Debate about work-life balance has mainly been concerned with the way in which work can be managed so that the worker can also have a life. In the more recent literature, disquiet has been founded not just on the traditional industrial society fear that, for the individual, there might be too much work and not enough life but also on a post-industrial society anxiety that work might insinuate itself into life. In an industrial society, where typically a complex production process is broken down into a myriad of simple tasks with each individual employee performing only one of them, an employer requires the labour of the worker. In a post-industrial society, because the employer requires employees to be multi-skilled and adaptable, thus putting at a premium their intellectual capabilities and psychological disposition, employees':

> 'values, attitudes and general orientation must mesh with organizational need . . . [with] the result that specific traits and attitudes that are useful to work are stimulated and reinforced. Those that are unnecessary or impede work are suppressed, thwarted and gradually weakened.[26]

In a post-industrial society the employer requires the employee's psyche as well as their body:

> [P]eople working in highly competitive and finely-structured corporations facing onerous daily demands to adapt to corporate culture can literally be driven crazy.[27]

[26] Casey, above n 20, at 36 and 84.
[27] Casey, above n 20, at 83.

Achieving a proper work-life balance, on this argument, thus involves not only preserving the time that the worker has for life but also preserving their mental well-being. In both instances the usual solution is perceived to be protecting the purity of life as from being infected by the taint of work.

Separating life from work in this manner is, however, in conflict with much that we know about workers. The Base-Line Study on work-life balance found that:

> [m]anagers and professionals, typically seek fulfillment through work, often working long hours but seek to fit family somewhere into their lives.[28]

Work for its own sake is an important part of their life. Moreover in the same study, whilst 62 per cent of employees said that they would not wish to work from home, very few of them said that this was because they wanted a clear separation between work and home.[29] 'For many work is a positive source of identification.'[30] Moreover:

> [f]or those whose work is a profession, a vocation, a calling or just really interesting, work and life merge into one. Work is life. Life is work. For those workers, work not only informs their identity—their values inform which job they do.[31]

Bourdain's description of life as a chef is hyperbole but nevertheless captures something of the essence of this view. 'Forget the loved ones. Forget the outside world. There *is* no life other than this life'.[32]

The straightforward prioritising of life over work is certainly in conflict with the way in which many academics, including academics in law schools, see their work. Those academics who 'live their physics,' who report 'total absorption' in their research or who 'can't help carting . . . work round' are unlikely to be impressed by the work-life dichotomy that is foundational to much discussion about this area.[33]

[28] Hogarth, Halsuck and Pierre with Winterbotham and Vivian, above n 22, at 265.

[29] *Ibid*, at 136.

[30] J Doyle, *New Community or New Slavery: the Emotional Division of Labour* (London, The Industrial Society, 2000) 7.

[31] Doyle, *ibid*, at 9.

[32] A Bourdain, *Kitchen Confidential* (London, Bloomsbury, 2000) 117 (emphasis in original).

[33] Becher and Trowler, above n 24, at 147–48. The empirical point that legal academics fail to separate out life and work can be explored in a number of different ways. For example Collier notes that 'for many (frequently younger) legal academics there may be little difference between "work" clothes and "home clothes" ' (Collier, above n 18, at 43). This point is explored in more detail in Cownie, above n 25.

Nor does the separation of work and life sit easily with the creative nature of academic life:

> Ideas occur to us when they please, not when it pleases us. The best ideas do indeed occur to one's mind in the way in which Ihering describes it: when smoking a cigar on the sofa; or as Helmoltz states himself with scientific exactitude: when taking a walk on a slowly ascending street; or in a similar way. In any case, ideas come when we do not expect them, and not when we are brooding and searching at our desks.[34]

Even more importantly, the notion of a clear-cut work-life division is in direct variance with those ideas that are central to the notion of a liberal education. What a liberal education requires is a personal response by the people engaged in it, whether they be academics or students. It is not merely a technical matter. The previous chapters of this book have stressed the need for individual involvement in teaching and research in the liberal law school. In the liberal law school academics focus their research on what they believe to be important, seeking what they believe to be the truth. In the end, whilst they might hope that others will recognise the value of their work, their work is validated by that personal belief alone. In their teaching they teach what they genuinely believe to be the truth. A liberal education is the education of the student as a person. The academic always continues to be a student; thus, they are themselves constantly being educated as a person. In this sense their work is deeply personal. To separate out work from life therefore becomes impossible because if work is personal how can it not also be life? And how can that which happens in work not constantly interact with life?

To advocate the unity of avocation and vocation is to argue that neither the family nor a life outside work necessarily is or need be the dominant source of individual self-affirmation and that neither the family nor life outside work should be entirely separable from work.[35] The psychological processes that, in part, determine why an individual becomes an academic and the intellectual processes that are involved in the way in which they research, teach and engage in administration also, in part, shape their emotional life, influencing who and how they

[34] M Weber, 'Science as a Vocation' in H Gerth and C Wright Mills (eds), *From Max Weber: Essays in Sociology* (London, Routledge, 1947) 136.

[35] 'The term "avocational" has never been precisely defined . . . "Avocational" carries with it two important connotations—as a quasi-religious calling and a task one does for love, rather than for the necessity of earning a living' (I Aron, 'Avocational Teaching; The Genesis and Diffusion of an Idea' (1997) 92 *Religious Education* 430 at 434).

love and how in turn they can be loved. The partner or child who is loved, is loved in the particular way that they are loved because of the intellectual capacities and psychological drives that the person brings to being an academic and they would be loved in a subtly or dramatically different way if the person did not have those capacities and drives.[36] The liberal law school cannot be an industrial factory and therefore its workers cannot leave at home their personalities and must perforce bring home the personalities that come from their work. Equally the liberal law school, if it is to remain true to its principles, must resist the corporatising tendencies of the post-industrial society work-place and allow each worker their own individuality.

Yet, notwithstanding the importance of the above, there has been one change between the Oxford or Cambridge of the nineteenth century and British university law schools in the twenty-first century. Collegiate life in the nineteenth century meant a life largely lived in college. In the modern day academics go home and some go home to partners, children or dependent relatives. Today Hamerton's 1929 description of academic life:

> [t]he professor may love his wife, and fully appreciate her qualities as a housekeeper, but he passes a more interesting evening with some male friend whose reading is equal to his own

makes one feel slightly sick.[37] What, however, does the failure to separate out life and work that is consequent on combining avocation and vocation mean 'in relation to how the temporal and spatial parameters of academic work relate to relationships of dependency and caring in individuals' "private" lives'?[38] Are Collier's forebodings accurate?

> Let us be clear, and to state what is, for many, now a 'common sense' fact about the nature of contemporary academic life. To be free to travel to national and international conferences, to 'work all hours' unconstrained by the demands (and pleasures) of family and friends, entails the presence of material and psychological networks of support which are not dissimilar from those associated with the well-documented 'commitment question' in

[36] This is not to argue that all academics will experience relationships in the same way or that their experience will necessarily be different from that of non-academics. Rather, it is to argue that the experience of your work as an academic and your family are necessarily infused into each other.

[37] Quoted in R Collier, 'Masculinism, Law and Law Teaching' (1991) 19 *International Journal of the Sociology of Law* 427 at 443.

[38] R Collier, 'The Changing University and the (Legal) Academic Career: Rethinking the Relationship between Woman, Men and the "Private Life" of the Law School' (2002) 22 *Legal Studies* 1 at 21.

> the careers of many practising lawyers. The flexibility of academic work in terms of contracted hours has traditionally been seen to have permitted some leeway around the negotiation of work-life conflict . . . Yet the very *indeterminacy* of academic labour in terms of time and commitment is proving double-edged within the new emotional economy which is being fostered by the corporatised university.[39]

Does uniting avocation and vocation in fact mean that partners, family and friends will simply be regularly ignored whilst the academic pursues their 'higher' calling? Will law schools be able to assume that they are:

> entitled to 'ideal (academic) workers' free from family responsibilities, and that both women and men should be expected to perform in a way regardless of any 'private life.'[40]

For the academic working in the liberal law school, the answer to these questions lies in Collier's use of the term 'corporatised university.' Collier's argument implicitly accepts that the university has been corporatised.[41] The argument in this book has been that, though there have been attempts to bureaucratise and corporatise the university, they have been resisted and can continue to be resisted. From this perspective thus, Collier's arguments are about what can happen not arguments about what must happen. The liberal law school remains a possibility in the twenty-first century and a law school that has liberal features remains an accurate description of many British university law schools.

The ideal of uniting avocation and vocation suggests a seamlessness and an intertwining to the academic's life. Psychologically no element of the academic's life can be completely separate from any other. Physically, however, there must be moments when domesticity or amity prevail. Given the huge demands on academics, when:

> the performance and research productivity of all legal academic staff has become crucial to the status, financial health and, perhaps, the very future of the law school itself

how can this life be managed in the liberal law school?[42] Here again the Base-Line study on work-life balance is instructive. In looking at the

[39] Collier, *ibid* (emphasis in original).
[40] Collier, *ibid*, 30.
[41] As, of course, do many other commentators.
[42] Collier, above n 38, at 15.

long hours culture that is found in many places of employment the study notes:

> [p]roviding a degree of flexibility about when those hours are worked can make all the difference between achieving a degree of balance in one's life and simply being overwhelmed by it.[43]

More specifically the study observes '[w]orking at home . . . may provide a degree of work flexibility with respect to, for instance, looking after children or aged relatives.'[44] Finally, the study argues that '[c]ommunication and consultation are important elements of workplace human resource policy.'[45] In formal terms no other group of employees have more flexibly working hours than those enjoyed by academics. Hochschild's pre-industrial revolution ideal where 'time with family overlapped and interwove with time at work' is a genuine possibility for academics in the liberal law school.[46] Equally, the collegial ethos of the liberal law school requires a greater degree of communication and consultation than that which is to be found in any other type of management structure. The environment of the liberal law school thus seems to be best placed to give academics an opportunity to satisfactorily manage their lives. There is, of course, always the danger of there being a gap between substance and form. The indeterminate nature of academic work means that every available hour can be used in a futile attempt to make the work determinate. But the solution to this lies partially in the hands of the individual academic. To manage one's life successfully requires constant attention to the way in which it is being lived as well as to, for example, the substance of one's teaching or research. A considered life has to be constantly reconsidered:

> Accidents of time and place shape options and opportunities for everyone, men and women, young and old. However for those with the necessary talents, it is more and more the case that the key factors are attitudinal; work-life performances, motivation, aspirations, and determination to achieve goals within the highly competitive public sphere of the marketplace, politics and other arenas.[47]

43 Hogarth, Halsuck and Pierre with Winterbotham and Vivian, above n 22, at 21.

44 *Ibid*, at 129.

45 *Ibid*, at 201.

46 A Hochschild, *The Time Bind: When Work Becomes Home and Home Becomes Work* (New York, Metropolitan Books, 1997) 47.

47 C Hakim, *Work-Lifestyle Choices in the 21st Century* (Oxford, Oxford University Press, 2000) 275.

How one does things, as well as what one does, is of consequence.[48] An academic who constantly works in the evenings and at week-ends and never takes time off in the week to be with family or friends is not an example of the successful conjunction of avocation and vocation. Instead, they have allowed themselves to become a poorly waged slave. Ideas occur anywhere and at any time and must be pursued as they come. At the same time, sometimes a long lunch hour and an extra bottle of wine are more important than another chapter of Weber. Individuals will make different choices about how they interweave work and life so as to make them one and the choices that they make will change over time but they need always to remember that the standard conditions of an academic contract make it possible for them to make those choices.[49]

In arguing for the possibility of successfully managing one's life if one works in a liberal law school I am not seeking to argue that this can be so for everybody. Not every bundle of expectations in terms of partner, children, friends, social life, hobbies or income level will be compatible with working in the liberal law school. Nor can the environment of the liberal law school change matters such as the fact that, given current resource levels, academic lives are highly pressurised or the fact that children are a major burden for their parents.[50] Nonetheless, working in a liberal law school and seeking to combine avocation and vocation offers the possibility of a way of life that is beyond the reach of most in modern society.

OF FAIRY RINGS

Writing about why he published poetry, Dylan Thomas recounted a story:

[48] Of course professional associations and those who, from time to time, hold offices such as head of department, dean or vice-chancellor also have a responsibility to ensure that individual academics have the freedom to manage their lives.

[49] Individual responsibility for these matters does not mean that the law school and its parent university has no responsibility in these matters. Academic life cannot be lived between 9.00 am and 5.00 pm but law schools can respect the complexity of academics' lives. Timetables, for example, should, in part, reflect the needs of individual academics. Equally universities should provide child-care and other facilities that reflect the commitment and flexibility that they expect of their academic staff. On this see further A Kolodny, *Failing the Future* (Durham, Duke University Press, 1998) ch 7.

[50] Though, of course, in some parents' eyes also a source of pleasure.

> I read somewhere of a shepherd who, when asked why he made, from within fairy rings, ritual observances to the moon to protect his flocks, replied: 'I'd be a damn' fool if I didn't!' These poems, with all their crudities, doubts, and confusions, are written for the love of Man and in praise of God, and I'd be a damn' fool if they weren't.[51]

In a more secular and sceptical age Thomas' remarks need slightly recasting but their spirit can be applied to the liberal law school. Work in the liberal law school should be done for love of the boundless possibilities that constitute the human condition. With all our crudities, doubts and confusions, we would be damn fools if we did anything else or did it for any other reason.

[51] 'Author's Note' in D Thomas, *Collected Poems: 1934–1952* (London, JM Dent, 1952).

Index

www.ingramcontent.com/pod-product-compliance
Ingram Content Group UK Ltd.
Pitfield, Milton Keynes, MK11 3LW, UK
UKHW020206290926
15470UKWH00001B/37

9 781841 132488